AF482138

Poverty among Immigrant Children in Europe

*Also by A.S. Bhalla*

BLENDING OF NEW AND TRADITIONAL TECHNOLOGIES (*co-editor*)

ECONOMIC TRANSITION IN HUNAN AND SOUTHERN CHINA

ENVIRONMENT, EMPLOYMENT AND DEVELOPMENT (*editor*) (*also in Portuguese*)

FACING THE TECHNOLOGICAL CHALLENGE

GLOBALIZATION, GROWTH AND MARGINALIZATION (*editor*) (*also in French*)
IN SEARCH OF ROOTS

MARKET OR GOVERNMENT FAILURES? An Asian Perspective

NEW TECHNOLOGIES AND DEVELOPMENT (*co-editor*)

POVERTY AND EXCLUSION IN A GLOBAL WORLD (*co-author*) (*also in Japanese*)

POVERTY AND INEQUALITY AMONG CHINESE MINORITIES (*co-author*)

REGIONAL BLOCS: Building Blocks or Stumbling Blocks? (*co-author*)

ROYAL TOMBS OF INDIA

SMALL AND MEDIUM ENTERPRISES: Technology Policies and Options (*editor*)

TECHNOLOGICAL TRANSFORMATION OF RURAL INDIA (*co-editor*)

TECHNOLOGY AND EMPLOYMENT IN INDUSTRY (*editor*) (*also in Spanish*)

THE EMPLOYMENT IMPACT OF CHINA'S WTO ACCESSION (*co-author*)

TOWARDS GLOBAL ACTION FOR APPROPRIATE TECHNOLOGY (*editor*)

UNEVEN DEVELOPMENT IN THE THIRD WORLD: A Study of China and India

*Also by Peter McCormick*

ECO-ETHICS AND CONTEMPORARY PHILOSOPHICAL REFLECTION

ECO-ETHICS AND AN ETHICS OF SUFFERING

THE NEGATIVE SUBLIME: Ethics, Warfare, and the Dark Borders of Reason

WHEN FAMINE RETURNS: Ethics, Identity, and the Deep Pathos of Things

MODERNITY, AESTHETICS, AND THE BOUNDS OF ART

FICTIONS, PHILOSOPHIES, AND THE PROBLEMS OF POETICS

HEIDEGGER AND THE LANGUAGE OF THE WORLD

ROMAN INGARDEN: Über das Wesen (*editor*)

STARMAKING: Realism, Anti-Realism, and Irrealism (*editor*)

THE AESTHETICS OF ROMAN INGARDEN (*editor*)

CONTEMPORARY ESSAYS ON ROMAN INGARDEN (*co-editor*)

ART AND ITS REASONS (*editor*)

HUSSERL: Shorter Works (*co-editor*)

HUSSERL: Expositions and Appraisals (*co-editor*)

GABRIEL MARCEL: Tragic Wisdom and Beyond (*translator*)

# Poverty among Immigrant Children in Europe

A.S. Bhalla

and

Peter McCormick

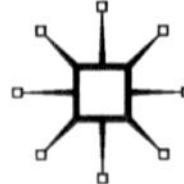



First published 2009 by
PALGRAVE MACMILLAN

Palgrave Macmillan in the UK is an imprint of Macmillan Publishers Limited, registered in England, company number 785998, of Houndmills, Basingstoke, Hampshire RG21 6XS.

Palgrave Macmillan in the US is a division of St Martin's Press LLC, 175 Fifth Avenue, New York, NY 10010.

Palgrave Macmillan is the global academic imprint of the above companies and has companies and representatives throughout the world.

Palgrave® and Macmillan® are registered trademarks in the United States, the United Kingdom, Europe and other countries

ISBN-13: 978–0–230–22104–8
ISBN-10: 0–230–22104–1

This book is printed on paper suitable for recycling and made from fully managed and sustained forest sources. Logging, pulping and manufacturing processes are expected to conform to the environmental regulations of the country of origin.

A catalogue record for this book is available from the British Library.

A catalog record for this book is available from the Library of Congress.

10   9   8   7   6   5   4   3   2   1
18   17   16   15   14   13   12   11   10   09

Printed and bound in Great Britain by
CPI Antony Rowe, Chippenham and Eastbourne

# Contents

# List of Tables

# List of Figures

# List of Boxes

# Preface

Why should child poverty exist in industrialized countries? This is a question to which there is at present no satisfactory answer. Child poverty is not only widely prevalent but it is particularly acute among the richest countries such as the USA, for example.

Our concern in this book is not child poverty in Europe as such because excellent work on the subject already exists, done partly by the UNICEF Innocenti Centre in Florence (Italy) and partly by individual scholars in European universities. Instead, our main concern is monetary and non-monetary poverty among immigrant children in Western Europe with special reference to Switzerland and France.

The choice of poverty among immigrant children is guided by several considerations. First, it is unacceptable that children of *legal* immigrants (who were welcomed for stimulating the host economies in times of severe labour shortages) should be denied basic needs such as food, education, health and access to decent housing. These children should enjoy moral and legal rights within the framework of the UN Convention of the Rights of Child ratified by a vast majority of countries. Second, there are humanitarian reasons for the public authorities and social services to attend to their well-being. Third, many immigrant children are citizens of the countries in which they live. They share acute poverty conditions with other non-immigrant children. Highlighting their economic and social plight is important as they form the future of their country of adoption along with non-immigrant children. Putting nation-building on a strong footing requires that children's well-being be assured through the fulfilment of their basic human needs.

Why Switzerland and France? The choice of these two countries is based on several factors. First, these are rich countries of Western Europe in which one does not expect significant and rising levels of poverty in general and among children in particular. Switzerland is the second richest country in Europe (after Luxembourg in terms of per capita income) where poverty, much less child poverty, was unheard of ten or 15 years ago. But the problem has now emerged and is growing from bad to worse as a result of a prolonged economic recession during the past decade or so. The Swiss Federal and cantonal authorities are increasingly concerned with the socio-economic problems of immigrant and their children considering that they form a substantial proportion (20 per cent) of the total population. Although the shares of immigrants and their children form a much smaller proportion of the French population, the absolute number of poor immigrant children is quite large.

Second, France and Switzerland are neighbouring countries with many similarities: democratic systems and political institutions, similar public expenditures on health and education, and literacy rates. But there are also differences in the size of the two countries and their immigrant populations. Therefore, it will be interesting to examine whether these differences account for any divergence in immigration policies and the treatment of immigrant children.

Third, these are the adopted countries of the two authors: one based in Geneva and the other in Paris. They have easy access to data and sources in these two countries.

In this book we are concerned primarily (but not exclusively) with poverty among immigrant children in two rich countries, namely, France and Switzerland. Generally, people in European cultures and societies today understand a child as any younger human being who has not yet reached physical maturity. And a young person's physical maturity is understood not just as his or her capacity for reproduction. Rather, physical maturity in this context refers to a state of being a physically full-grown adult human being as well as possessing a habitual capacity for exhibiting adult mental and emotional development (even though development may continue throughout most of one's lifetime). Sometimes, however, a child is understood as someone who has not yet reached legal age. Legal age, however, varies in European countries more than the usual age at which a young person reaches his or her physical maturity.

Child poverty of these young people is defined in terms of the concepts of deprivation, poverty, extreme poverty or destitution. The notion of deprived children captures those who are handicapped living normally with their parents but lacking regular access to special schooling, for example. It may also include poor or 'indigent children', for example, vulnerable children like some victims of paedophilia in France living with single parents (see Harris-White, 2002; Devereux, 2003a).

The notion of 'precariousness' discussed in the book is distinct from poverty but closely related to it. The French word, *'précarité'*, refers mainly to a state or condition that is a precursor of poverty rather than to poverty itself. Thus, in the case of individuals rather than groups, current French newspapers and French social science research may sometimes describe a young person's position as *'précaire'* in the sense that the person lacks any stable employment, stable income or stable housing. And any one of these or any one of their combinations may lead to a different state, namely, poverty and social exclusion.

France and Switzerland, the two countries with which we are concerned have a large number of poor and immigrant children from various religious and ethnic backgrounds. These countries are rich with exceptional resources. Yet the persisting economic, social and psychological problems of immigrant children are enormous. Someone might object that neither France nor Switzerland has noteworthy problems concerning child poverty. While this may be so, child poverty is growing in both the countries, as we discuss in detail in Chapters 3 to 5. Poverty among immigrant children has been relatively neglected so far. We believe that our modest attempt to study the problem will fill a gap.

Chapter 1 discusses the meaning and concepts of poverty and well-being. We show that well-being embraces not just minimum reasonable incomes, which are a *necessary* but not a *sufficient* condition of well-being. As we discuss in subsequent chapters, well-being includes satisfaction of basic needs and children's rights, such as access to proper health care, education and decent housing.

Three essential aspects of the conditions affecting immigrant poor children are explored. The first has to do with injustices, the second with lack of capabilities and the last with breaches of (human) rights. We examine whether the national policies towards poor immigrant children violate the United Nations Convention on the Rights of the Child adopted on 20 November 1989 by the General Assembly Resolution 44/25. Throughout the book we do our best to remain very close to the available empirical data while keeping in mind the much larger non-empirical concerns that motivate this work just as much as its distinguished precursors.

Chapter 2 provides a brief quantitative sketch of the magnitude of immigrant children in Europe and their income and non-income poverty situation compared to non-immigrant children.

Chapter 3 discusses the viewpoints of the critics and protagonists of European immigration with special reference to the plight of immigrant children. The policy of family reunification and how it has become more strict now in most European countries is discussed.

Chapter 4 and 5 discuss poverty among immigrant children in Switzerland and France in the context of child poverty in Europe in general. Poverty is defined in terms of both monetary (income) poverty and non-monetary poverty in terms of lack of access to goods and public services such as education and housing. These two chapters will explore the links between (a) income poverty and non-income poverty (education, health, employment and housing) and (b) legal status in terms of the nature of residence permits and the different types of poverty. The chapters will attempt to determine whether the former determine children's access to education, health services and employment.

The data and estimates of absolute and relative child poverty are generally based mainly on income poverty, which does not take account of deprivation and extreme poverty. While attempts to look for non-monetary indicators of poverty are an improvement, they also suffer from a subjective bias. Perceptions of basic necessities vary across families and household. But a fundamental conceptual problem is the failure to measure child poverty directly. Most measures are based on economic and social conditions of the households and children's parents, not on children themselves. This indirect approach to measuring child poverty may fail to address many problems of children's health and schooling and other forms of social exclusion. We shall, therefore, explore direct indicators of children's poverty. For example, can the teenage pregnancy of girls be used as a proxy for their poor socio-economic situation and breakdown of their families?

Chapter 6 undertakes an in-depth analysis of the problems of housing of immigrant children in France, a problem more serious there than in Switzerland. Access to decent housing of immigrant children is a precondition for their healthy development and proper education/schooling. While the general housing situation in France has improved, gaining access to proper housing remains quite difficult for many immigrants, particularly from the Maghreb (Algeria, Morocco, Tunisia) and other parts of Africa compared to immigrants from within Europe.

Poor housing conditions, limited floor space and lack of privacy in co-habitation (with family and friends) militate against raising a family, devoting adequate time to studies and professional pursuits and so on. Children living in poor families in overcrowded housing are much more exposed in their daily lives to such serious problems as insecurity, excessive noise, vandalism and surrounding violence. This is particularly true of the suburban ghettoes of Paris. The degree of difficulty experienced by children is relative to the types of housing in which they live. A substantial number of these children live in social housing as well as in tenement housing, often located in difficult urban areas.

Chapter 7 provides a comparative analysis of the situation of immigrant children in Switzerland and France. Following the UNICEF approach (2007) it quantifies the well-being of children in the two countries on the basis of a number of indicators.

In principle, child maltreatment and abuse is a useful indicator of a lack of well-being because it is associated with other symptoms of this state such as poverty and deprivation, single parenthood, family breakdown, unemployment and drug abuse. However, in practice it is difficult to determine the causes of maltreatment. Any single factor noted above is unlikely to explain maltreatment in isolation of other factors. It is poverty and mental stress resulting from, for example, unemployment and single parenthood that may raise the risk of child abuse.

The final chapter summarizes the main highlights of the book, notably the economic and social as well as the legal and political status of immigrant children, which affect their poverty and well-being.

*Commugny, Switzerland*          A. S. BHALLA
*Paris, France*          PETER MCCORMICK

# Acknowledgements

The authors and publishers are grateful to the following for permission to reproduce or use the following copyright material:

1. Cambridge University Press and Ann Morissens, the author, for using Table 2.3 (Chapter 2) taken from her chapter 'Immigrants, Unemployment and Europe's Varying Welfare Regimes' in C. Parsons and T. Smeeding (eds) (2006) *Immigration and the Transformation of Europe* (Cambridge: Cambridge University Press).
2. Joseph Rowntree Foundation (UK) and Democratic Dialogue (Northern Ireland) for using Table 2.6 in Chapter 2 from *Poverty and Social Exclusion in Britain* by Gordon *et al.* published in 2000; and from '[Bare Necessities Poverty and Social Exclusion in Northern Ireland: Key Findings'] by Hillyard *et al.* published in 2003 by *Democratic Dialogue*. Reproduced by permission of the Joseph Rowntree Foundation and *Democratic Dialogue*.
3. Blackwell Publishing and Simon Hix and Abdul Noury, the authors, for Table 3.1 in Chapter 3, taken from their article. 'Politics, Not Economic Interests: Determination of Migration Policies in the European Union', *International Migration Review*, vol. 41, no. 1.
4. The Swiss Federal Office of Statistics (OFS) for Figures 4.1 and 4.2 in Chapter 4.
5. The National Institute of Statistics and Economic Studies (INSEE, Paris) for using Tables 5.1 and 5.4 in Chapter 5 and Table 6.2 in Chapter 6.
6. The Council for Employment, Income and Social Cohesion (CERC, Paris) for using Table 5.2 in Chapter 5.
7. Blackwell Publishing and Marco Giugni and Florence Passy, the authors, for Table 7.3 in Chapter 7 taken from their article 'Migrant Mobilization between Political Institutions and Citizenship Regimes: A Comparison of France and Switzerland', *European Journal of Political Research*, vol.43, 2004.

We owe a debt of gratitude to a number of persons and institutions: in Switzerland, Rosita Fibbi of the University of Neuchâtel, and member of the Swiss Forum for Migration and Population Studies (SFM); Jean-Marc

Falter, University of Geneva; Jean-Pierre Boillat (responsible for registering clandestine immigrant children at public schools) of the Centre for Contact between Swiss and Immigrants (CCSI), Geneva, for supplying data on which Figure 4.3 in Chapter 4 is based; Rainer Winkelman, Socio-economic Institute, University of Zurich; and Sybille Bayard of the Jacobs Centre for Productive Youth Development, University of Zurich; in France, Jean-Paul Caille, Ministry of National Education and Research; in Italy, Eva Jesperson, Chief, Social and Economic Policy Analysis, UNICEF Innocenti Research Centre (Florence); and in the UK, Professor Anthony Atkinson of Nuffield College, Oxford, and holder of a Blaise Pascal Chair at the Paris School of Economics.

A. S. BHALLA<br>PETER MCCORMICK

# List of Abbreviations

| | |
|---|---|
| AFD | Swiss Corps of Frontier Guards (*Corps des gardes-frontière*) |
| AGDREF | Computer Applications for the Monitoring of Foreigners in France (*Application informatique de gestion des ressortissants étrangers en France*) |
| AME | State Medical Aid (France) |
| ANAEM | National Agency for Foreigners and Migration (*Agence nationale d'accueil des étrangers et migrations*) |
| ANAFE | National Association for Assistance to Foreigners at the Borders (*Association nationale d'assistance aux frontières pour les étrangers*) |
| ANAH | National Agency for the Improvement of Housing (*Agence nationale pour l'amélioration de l'habitat*) |
| ANIL | National Agency for Information on Housing (*Agence nationale d'information pour le logement*) |
| ANPL | National Agency for the Protection of Housing (*Agence nationale pour la protection de l'habitat*) |
| ANRU | National Agency for Urban Renewal (*Agence national pour la renovation urbaine*) |
| ASE | Child Welfare Assistance (*Aide sociale à l'enfance*) |
| ASPE | Swiss Agency for Child Protection |
| BASS | Bureau of Labour and Social Policy Studies (*Bureau d'études de politique du travail et de politique social*) |
| BEP | Apprenticeship Certificate (*Brevet d'études professionnelle*) |
| BEPC | Secondary School Certificate (*Brevet d'étude de premier cycle*) |
| CADA | Reception Centre for Asylum-seekers (*Centre d'accueil pour demandeurs d'asile*) |
| CAOMIDA | Reception and Orientation Centre for Separated Children seeking Asylum |
| CAP | Certificate of Vocational Aptitude |
| CASE | Centre for the Analysis of Social Exclusion |
| CCSI | Centre for Contact Between Swiss and Immigrants |
| CEPR | Centre for Economic Policy Research (UK) |
| CERC | Council for Employment, Income and Social Cohesion (France) (*Conseil d'emploi, revenue et de la cohésion sociale*) |
| CFEJ | Swiss Federal Commission for Children and Youth |
| CGP | French Planning Commission (*Commisariat Général du Plan*) |

| | |
|---|---|
| CHRS | Accommodation and Reintegration Centre (*Centre d'hébergement et de réinsertion sociale*) |
| CIMADE | Committee for the Rehabilitation of Displaced Persons (*Comité inter-mouvements auprès des évacués*) |
| CNAF | National Fund for Family Benefits (*Caisses nationales d'allocations familiales*) |
| CNIL | National Commission for Information Technology and Freedom |
| COFF | Federal Commission for the Coordination of Family-related Issues |
| CPAG | Child Policy Action Group |
| CREDES | Centre for Research, Study and Documentation in Economics of Health (*Centre de recherche, d'étude et de documentation en économie de la santé*) |
| CREDOC | Research Centre for the Study of Living Conditions (France) |
| CRS | The French Riot Police |
| CRSP | Centre for Research in Social Policy |
| CSLS | Centre for the Study of Living Standards |
| CSO | Central Statistical Office (Ireland) |
| DAL | Law concerning the Right to Housing (*Loi sur le droit au logement opposable*) |
| DEP | Department of Economics and Politics |
| DLPAJ | Directorate for Civic Liberties and Legal Affairs (*Direction de libertés publiques et des affaires juridiques*) |
| DPM | Directorate for Population and Migration |
| DREES | Directorate for Research, Studies, Evaluation and Statistics (France) |
| DSD | Department of Social Development (UK) |
| ECHP | European Community Household Panel |
| ECRI | European Commission against Racism and Intolerance |
| EDQ | *Les Enfants de Don Quichotte* (France) |
| EFFNATIS | Effectiveness of National Integration Strategies (towards second-generation migration youth) (an EU project) |
| EFTA | European Free Trade Area |
| EMU | European Monetary Union |
| EP | European Parliament |
| ESPS | Survey of Health and Social Protection (*Enquête santé et protection social*) (Switzerland) |
| ESS | Swiss Survey of Public Health (*Enquête Suisse sur la santé*) |
| EU | European Union |
| EURONET | European Children's Network |

EUROSTAT   Statistical Office of the European Communities
FASILD   Association for Integration and Fight against Discrimination (*Fond d'action et de soutien pour l'intégration et la lutte contre des discriminations*)
FEANTSA   European Federation of National Associations working with the Homeless (*Fédération européenne d'associations nationales travaillant avec les sans abri*)
FNAIM   National Federation of Real Estate Agents (*Fédération nationale des agents immobilières*)
FNARS   National Federation of Associations for Social Reintegration (*Fédération nationale des associations d'accueil et de réinsertion sociale*)
GDP   Gross Domestic product
GISTI   Information Network for the Support of Immigrant Workers (*Groupe d'information et soutien des travailleurs immigrés*)
GRETA   Enterprise Networks for Adult Training (*Les groupements des établissements pour la formation continue*)
HALDE   High Commission for Fight Against Discrimination and for Equality (*Haute autorité de lutter contre les discriminations et pour l'égalité*)
HCR   Head-count Ratio
HLM   Low-income Housing (*Habitation loyer modéré*)
IDS   Institute of Development Studies (UK)
IFOP   French Institute for Public Opinion (*Institut français pour les opinions publiques*)
IGAS   Inspectorate General for Social Affairs (*Inspection générale des affaires sociales*) (France)
IMES   Swiss Federal Office for Immigration, Integration and Emigration (*Office fédérale de l'immigration, intégration et émigration*)
INED   National Institute of Demographic Studies (*Institut national d'études démographiques*)
INSEE   National Institute of Statistics and Economic Studies (*Institut national de la statistique et des études économiques*)
IOM   International Organization for Migration
IRC   Innocenti Research Centre (UNICEF, Florence)
ISEW   Index of Sustainable Economic Welfare
LAO   Reception and Orientation Centre (*Lieu d'accueil et d'orientation*)
LIS   Luxembourg Income Study
MDM   *Médecins du Monde*

| | |
|---|---|
| MEP | Member of European Parliament |
| MERCI | Mobilization on Ethnic Relations, Citizenship and Immigration |
| MFI | Median Family Income |
| MGIEN | Programme for the Promotion of National Education (*Mission générale à l'insertion de l'éducation national*) |
| MRAP | Association against Racism and for Friendship between People (*Mouvement contre le racisme et pour l'amitié entre les peuples*) |
| NSPCC | National Society for the Prevention of Cruelty to Children (UK) |
| ODAS | Decentralized Network for Monitoring Social Action (*Observatoire décentralisé de l'action sociale*) |
| ODR | Swiss Federal Office for Refugees |
| OECD | Organisation for Economic Co-operation and Development |
| OFM | Swiss Federal Office of Migration |
| OFPRA | French Office for the Protection of Refugees and Stateless Persons (*Office français de protection des réfugiés et apatrides*) |
| OFS | Swiss Federal Statistical Office |
| OFSP | Swiss Federal Office for Public Health (*Office fédéral pour la santé publique*) |
| OMI | International Migration Office (France) |
| OMISTAT | OMI Annual Statistics |
| ONED | National Network for Children in Danger (*Observatoire national de l'enfance en danger*) |
| ONPES | National Monitoring Network of Poverty and Social Exclusion (*Observatoire national de la pauvreté et de l'exclusion sociale*) |
| OSEO | Swiss Labour Assistance Agency (*Œuvre Suisse d'entraide ouvrière*) |
| PAF | French Border Police (*Police de l'air et des frontières*) |
| PISA | Programme for International Student Assessment (OECD) |
| PJJ | Legal Protection of Youth (*Protection juridique de la jeunesse*) |
| PNR | National Programme for Research (*Programme Nationale de Recherche*) |
| PPP | Purchasing Power Parity |
| PSE | Poverty and Social Exclusion |
| PSENI | Poverty and Social Exclusion in Northern Ireland |
| PTZ | Housing Loans without Interest (France) |
| QUB | Queen's University, Belfast |
| RCV | Roll Call Vote |
| SDF | Without Fixed Domicile (*Sans domicile fixe*) |
| SFM | Swiss Forum for Migration and Population Studies |
| SIES | Swiss Income and Expenditure Survey |
| SILC | Community Statistics on Income and Living Conditions (EU) |

| | |
|---|---|
| SIS | Schengen Information System |
| SIT | Geneva Professional Workers Trade Union |
| SMEs | Small and Medium Enterprises |
| SMEW | Sustainable Measure of Economic Well-being |
| SMIC | Minimum Income Scheme (*Salaire minimum interprofessionel de croissance*) (France) |
| SOPEMI | OECD Permanent Monitoring System (*Système d'observation permanente de l'OCDE*) |
| TNS SOFRES | Institute for Studies on Marketing and Public Opinion (France) |
| UNDP | United Nations Development Programme |
| UNESCO | United Nations Educational, Scientific and Cultural Organization |
| UNICEF | United Nations Children's Fund |
| UNRISD | United Nations Research Institute for Social Development |
| ZEP | Geographical Area for Educational Priority (*Zone d'éducation prioritaire*) |
| ZUS | Difficult Urban Area (*Zones urbaines sensibles*) |

# 1
## Child Poverty and Well-Being

In January 2008 the European Commission released a report on child poverty and well-being (European Commission, 2008). It reports that there are a substantial number of poor children in the European Union (EU) countries. They are living poorly in the midst of Europe's wealthy citizens. The situation of these children is worse than that of the general population.[1] In some countries, one out of four children are poor. The most vulnerable are the immigrant children living in migrant households (in which at least one parent is born abroad). They suffer from a much higher risk of poverty than others whose parents were born in the host country. The risk for these children 'is two to five times higher' (European Commission, 2008, p. 63). This higher risk is often due to joblessness and larger size of households. In some countries, other factors – namely, lower wages and poor working conditions – are more important.

Immigrant child poverty is our concern here. We examine such poverty initially as a lack of well-being. After considering possible applications of different approaches to immigrant child poverty (namely, a justice-as-fairness approach and a capability approach), we sketch our own approach in terms of a particular understanding of the nature and requirements of children's rights and social justice. We shall refer to these approaches in the following chapters.

Three important issues concerning poor immigrant children in Europe relate to their rights, personal dignity and social justice (Bernard, 2002; Galland, 2002; van Eeckhout, 2007). We deal with these issues here in their economic, political and judicial contexts (Bouchet-Saulnier, 2006; Martinetti, 2002; and Dekeuwer-Défossez, 2006).[2] Insufficient attention to these issues reflects persistent failures in legal, social and moral responsibility on the part of resourceful, knowledgeable and powerful European elites. More broadly these failures consist in neglecting to adequately uphold the human rights of the poor generally and of poor immigrant children in particular. Despite some initiatives European elites have repeatedly failed to institutionalize effective social justice, children's rights and human rights programmes (Clayton and Williams, 2000; Krugman, 2008).

European elites are *resourceful.* Hence they have at their disposal a wealth of means to remedy deficiencies in children's well-being (involving nutrition, health care, education, housing and employment) that continue to affect poor immigrant children and youth. They are *knowledgeable* and know how pernicious the persistence of such poverty among all poor people, and especially among these children, really is (Fricker, 2007). They are also *powerful* and hence fully capable of helping to mitigate such crippling impoverishment (Klugman, 2002). Immigrant children are less numerous than poor people generally. In devoting more resources at their disposal in their wealthy societies to assist them, the elites face no sufficiently powerful counter forces that could effectively block persistent efforts at major social reforms.

In the following pages, we first discuss the general notion of poverty, deprivation and destitution. We spell out a general understanding of poverty as a lack of well-being. We examine what poor immigrant children's lack of 'well-being' means. We also discuss the persisting problems of poor immigrant children in Europe with special reference to Switzerland and France.[3]

Two accounts in particular will occupy us here. The first refers to the suitability of a justice-as-fairness approach to an understanding of immigrant child poverty. The second centres on the applicability of a capability approach. We find both these general approaches helpful. However, neither of them is sufficiently adequate for our purposes.

In the concluding section we briefly sketch our alternative approach to a fuller understanding of immigrant child poverty. This approach is based on particular notions of social justice. It assigns major weight to the interrelated notions of personal dignity, social integration and human solidarity.

## Poverty, deprivation and destitution

The *New Oxford Dictionary of English* defines the terms 'poverty', 'deprivation' and 'destitution' as follows: (1) *poverty*: 'the state of being extremely poor'; (2) *deprivation*: 'the damaging lack of material benefits considered to be basic necessities in a society'; and (3) *destitution*: the state of being 'without the basic necessities of life'.

There are several problems with these dictionary definitions. First, these definitions include three categories that overlap. For example, the definitions of deprivation and destitution are almost the same, except that deprivation is considered damaging whereas destitution is not. Second, the definitions do not tell us anything about the different *degrees* of poverty. Thus, persons who are living just below any particular poverty line are given the same weight as the very poor living far below the poverty line. Moreover, these persons are also given the same weight as those who have little hope of reaching such a line or ever rising above it. Thus, the definitions are also silent on the *intensity* of poverty.

Furthermore, the main focus in the dictionary definitions seems to be on basic necessities of life within a particular society without which a person would be considered deprived or destitute. But these basic necessities are likely to differ with time and place. Even within a given society inter-personal welfare comparisons are difficult to make. Such comparisons become almost impossible across different societies in different parts of the world and at different stages of development. Finally, stress on basic necessities of life in defining poverty may imply a lack not only of material but also of non-material necessities such as adequate opportunities for self-development.

A key issue here is who decides what is basic or not for an individual or a household. Many children themselves are often not able to decide on what their basic needs are and what their preferences among these basic needs should be. They will tend to rely on their parents and guardians for guidance on this point.

Basic needs differ from one child to another, whatever the head of a household may decide. Further, such decisions often depend not on what a child's needs are, but on what the household head believes they are or should be. These beliefs incorporate value judgements involved in a household head's decisions about what makes up an appropriate bundle of material and non-material necessities of life. Moreover, the same head of household may also decide how these basic needs should be met. For example, he or she may decide whether one child should receive more material and non-material benefits than another depending on gender, age and other factors. In short, child poverty is really not child poverty as such, but the poverty of parents and families to which children belong.

Nonetheless, there are common norms rather than simply the beliefs of a household head about what constitutes a decent level of food and nutrition, clothing and shelter, and other material and non-material necessities. Besides these common norms, there are also multiple indicators of poverty and their varying assigned weights (see, for example, the six-year longitudinal study of varying assigned weights for 12 of these indicators in Dorval, 2008, p. 37).

Many human goods are unambiguously objective (Moore, 2000). Accordingly, in philosophical and ethical domains the well-being of a child may be considered in terms of his or her right to enjoy access to some basic minimum of nutrition, health and education below which it would simply be immoral to let a child fall (Birdsall, 2001). In economic and public policy prescriptions and analyzes, operationally meaningful distinctions between the notions of poverty, deprivation and destitution are required.

For example, destitution may be regarded as an extreme form of poverty. It may be considered not only as a lack of adequate incomes, but also as a lack of material and non-material goods, capabilities and even human rights. In such Western European countries as Spain and Italy, strong family support systems and social networks are a form of social security to overcome extreme hardships, for example, those caused by long-term unemployment. But these systems, quite common in developing countries, are rare in Europe. Child poverty would probably be much worse in these countries without the informal support systems and social safety nets.

Table 1.1 gives a typology of some distinguishing features of the interrelated but distinct notions of poverty, deprivation and destitution.

The above definitions differ somewhat from those many economists usually adopt. Thus, economists generally define destitution as an extreme form of poverty and the destitute as 'the extremely poor' or 'the poorest'. For example, Khan and Riskin (2001), in the particular contexts of their study of China, distinguish between three categories: broad poverty, deep poverty and extreme poverty. Presumably this last category is close to the notion of destitution adopted here. Essentially, they distinguish between the three categories in terms of different levels of income or consumption thresholds.

This approach to defining the notions of poverty, deprivation and destitution is operationally simple. However, it is conceptually poor. By contrast, Dasgupta (1993, p. 10) defines 'the phenomenon of destitution as an extreme condition of ill-being'. He also notes: 'even though much has been written in recent years on poverty and destitution, the analytical economics of chronic, or even of sharp and fatal, deprivation has remained an underdeveloped subject. What is currently on offer is mostly policy without the backing of theory.' This is true particularly of much of the literature on child poverty in Europe and North America. Despite some excellent empirical work, one does not come across any

*Table 1.1*   Some distinguishing features of the notions of poverty, deprivation, and destitution

| Poverty | Deprivation | Destitution |
| --- | --- | --- |
| – absolute and relative concept | – absolute and relative concept | – absolute concept? |
| – transitory or persistent phenomenon | – transitory or persistent phenomenon | – persistent phenomenon |
| – lack of income | – lack of access to basic goods | – extreme lack of access to goods and services |
| – lack of employment may be the main cause of lack of incomes | – lack of employment may or may not be important for explaining deprivation | – lack of employment and incomes |
| – lack of entitlements | – serious lack of entitlements | – absence of entitlements |
| – some material assets apart from potential labour power | – very few material assets | – absence of assets |
| – sporadic risk of failing to meet basic needs | – failure to meet at least some basic needs | – systemic risks and failure to meet basic needs, resulting in undernourishment and even starvation |
| – social welfare or income transfers may or may not be a solution to the transient poverty problem | – some income transfers may be necessary | – state action in the form of social welfare and charity may be the only solutions to destitution |

rigorous analytical framework and conceptual analysis underlying this empiricism.

Poverty is a necessary but not a sufficient concept to determine the ill-being of immigrant children (mainly those between five and 18) on whom we focus. Unless they are orphans, most poor children are poor because their parents are poor. But this derived sense of child poverty fails to capture the true nature of poor children's ill-being.

Dasgupta (1993) analyzes poverty and deprivation in terms of what he calls economic disenfranchisement. This concept is somewhat similar to Sen's concept of entitlement and capabilities, which we discuss below. Dasgupta argues that the poor suffer from a failure of entitlements owing to lack of incomes, assets or employment. Their capabilities to command employment and access to resources can be improved if they can convert their *potential* asset of labour power into *actual* labour power. But this conversion is possible only if the poor have regular access to at least some proper food so as to satisfy their minimum nutritional requirements.

However, Dasgupta's concept of economic disenfranchisement is not applicable to the notion of child poverty since children (below 16 years) are legally outside the labour force or should be. It is true that in developing countries poverty often forces poor people to send out their children to earn and supplement their parents' income. This is a phenomenon, as we discuss in Chapters 4 and 5, that also characterizes some family situations in several former Eastern European countries such as Romania and Bulgaria.

Devereux (2003, p. 9) remarks: 'One way in which destitution is fundamentally distinct from income or consumption-based measures of poverty is in its focus on assets and assetlessness.' Lack of assets essentially boils down to what Dasgupta calls 'economic disenfranchisement' and Sen calls 'lack of entitlements and capability'.

Our concern in this book is not destitution per se, but destitute immigrant children in Europe and their expectations from affluent European societies. How does deprivation and destitution affect their principal or primary as opposed to their derived or secondary poverty? And what norms, economic, social and moral, should govern their precarious state (Dancy, 2000; Raz, 2000)?

As noted above, poor immigrant children are deprived or destitute because their parents are destitute. When the parents are destitute, much of their time and effort is devoted to finding a survival strategy. This situation forces them to send children to work to eke out a living, giving rise to a phenomenon of child labour and child crime, for example, that of Roma children living in appalling conditions in the streets of Geneva and Paris (see Chapters 4 and 5). Inability to complete their education or the need for them to work prematurely leads to a situation of poor employability for such children in later life. The destitution of parents also leads to the severe undernourishment of their children. Their children will in turn pass on their unemployability and undernourishment to their children and to future generations once they become adults.

Immigrant children and their parents or guardians suffer from an additional disadvantage owing to their often uncertain and ill-defined legal status. This legal status is continually changing as the European Union struggles to arrive at a common immigration policy (see Chapter 3). As we discuss in Chapter 4 on Switzerland, such children lack access to proper schools and the job market because they possess short-term residence permits or are staying in the country illegally. This is also the case to a lesser degree in France where Roma children in particular lack access to proper schools. This situation may mainly reflect the fact that they are disadvantaged because of their precarious legal status, not necessarily because of their poverty. One can be disadvantaged in some respects without necessarily being poor economically or financially speaking.

Having discussed briefly several notions of poverty, deprivation and destitution, we now turn to some related notions of well-being and ill-being that enable us better to understand poverty.

## The notions of well-being and ill-being

In ordinary British English today, people generally use the expression 'well-being' to denote what the *Oxford Dictionary of English* calls 'the state of being comfortable, healthy, or happy'.[4] To illustrate, the dictionary cites a familiar English phrase from medical contexts, 'an improvement in the patient's well-being'. The sense here is that an ill person now under medical treatment is doing well. The opposite of well-being, namely 'ill-being', is that the same person is not doing well, or is doing poorly. Accordingly, in our special context here we might say that a poor person, such as a poor immigrant child in France or Switzerland, may be said to be suffering from ill-being or a lack of well-being in the ordinary sense of being in poor health, or, generally, of lacking normal comfort, or, even more generally, of being unhappy (Diener *et al.*, 1999). The terms 'ill-being' or 'lacking in well-being' may also refer not just to the unhealthy, uncomfortable, or unhappy particular situation of individuals, but also to their general situation as members of a social group.

To conclude, the terms 'ill-being' or 'lack of well-being' may refer to three situations of a person or a child: (a) lacking normal comfort, good health and happiness; (b) in a negative situation, lacking these not just as an individual but also as a member of a group of similar individuals; (c) lacking certain material and non-material goods (including moral, political and financial goods) satisfying basic needs, as well as lacking the feeling of a general sense of serenity that follows from the satisfaction of basic needs (Sumner, 1996).

The next relevant question is whether individual or aggregate social well-being can be measured and properly assessed. Dasgupta (2007) distinguishes between assessing well-being directly and indirectly. Some aspects of well-being, such as the medical, nutrition and education needs of people, can be measured objectively and directly. By contrast, other aspects of well-being can be assessed only indirectly. Here, instead of objective measurement techniques, the usual methods are those of persons 'revealed preferences', say the assessment of persons' needs from what can be reasonably inferred from their patterns of consumption.

However, each of these approaches to assessing well-being remains controversial. For example, direct assessment by objective measurement sometimes has to rely on persons actually stating what their needs are, which introduces an element of subjective judgement. But often such an assessment occurs in 'cases where the determinants [of well-being] are goods and services on which people are unable to express their preferences and interests because there is no opportunity for them to do so' (*ibid.*, p. 144). Even in cases where persons do succeed in stating their preferences, the obvious problem remains that, when asked to state their preferences, they do not always reply truthfully. Moreover, as we noted above, many immigrant children are unable to express their preferences independently of their parents and guardians.

In Chapter 7 we describe how the UNICEF Innocenti Research Centre assesses child well-being quantitatively on the basis of a survey of children's own perceptions about their well-being or ill-being. These subjective judgements about the components and determinants of well-being, we show, can vary a great deal. And these variances help explain, *inter alia*, the wide variations in the rankings of child well-being in France and Switzerland. Children at a young age can hardly be expected to give reliable and accurate answers concerning their well-being.

The UNICEF Innocenti Research Centre's attempt at assessing the subjective judgements of children about their own well-being are bold but flawed (see Chapter 7). The results of such subjective judgements cannot be accepted uncritically. Indirect assessments of well-being, for example those based on inferences from consumption patterns, also face serious difficulties. These assessments find it difficult to account for such goods as democracy or human rights.

What strikes us is the relevance to the situation of poor immigrant children in Europe of what Dasgupta has in mind when he talks of a 'natural recursion rate'. Thus Dasgupta notes:

> Considerate parents take into account the well-being of their children when choosing their family size and deciding how much to save. If they are in addition thoughtful parents, they know that the welfare of their children will depend upon the well-being of their grandchildren, that the welfare of their grandchildren will in turn depend upon the welfare of *their* children, and so on, down the generations. In short, there is a natural recursion of well-being interests along a family line. (Dasgupta, 1993, p. 378)

As we discuss in Chapters 4 to 6, this is precisely the kind of well-being that poor immigrant children lack. The well-being at issue there is specifically that of children's rights to proper health care, education and housing, now and not just in the future.

## Well-being vs deprivation

A study of the well-being of children in Germany (Holz, 2007) shows a link between well-being and deprivation. It estimates the living conditions of children aged six and ten on the basis of three types of situations: well-being, disadvantage and multiple deprivation (see Table 1.2).

*Table 1.2*   Living conditions of children aged six and ten in Germany (%)

| Type of situation | Children aged 6 (1999) N = 893 | | Children aged 10 (2003/04) N = 500 | |
|---|---|---|---|---|
| | *Poor children* | *Non-poor children* | *Poor children* | *Non-poor children* |
| Well-being | 23.6 | 46.4 | 15.1 | 47.5 |
| Disadvantage | 40.3 | 39.8 | 46.5 | 41.9 |
| Multiple deprivation | 36.1 | 13.7 | 38.4 | 10.6 |
| Total | 100.0 | 100.0 | 100.0 | 100.0 |

*Source*: Holz (2007), p. 30.

This longitudinal study shows that the living condition of a child changes rapidly between the ages of six and ten. Therefore, it would be inappropriate to describe his or her condition as one of being 'poor one day, and poor forever'. The situation will vary depending on whether a child is living in a poor or a non-poor household. In the former case, the situation may become more vulnerable over time changing from that of 'disadvantage' to one of 'multiple deprivation'. However, in the latter case it may move in the opposite direction of greater well-being and welfare.

Thus, poverty affects not only children's well-being but also what CERC (2005, p. 6) calls their 'well-becoming' (*bien devenir*) in the future. This issue of dynamic and intergenerational poverty and well-being is of particular relevance to children because it affects the development of their capabilities (see below and Chapter 2).

Having discussed notions of poverty, deprivation and well-being, we now turn to two outstanding reflections on poverty, those of Rawls and his one-time colleague, Sen.

## A justice-as-fairness approach to poverty

In this section we discuss the first of the two quite general approaches to questions of poverty. We wish to examine whether either one of these approaches can be applied fruitfully to poverty among immigrant children in affluent European countries. We begin with the views of Rawls.

One key to appreciating Rawls's justice-as-fairness approach to poverty is to understand the inadequacies of utilitarianism in politics, economics and, to a lesser degree, in political and social philosophy (Smart and Williams, 1973). Of course, utilitarianism is more than one doctrine: it comprises many contemporary versions as well, including sophisticated versions of consequentialism (Scanlon, 1998).[5]

The utilitarianism that Rawls himself initially espoused had two elements: first, that the sole central element in human happiness or well-being understood as 'a person's good' is utility, where 'utility' is itself taken as desire-satisfaction or, more carefully, as the ordering of preferences; and, second, that the moral rightness of actions is a function solely of their producing at least as much utility for all persons affected as any feasible alternative would.

'The main idea', as Rawls states, 'is that a person's good is determined by what is for him the most rational long-term plan of life given reasonably favourable circumstances. A man is happy when he is more or less successful in the way of carrying out this plan' (Rawls, 1999).[6]

More importantly, Rawls also added a basic correction to his 1971 understanding of the crucial notion of the nature of 'primary goods'. In their original version, 'primary goods' were to be understood as 'things that rational persons want whatever else they want, and what these were and why they were to be explained by the account of goodness' (p. 79). Thus, primary goods were those that many first understood as needing to be distributed fairly and justly, the goods poor immigrant children may be lacking.

Rawls later understood primary goods as 'what persons need in their status as free and equal citizens, and as normal and fully cooperating members of society over a complete life'. He wrote: 'Interpersonal comparisons for purposes of political justice are to be made in terms of citizens' index of primary goods and these goods are seen as answering to their needs as citizens as opposed to their preferences and desires' (Rawls, 1999, p. xiii).

In general, 'the chief primary [social] goods', Rawls wrote, 'are rights, liberties, and opportunities, and income and wealth' (*ibid*), and the central primary social good is self-respect. In particular, he specified primary goods at length as '(i) basic rights and liberties; freedom of thought and liberty of conscience... (ii) freedom of movement and free choice of occupation against a background of diverse opportunities... (iii) powers and prerogatives of offices and positions of authority and responsibility [in the political and economic institutions of the basic structure]. (iv) income and wealth understood as all-purpose means... generally needed to achieve a wide range of ends whatever they may be. [And] (v) the social basis of self-respect, understood as those aspects of basic institutions normally essential if citizens are to have a lively sense of their worth as persons and to be able to advance their ends with self-confidence' (Rawls, 1993; 2001).

Sen is critical of Rawls's notion of primary goods. For, even with a fairer distribution of primary goods within a particular society, many people will still be unequal with respect to their capabilities to lead the kinds of life they aspire to lead. Thus, 'people who differ with respect to disease, disability, nutritional needs, or gender, will convert the same package of primary social goods into different sets of capabilities; they will remain unequal in ways that matter to justice' (Sen, 1992, p. 256).

Sen (2002, pp. 83–5; 309) believes that Rawls's notion of primary goods left unaddressed certain kinds of care that some people provide for others. For example, Rawls's notion included much about citizens but, as we also observed, virtually nothing about children. It was, in short, insensitive to the dependence of the needy. Thus, Rawls's 'account of the primary goods, introduced . . . as an account of the needs of citizens who are characterized by the two moral powers and by the capacity to be "fully cooperating", has no place for the need of many real people for the kind of care we give to people who are not independent' (Nussbaum, 2003, p. 512). Finally, Sen noted that Rawls's idea of primary goods was abstract (Walzer, 1983). As several philosophers summarized the issue, 'Rawls's theory of justice was designed to apply universally and thus failed to attend to the ways in which different cultures embody different values and practices. . . . [His] conception of the social resources of which justice demands a principled distribution is conceptually incoherent.'

On the surface, Rawls's account above may seem to be helpful in discussing the situation of poor immigrant children. Yet, at least three basic presuppositions underlying this thoughtful account raise difficulties. First, his assumption of rationality vitiates such an approach. As Chapters 4 to 6 show, children are not capable of the kinds of mature, adult rationality that such an approach presupposes. Neither are poor children capable of what the second presupposition assumes, namely, that persons always enjoy the two central moral capacities of a sense of justice and a comprehensive conception of the good. Children's poverty has prevented them from properly developing such powers. A third presupposition that most people are citizens also does not apply to immigrant children who are generally not 'citizens', properly speaking.

Thus, we doubt that a justice-as-fairness approach is satisfactory for elucidating the well-being of poor immigrant children.


## A capability approach to poverty

The capability approach associated with Sen defines poverty as a failure of some members of society to enjoy a certain minimum of capabilities (Sen, 1999, pp. 20; 87–110).[7] These capabilities include being free from starvation, being adequately sheltered, being free to visit friends and so on. Sen writes: 'The role of income and wealth – important as it is along with other influences – has to be integrated . . . into a broader and fuller picture of success and deprivation' (*ibid.*, p. 20).

The term 'capability' refers to the opportunity to achieve valuable combinations of human functionings. A person's 'capability set' represents the alternative combinations of functionings that are within a person's reach (and which are therefore feasible) and over which a person has freedom of effective choice (regardless of what he or she actually decides to choose) (*ibid.*, p. 18).

By combining capability with freedom to act this approach moves closer to a rights-based approach (see below). 'Freedom from want' that entitles individuals to enjoy income and material goods needs to be distinguished from 'freedom to act' or an individual's choice set that enhances his or her capability.[8] The entitlement to income and commodities is a necessary but not a sufficient condition to enlarge one's choice set. Individual abilities to convert goods into capabilities will differ a great deal depending on one's natural and social environment, gender, age and access to health care, education, housing, employment and other resources.

An able-bodied individual in his or her mid-30s is likely to command greater resources, freedom to act and abilities than a teenager of say, 15, who is dependent on his parents for financial means, moral support and guidance, and a choice set. Capabilities depend only partly on individual characteristics; they also depend on resources and opportunities offered by families and households, social organizations, the government and society at large. Within households, the well-being of children depends on the income of others – parents, uncles and other income-earning family members (see Gore, 1993).

We discuss some of these distinctive features of children's poverty in Chapters 4 and 5. These features constitute qualitatively different kinds of poverty than the poverty of adults. Thus, it is not evident that one can simply extend the capability approach developed on the basis of adult poverty to child poverty generally and specifically to the poverty of immigrant children. Is the case of poor children in fact different enough from that of poor adults to make the capability approach less applicable? On the evidence adduced in subsequent chapters, we believe it is (however, see Sen, 1982, and Nussbaum and Sen, 1993).

Children are different from adults in several fundamental ways, for example, in cognitive ability and comprehension (see Ben-Arieh, 2006, pp. 20–1). These differences may be partly age-specific within the different phases of childhood. The younger the children, the less independent they are of their parents. Still, many of these differences remain distinctive of childhood as a whole.

It is true that considering a child's well-being independently of that of his or her parents may not always be appropriate. A child is not responsible for all of his or her actions. And the onus for exploiting his or her capability potential is less on the child and more on the external agents (for example, parents and governmental and non-governmental welfare agencies) who may have to be responsible for his or her well-being. Most children are generally not mature enough to judge for themselves (that is, they lack capabilities) what is good or bad for them and what sort of life they value most. A child's capability potential will remain latent until it is exploited consciously through physical and mental development in a healthy environment.

As we discussed above, parents take decisions within households, which concern their children. These decisions are likely to influence children's capability development besides hereditary factors and others, such as parents' education. The decisions may relate to the generation of income and its distribution within the household, consumption, savings, leisure and allocation of time to children. Other parental choices relate to type of lodgings to live in, their location (type of neighbourhood), the size of family (number of children to have) and so on. Along with income, all these factors will influence children's educational and professional attainment as we discuss in Chapters 4 to 6.

Parents and older siblings are primary role models for young children. Their behaviour, values and educational expectations can directly affect the 'cognitive and social-psychological development of children'. The relationship between the two parents (harmonious or confrontational) and separation and divorce would also affect the development of a child depending on his or her age. This situation combined with their employment status can create 'emotional uncertainties' that may hinder the normal development of a child. The development of capability of children who grow up in poverty is likely to be hindered. Other things being equal, children from low-income families with low education of parents are likely to be under-achievers in school and the job market (Haveman and Wolfe, 1995, pp. 1835–7).

Haveman and Wolfe (*ibid.*, p.1836) note the following three choices affecting children's capability development: (i) choices made by society (government), (ii) those made by parents regarding investment in children and (iii) those made by children themselves 'given the investments in and opportunities available to them'.

## Capacities vs capabilities

We need to distinguish between 'capacities' and 'capabilities'. The capacities of an agent 'are not to be identified with their individual capacities or with their aggregate power ... agents and agencies must dispose not only of capacities which they could deploy if circumstances were favourable, but of capabilities, that is to say, of *specific, effectively resourced capacities which they can deploy in actual circumstances*. Capabilities are to capacities or abilities as effective demand is to demand: it is the specific capabilities of agents and agencies in specific situations, rather than their abstract capacities or their aggregate power, that are relevant to determining which obligations of justice they can hold and discharge – and which they will be unable to discharge' (O'Neill, 2001, p. 197).

An example illustrates this crucial difference between abstract capacities and concrete capabilities. Thus,

> a person may have various capacities or abilities to act. For example, a person may have the capacity to work as an agricultural labourer or an ability to organize family resources to last from harvest to harvest; a development agency may have the capacity to distribute resources to the needy in a given area. However, when a social and economic structure provides no work for agricultural labourers or no resources for a given family to subsist on or for an agency to distribute, these capacities lie barren. (*Ibid.*)

## An assessment

In the light of the above discussion, we now offer a brief assessment of Sen's capability approach in more detail. Our objective is to examine its usefulness for studying immigrant child poverty.

First, we need to note a distinction between a person's entitlements, say his/her 'command over commodities', and a person's capacities, say his/her ability to realize 'valuable functionings' (Vizard, 2006, pp. 108–9). The point of this distinction is that the relation between someone's control over certain resources and his or her capacity to convert those resources into things of value depends on certain general constraints. Among these constraints are such matters as environment, gender, body-type, age and so on. In the case of children, these constraints are magnified. This distinction helps us see better how Sen challenged several central behavioural assumptions behind the classic utilitarian methodologies aimed at the maximization of utilities.

Sen's basic objections are summarized below:

> First, the behavioural assumptions relating to the choice of a maximal element in a given set of alternatives may be inappropriate. An individual may not seek to maximize personal well-being[,] and individual choice may be motivated by broader objectives (for example, other people's well-being) and other objectives (including obligations and commitments to others). Secondly, personal well-being may not be independent of freedom of the range and adequacy of choices

> available. If autonomy and freedom of choice affect personal well-being, then the possibility of choice and the number of alternatives in a set (intrinsic valuation of the freedom to choose) as well as, perhaps, the range (or diversity) and the quality (or adequacy) of these alternatives also affect personal well-being. (*Ibid.*, p. 110)

In short, there are two different kinds of basic constraints on freedom of choice for persons.

The freedom at issue here comprises mainly two elements. The first element has to do with a person's freedom to take decisions autonomously, that is, by oneself independently of interference by others or by institutions. Sen calls this element 'the process aspect of freedom'. The second element has to do with whether or not a person enjoys sufficient occasions for taking such autonomous decisions, that is, given the nature of those occasions and their relations to the person's goals and objectives. Sen calls this element 'the opportunity aspect of freedom' (*ibid.*, pp. 67–8).

For each of the two types of freedom of choice a person may be said to enjoy, there is a typical kind of constraint on that freedom. In the case of the constraints on process freedom, Sen proposes the idea of a 'chooser dependence'. And in the case of those on opportunity freedom he suggests the idea of a 'menu dependence'. When we take freedom, then, as an essential part of a person's well-being, it follows that persons may lack well-being as a function both of their chooser dependence, the constraints on their process freedom, and their menu dependence, the constraints on their opportunity freedom.

We now briefly assess the possible fruitfulness of Sen's capability approach for studying the particular kinds of poverty experienced by poor immigrant children. We appreciate much of the comprehensiveness, power and value of Sen's capability approach. We also appreciate the relevance to our study of several of its elements, such as a distinction between abstract capacities and concrete capabilities. Still, we find that the main difficulty in applying the capability approach to poor immigrant children does not lie, as in Rawls, either in undue abstraction or in assigning too central an importance to the developed moral powers of citizens. Instead, the difficulty lies with Sen's insistence on a very high level of rationality in agent freedoms.

Ryan (2003, p. 44) notes:

> Sen's guiding principle is that we have to think about human beings in ways that do justice to the complexity of their values and beliefs.

If they in fact guide their conduct by high principle, a passion for justice or freedom, simple compassion for the badly off, or whatever else, there is nothing to be said for theories that represent "rationality" as the single-minded pursuit of self-interest defined in the narrowest possible terms.

Granted that Sen's broader view of rationality is a substantial improvement on traditional interpretation of rationality in economic analyses, it still remains too idealistic for a better understanding of child poverty (Harsanyi, 1977). How could poor immigrant children be expected to subject the quite minimal choices they actually have to 'reasoned scrutiny'? Their peculiar and especially debilitating species of poverty (given their age) has mired them all too often in situations where few if any are able to learn to reason about anything whatsoever (Krugman, 2008).

As our detailed discussion of the situations of poor immigrant children in Switzerland and France (Chapters 4 and 5) shows, many of those children enjoy virtually no freedom of choice. Whatever freedom they may have is much more a freedom to receive something from others than a freedom from constraints on doing something for themselves.

We believe that a more pertinent analysis of their situation is not in terms of freedom of choice or freedom *tout court*. The freedom of poor (immigrant) children is derived from that of their parents. Consequently, it largely depends on the willingness of how much freedom their parents allow them.

True, such immigrant children may indeed lack both concrete capabilities and abstract capacities. We believe that much more to the point than 'process freedom' and 'opportunity freedom' and 'rationality' is to understand better two basic issues. The first is understanding how individuals and societies in affluent countries are to assume their social, political and moral responsibilities in assisting poor immigrant children in incorporating fully their rights and dignity as children and persons (Brink, 1993). And the second is understanding just how such individuals and societies are to respond to the specific demands of social justice in properly integrating such children into their societies (Schnapper, 2007).

Thus, we believe that elucidating the situation of such children's ill-being is better fostered by analyzing not what they lack in terms of personal freedoms to choose but what others may offer them in terms of dignity, justice and the common good.

We now turn to a brief discussion of such basic issues as immigrant children's rights and the demands of social justice.

## Children's rights and social justice

Our discussion has highlighted at least three essential aspects of the conditions affecting immigrant children. The first has to do with injustices, the second with lack of capabilities, and the last with breaches of human rights. The extension of human rights to children accepts the notion that they are as much human beings as are adults. Hence children deserve the same respect as adults and are equally endowed with the same basic human dignity. This last aspect is what concerns us in this section.

Reflection on human rights has a long history (Hunt, 2007). However, it was little more than 60 years ago, in 1948, that the United Nations General Assembly approved the Universal Declaration on Human Rights, historically the first such truly universal convention. Further, on 16 December 1966, the General Assembly approved two supplementary treaties as additions to the 1948 Declaration.

### The UN Convention on the Rights of the Child

The United Nations adopted the more specific Convention on the Rights of the Child on 20 November 1989 in the General Assembly Resolution 44/25. This Convention came into force in September 1990.[9] (192 states ratified the Convention. The only two countries failing to do so were Somalia and the USA.)

The Convention defines 'children' as, generally, all persons from their ages of birth up to their 18th birthday but not above. In this book, while we generally define children as those below 18, we also consider youth (18 to 24) who are either studying or working. We generally exclude from our analysis the situations of children up to their fifth birthday. Among other advantages, this restriction allows us to set aside the complicated issues concerning such matters as birth control policies, child mortality, early school training and so on, which, while relevant and indeed important matters, are somewhat peripheral to our central theme concerning the poverty of immigrant children and youth.

Not all legal systems use the same judicial category for describing children. In some legal systems a 16-year-old may be properly categorized in certain legal contexts as a 'minor' and thereby may qualify for reduced sentencing if convicted of a crime. In other systems, however, only a juvenile 14 years or younger can qualify for the status of 'minor' (Bouchet-Saulnier, 2006, pp. 230–1). Moreover, the scope for the legal uses of the term 'minor' continues to change depending on political circumstances. For example, in France the previous legal impunity of some very violent adolescents is now being challenged.

Despite differences in the judicial treatment of children, the Convention has nonetheless reinforced the widespread conviction that proper protection and promotion of children's freedoms and rights require external intervention. Such protection and promotion cannot be left entirely to the quite limited autonomy, if any, of the children themselves.

The Convention covers both the material and non-material well-being of children. It calls upon member states to provide children with a decent standard of living, education, health and housing. It also calls upon them to pay particular attention to disadvantaged and disabled children.

We present below a summary of the main articles that we believe are particularly relevant to the condition of poor immigrant children discussed in later chapters (Dekeuwer-Défossez, 2006). Many of these articles evidently incorporate fundamental freedoms and rights from the general 1968 Convention on Human Rights.

Under the material aspects of children's well-being, the Convention holds that:

1. 'State Parties', that is, those states that have ratified the Convention, should take appropriate measures to protect the child 'against all forms of discrimination or punishment on the basis of the status, activities, expressed opinions, or beliefs of the child's parents, legal guardians, or family members' (Article 2).
2. 'Applications by a child or his or her parents to enter or leave a State Party for the purpose of family reunification shall be dealt with by States Parties in a positive, humane and expeditious manner' (Article 10).
3. States 'shall take measures to combat the illicit transfer and non-return of children abroad' (Article 11).
4. States should 'ensure the provision of necessary medical assistance and health care to all children with emphasis on the development of primary health care' (Article 24).
5. States should 'recognize the right of every child to a standard of living adequate for the child's physical, mental, spiritual, moral and social development' and 'in case of need provide material assistance and support programmes, particularly with regard to nutrition, clothing and housing' (Article 27).
6. States should 'recognize the right of the child to education' and to achieve this right 'to make primary education compulsory and available free to all' (Article 28).

Under the non-material aspects of children's well-being, the Convention holds that:

 7. States should undertake to respect the right of the child to preserve his or her identity (Article 8).
 8. States should respect the right of the child 'to maintain personal relations and direct contact with both parents on a regular basis' (Articles 9 and 10).
 9. Those States that have ethnic, religious or linguistic minorities should ensure that minority children are not denied the right 'to enjoy his or her culture, to profess and practice his or her own religion, or to use his or her own language' (Article 30).
10. The States should ensure that 'every child deprived of liberty shall be treated with humanity and respect for the inherent dignity of the human person' (Article 37).

The UNICEF Innocenti Research Centre (2004) has studied the impact of the implementation of the Convention by the UN member states. The study notes that the impact has been favourable in respect of the following: introduction of legal reforms which will act as a catalyst for cultural changes concerning the role of children in family and society; prohibition of the recruitment of children under 18 into armed conflicts; protection of children against all forms of violence, abuse and neglect; and children's enjoyment of the right to health, education and social services. For example, the UNICEF Innocenti Research Centre (*ibid.*, p. 5) cites the Italian Charter on the Rights of secondary school students adopted by a Presidential Decree in May 1998 which states that 'each person, with equal dignity and in a diversity of roles, works to guarantee a training in citizenship, the realization of right to study, the development of each child's potential and the overcoming of situations of disadvantage'. It also notes that, 'in 2000 Germany reformed its Civil Code, recognizing children's right to a non-violent upbringing and prohibiting corporal punishment, psychological injuries and other humiliating measures' (*ibid.*, p. 6).

However, despite the adoption of the Convention on child rights and progress in its implementation noted above, we show that even many developed countries do not necessarily guarantee the implementation of these rights, not to speak of developing ones. For example, increasing restrictions in both Switzerland and France on the reunification of children with their parents and other family members (see Chapters 4 to 6) do not appear to be in conformity with the relevant articles of the Convention.

As we discuss in Chapter 4, in Switzerland recent referendums on young immigrants and asylum-seekers have resulted in laws that discriminate against non-European children as compared to those from within Europe. The new law concerning asylum-seekers is inhumane in the sense that it does not exempt children under 15 from detention.

Moreover, as we discuss in Chapter 5, recent changes (introduced in 2007) in French immigration laws have drastically reduced the number of children eligible for legal entry into France on the grounds of family reunification (Chapter 7 and van Eeckhout, 2007). Furthermore, these new laws also include a number of measures that increase the ease with which poor immigrant children who are in France illegally may be expelled, with or without their parents. These new laws remain to be tested in the courts.

## The European Social Charter

Even before the adoption of the UN Convention on the Rights of the Child discussed above, in 1961 the Council of Europe adopted a European Social Charter, which was revised in 1996. In its Preamble, it noted that 'the enjoyment of social rights should be secured without discrimination on grounds of race, colour, sex, religion, political opinion, national extraction or social origin'. The body of the Social Charter has 19 articles dealing with economic and social rights of people and workers. One such Article (no. 7) is on the 'Right of children and young persons to protection'. The bulk of the article covers such issues as minimum age of admission to employment, conditions of work and education. The following clauses are relevant to the issues concerning (immigrant) children discussed in this book:

(i) 'to provide that persons who are still subject to compulsory education shall not be employed in such work as would deprive them of the full benefit of their education'.
(ii) 'to provide that the minimum age of admission to employment shall be 15 years, subject to exceptions for children employed in prescribed light work without harm to their health, morals or education'.
(iii) 'to recognise the right of young workers and apprentices to a fair wage or other appropriate allowances'.
(iv) 'to ensure special protection against physical and moral dangers to which children and young persons are exposed, and particularly against those resulting directly or indirectly from their work'.

Article 19 of the European Social Charter deals with the 'right of migrant workers and their families to protection and assistance'. The subjects covered in the Article include the provision of appropriate services for health, medical attention and good hygienic conditions, the reunion of the family of a foreign worker, and equally favourable treatment to him or her in respect of remuneration and other employment and working conditions.


**Children and social justice**

Before concluding this chapter, we need to specify our approach to the situations of poor immigrant children in affluent European countries. We do not offer a theory of social justice. Nor do we try to offer anything like comprehensive accounts of human well-being such as those discussed above. However, we do write in this book from a distinctive perspective, which is described below.

We recall briefly Max Weber's classical sociological distinction among three kinds of inequality: economic, political and social inequality. If we accept that there are only these three basic levels in which human societies are stratified, then, whatever inequalities a society might exhibit, we must basically categorize them accordingly (Runciman, 1966, p. 37). On this classical account all inequalities, including those affecting poor immigrant children in affluent European countries, are either economic, or political, or social. But should we accept this tripartite distinction?

Historically, many scholars were quick to challenge such an overly general basic trichotomy. Thus, many Marxist sociologists proposed that Weber's own categories of class, status and power inequalities should be used to replace his initial categories of economic, political and social inequalities (Weber, 1976, pp. 177–9). Other sociologists of today such as Giddens, Touraine, Bourdieu and Luhmann proposed other categories altogether (Corcuff, 2007).

If we stay with the Marxist set of Weber's categories for now, we see that Weber considers class inequalities as those that derive from a person's situation in the production, distribution and exchange processes with respect to other persons involved in the same processes. Thus, class inequalities comprise such matters as income differences among persons in different occupations, opportunity differences with respect to professional advancement, retirement plans, employment security, and social relationships deriving from one's profession.

Status inequalities are closely related to class inequalities. However, unlike class inequalities status inequalities derive not from a person's situation. Rather they derive from how and where that person's society places his or her prestige in a prestige ranking. Thus, even though belonging to the same class as other persons, some persons may suffer from lower status, that is, they may belong to the same professional class as other persons, but belong to different status groups 'according to social origin or secondary education or manner of speech' or way of life or social contacts (Runciman, 1966, p. 38).[10]

Power inequalities, like those of both class and status, are interrelated with the other two basic kinds of inequality. Nonetheless, these inequalities also differ importantly from the other inequalities. They are often visible in judicial situations. Because of the relatively different economic levels of the jurisdictions in which courts are located, many poor persons brought to trial wind up not having fair access to the same levels of judicial attention and competence.

We need to recognize that the above three-part classical sociological division among basic kinds of inequalities depends mainly on the assumption that people 'can be collectively ranked in any one, or all, of the three dimensions of social inequality' (*ibid.*, p. 43). However, with respect to our central theme such rankings are most often inapplicable to poor immigrant children. Even in the case of the poor immigrant parents of such children, such rankings are applicable only with increasing difficulty. In both such cases the classical sociological triads are intrinsically problematic (Ringer, 2004, pp. 225–30).

Thus, inequalities facing poor immigrant parents are relatively easy to specify as power inequalities. But the specific inequalities that their poor children face are of a different kind altogether. These inequalities depend far more on their condition as children than on their condition as children of poor immigrant parents.

Continuing to use classical sociological categories for describing the nature of the social injustices faced by immigrant children does not prove helpful. Hence, we rely more on recent sociological notions such as 'action' and 'collective action', 'convention', 'situation' and so on (see Ogien and Quéré, 2005), as well as on standard philosophical terms in English (see Blackburn, 2005b; Honderich, 2005). Thus, we try to understand these social injustices in less traditional terms than those of either the overly general triad of economic, social and political inequality or of the overly problematic triad of class, status and power. We interpret the situation of these children as that of social injustice that continues to violate their rights, their integrity and their dignity both as human beings and as children.

# 2
# Immigrant Child Poverty in Europe

Why should one be concerned with child poverty rather than with poverty in general? After all, child poverty is derived from poverty of families and heads of households in which poor children live. But highlighting children is important as they are the future of nations. Moreover, as we discussed in Chapter 1, it is unfair and unacceptable to leave child poverty unaddressed properly in the midst of overall prosperity in Europe.

The economic and social conditions of poor and destitute children in Europe has become worse. In 17 out of 24 OECD countries their situation worsened during the past two decades (UNICEF Innocenti Research Centre, 2005). The highest rates of absolute and relative poverty are found in such countries as the United Kingdom (UK), whose income levels are high. Thus there is no direct and positive correlation between child poverty and the wealth of a nation.

The European Commission is currently (2008) busy working out a strategy for children and development. But this strategy is for poor children in developing countries, not those in Europe's own backyard. The latter is not the responsibility of the Commission (at least, so it would claim) but that of the national governments in Europe, which are much richer than those of the poor developing countries. There is no doubt that poor children in rich countries enjoy better incomes and opportunities (level of capability *à la* Sen, discussed in Chapter 1) than their opposite numbers in poor countries.[1]

In the following pages, we first provide information on the numbers and proportions of immigrants and their children. We then consider their poverty situation in terms of income and non-income aspects. The latter embrace access to education, health care and housing as well as human rights and dignity. The final section discusses the EU policy on child poverty and explores whether any special attention is paid to alleviate poverty among immigrant children.

## Adult immigrants and children in Europe

The numbers of immigrants in Western Europe are far greater than those in Eastern Europe (see Table 2.1). Between 1990 and 2004, their number continued to rise in Germany (which has the highest figures in each of the intervening years) followed by France and the UK. In Eastern Europe, Hungary and Poland are the main countries of immigration. However, compared to Western Europe this region is an example more of out-migration than in-migration.

In the EU-25 during 1960–2004, net migration led to an increase of 20 million people. However, the experience of EU-15 was different. There

*Table 2.1* Number of immigrants (non-nationals) in Europe over time (1990–2004) (thousands)

| Country | Year | | | | |
|---|---|---|---|---|---|
| | 1990 | 1995 | 2000 | 2003 | 2004 |
| *Western Europe* | | | | | |
| Denmark | 151 | 197 | 259 | 265 | 271 |
| Finland | 21 | 62 | 88 | 104 | 107 |
| Norway | – | – | – | 198 | 205 |
| Sweden | 456 | 537 | 487 | 474 | 476 |
| Switzerland | – | – | – | 1,485 | 1,501 |
| France | 3,597 | – | 3,263 | – | – |
| Belgium | 881 | 922 | 897 | 850 | 860 |
| Luxembourg | 109 | 133 | 159 | – | 174 |
| Netherlands | 642 | 757 | 652 | 700 | 702 |
| Germany | 4,846 | 7,118 | 7,336 | 7,348 | 7,342 |
| Austria | 434 | 677 | 699 | 709 | 765 |
| Spain | 398 | 461 | 924 | 2,673 | 2,772 |
| United Kingdom | 2,416 | – | 2,460 | 2,760 | 2,941 |
| Ireland | 81 | 96 | 127 | 215 | 215 |
| Italy | – | 685 | 1,271 | – | 1,990 |
| *Eastern Europe* | | | | | |
| Slovakia | – | – | – | – | 30 |
| Poland | – | – | – | 700** | – |
| Hungary | – | 138 | 153 | 116 | 130 |
| Czech Republic | – | – | 239 | 179 | 195 |

*Source*: EUROSTAT (2006). *-2003. **-2002.

was a positive net migration into these countries, resulting in a nearly 22 million increase in population (EUROSTAT, 2006). These figures do not include undocumented or illegal immigration into the EU, which can be substantial depending on the country.

In the EU and Europe in general, a renewed interest in international migration is explained by an increase in the number of asylum-seekers in the wake of political and social strife in the former Yugoslavia. In the EU-25 nearly 6 million persons applied for asylum during 1990–2004. The bulk of applications were made in the EU-15. The distribution of asylum-seekers across Western Europe is quite uneven. The share in Germany fell from 55 per cent during 1990–4 to 18 per cent during 2000–4, whereas the shares of France and the UK increased significantly. As we shall discuss in Chapters 4 and 5, the number of asylum-seekers has declined from 2004 onwards in both France and Switzerland.

A significant proportion of young immigrants in Europe are in the age groups 15–19 and 20–4 (see Table 2.2), that is, youth in educational institutions or in the labour market. This is true particularly in Germany (1,072,000), Poland (108,000), Spain (428,000) and Switzerland (187,000). Therefore, in Europe the issues of education and employment of immigrant youth have become particularly important.

## Poverty incidence among immigrants and children

### The poverty concept

Poverty is defined and measured in different ways (see Bhalla and Qiu, 2006; Kehrli and Knöpfel, 2007; UNICEF Innocenti Research Centre, 2005). This is partly because poverty is a multi-dimensional concept. People with different socio-economic and cultural backgrounds and value judgements can view it quite differently. However, a clear and common understanding of the concept is essential for determining the magnitude of poverty on a comparable cross-country basis. But even when a suitable definition of poverty is found, its measurement may remain problematic. It is not our intention to go into the measurement and methodological problems here, especially as several studies on the subject exist (for example, see Bradbury, Jenkins and Micklewright, 2001b; Callan and Nolan, 1991).

Poverty is generally defined in terms of a 'poverty line' (a low-income threshold) below which an individual, parent, child or a household would be considered 'poor'. A child is considered poor if he or she belongs to a household or parents who are below the 'poverty' line. The underlying premise of the above definition is that income and standard

*Table 2.2* Immigrant children and youth in Europe (1 January 2004) (thousands)

| Country | 0–4 | 5–9 | 10–14 | 15–19 | 20–4 | Total no. of children and youth | Total no. of immigrants |
|---|---|---|---|---|---|---|---|
| *Western Europe* | | | | | | | |
| Denmark | 18.2 | 18.5 | 18.2 | 17.1 | 23.9 | 95.9 | 271 |
| | (19.0) | (19.3) | (19.0) | (17.8) | (24.9) | (100.0) | |
| Finland | 6.1 | 6.0 | 6.3 | 6.9 | 8.2 | 33.5 | 107 |
| | (18.2) | (17.9) | (18.8) | (20.6) | (24.5) | (100.0) | |
| Norway | 12.7 | 11.7 | 11.2 | 11.2 | 17.3 | 64.1 | 205 |
| | (19.8) | (18.2) | (17.5) | (17.5) | (27.0) | (100.0) | |
| Sweden | 23.0 | 24.7 | 26.5 | 24.7 | 34.5 | 133.4 | 476 |
| | (17.2) | (18.5) | (19.9) | (18.5) | (25.9) | (100.0) | |
| Switzerland | 95.5 | 95.3 | 93.1 | 84.1 | 102.8 | 470.8 | 1,501 |
| | (20.3) | (20.2) | (19.8) | (17.9) | (21.8) | (100.0) | |
| France | – | – | – | – | – | – | – |
| Belgium | – | – | – | – | – | – | 860 |
| Luxembourg | 16.5 | 12.4 | 10.8 | 9.7 | 10.7 | 60.1 | 174 |
| | (27.4) | (20.6) | (18.0) | (16.1) | (17.8) | (100.0) | |
| Netherlands | 37.3 | 36.7 | 39.0 | 48.9 | 70.1 | 232.0 | 702 |
| | (16.1) | (15.8) | (16.8) | (21.1) | (30.2) | (100.0) | |
| Germany | 228.7 | 421.2 | 433.4 | 427.7 | 644.6 | 2,155.6 | 7,342 |
| | (10.6) | (19.6) | (20.1) | (19.8) | (29.9) | (100.0) | |
| Austria | 46.6 | 47.9 | 44.1 | 46.3 | 67.2 | 252.1 | 765 |
| | (18.5) | (19.0) | (17.4) | (18.4) | (26.7) | (100.0) | |
| Spain | 148.7 | 141.7 | 137.8 | 142.4 | 285.2 | 855.8 | 2,772 |
| | (17.4) | (16.5) | (16.2) | (16.6) | (33.3) | (100.0) | |
| United Kingdom | 113.6 | 119.9 | 134.4 | 94.7 | 287.0 | 749.6 | 2,941 |
| | (15.1) | (16.1) | (17.9) | (12.6) | (38.3) | (100.0) | |
| Ireland | – | – | – | – | – | – | 215 |
| Italy | 106.9 | 76.7 | 64.3 | 63.9 | 99.4 | 411.2 | 1,990 |
| | (26.0) | (18.6) | (15.6) | (15.5) | (24.2) | (100.0) | |
| *Eastern Europe* | | | | | | | |
| Slovakia | 0.4 | 0.4 | 0.4 | 1.0 | 2.5 | 4.7 | 30 |
| | (8.5) | (8.5) | (8.5) | (21.3) | (53.2) | (100.0) | |
| Poland | 27.6 | 28.8 | 34.4 | 49.4 | 59.1 | 199.3 | 700* |
| | (13.8) | (14.4) | (17.3) | (24.8) | (29.7) | (100.0) | |
| Hungary | 3.1 | 4.2 | 4.8 | 6.8 | 11.4 | 30.3 | 130 |
| | (10.2) | (13.9) | (15.9) | (22.4) | (37.6) | (100.0) | |
| Czech Republic | 3.9 | 6.2 | 7.3 | 7.2 | 15.0 | 39.6 | 195 |
| | (9.8) | (15.6) | (18.4) | (18.2) | (37.9) | (100.0) | |

*Note*: Figures in brackets are percentages of the total number of children.
*Source*: EUROSTAT (2006). *-2003.

of living of individuals and households are persistently below a certain level required physically for sustaining human life according to some accepted norms. Such a definition can be interpreted in two ways. First, it may mean that the resources over which some people enjoy command are inadequate to enable them to be alive. The second interpretation may refer to a situation in which resources or means are not sufficient to allow an individual or household concerned to lead a life that is considered 'decent' in a given society. The first interpretation refers to so-called 'absolute' poverty and the second to 'relative' poverty. Sen's concept of poverty (discussed in Chapter 1) in terms of a failure of some people to enjoy a certain minimum of 'capabilities' is an absolute concept in the sense that people's deprivations are judged absolutely, not simply in comparison with deprivations of others.

In this and subsequent chapters we discuss immigrant child poverty in three different ways. First, poverty is defined as income or monetary poverty in terms of being below a 'poverty' line. At the European Union (EU) level, this income threshold is 60 per cent of the median income. However, in such member countries as France the threshold of 50 per cent of the median income is adopted. The French statistical agencies have also started estimating poverty as below 60 per cent income threshold to make national estimates comparable to those of the EU (see Chapter 5).

However, the above 'poverty line' measure is open to question, especially regarding child poverty. The definition equates children with adults (parents). Yet as we noted in Chapter 1 the particular characteristics of children set them apart. Furthermore, it assumes equal distribution of resources of households among different members and children. In practice, there will be altruistic and non-altruistic households. In the former, children are likely to suffer from less poverty than their parents. However, a reverse situation may obtain in non-altruistic households.

Second, immigrant child poverty is defined in terms of a certain number of physical deprivations (the concepts of deprivation and destitution are discussed in Chapter 1). There are some critical levels of consumption of goods and services (mainly food, clothing and shelter) below which children will persistently suffer. Apart from the critical levels, it is also considered desirable for children to enjoy some holidays and leisure activities besides having friends over for social interaction.

Third, immigrant child poverty is defined in non-income terms such as access to health, education, employment and housing. Clearly income and non-income aspects of poverty are interrelated. Low incomes of parents often prevent children from enjoying access to various goods and services. Children from poorer households tend to go to low-standard schools, suffer from higher drop-out rates and often find difficulties in joining the labour market. Low incomes of parents may also prevent them from gaining access to health services and to decent housing (see Chapters 4 to 6).

Fourth, child poverty is defined in broader terms to include material (food, clothing, housing and so on) as well as non-material or social deprivation (for example, family, recreational and educational). The broader approach to poverty, popular at the EU-level, includes failures in social interaction, a lack of public participation (see Chapter 7) and violation of children's rights discussed in Chapter 1. The approach to deprivation of immigrant children is designed in part to study their exclusion from social, human and political rights (see Bhalla and Lapeyre, 2004; Townsend, 1979). In Western European countries, a shift in thinking from poverty to social exclusion resulted from a growing concern with the structural and multi-dimensional processes by which individuals are actually excluded from 'the social exchanges, practices and rights which are an intrinsic part of social and economic integration' (European Commission, 1989, p. 43).

Other relevant aspects of child poverty are its static and dynamic dimensions. For example, immigrant children may be poor in a *static* sense of being poor in a given time period. They may suffer from 'transitory' poverty moving into and out of it from time to time, or from 'persistent' poverty over long periods of time. They may grow from being poor children to being poor adults. However, immigrant children are generally more vulnerable and may suffer more from persistent poverty than transitory poverty, unlike native children. Bradbury, Jenkins and Micklewright (2001a, p. 283) show wide variations in the persistence of poverty: 'in Britain and the USA over 15 per cent of children were poor for two consecutive years, and nearly 10 per cent or more were poor for five years out of five...in Hungary and Germany only about 4 per cent were poor even two consecutive years and just 2 per cent of children were poor for five straight years'. Could the much higher rates for the UK and the USA be due to a much higher proportion of immigrant children in these two countries? It is not possible to answer this question since children are not separated by nationality or ethnic origin. In Europe, several studies also exist on the intergenerational transmission of poverty, which are discussed below.

*Table 2.3*   Poverty incidence among immigrants and non-immigrants in selected European countries

| Country | Year | Poverty ratio: immigrant/ non-immigrant | Poverty incidence among households in receipt of unemployment benefits (%) | | |
|---|---|---|---|---|---|
| | | | Immigrants | Non-immigrants | Ratio: immigrant/ non-immigrant |
| Norway | 2000 | 2.6 | 3.7 | 3.6 | 1.02 |
| Germany | 2000 | 2.2 | 20.6 | 9.7 | 2.1 |
| United Kingdom | 1999 | 2.1 | 29.3 | 29.9 | 0.98 |
| Sweden | 2000 | 1.9 | 8.3 | 4.7 | 1.8 |

*Source*: Morissens (2006), pp. 180, 185. Based on Luxembourg Income Study (LIS).

## Evidence on immigrant child poverty

As discussed in Chapter 1, immigrant child poverty is really derived from the poverty situation of children's parents. It is therefore appropriate to start our discussion of child poverty with an account of poverty among immigrant parents compared to non-immigrants.

Several studies (for example, Platt, 2002; Blume *et al.*, 2003; Morrisens, 2006) have shown that poverty risk is much greater among immigrants than non-immigrants in most countries in Europe. Immigrant poverty rate is the lowest in Sweden (about 10 per cent) and the highest in the UK (over 21 per cent). Germany and Norway have similar immigrant poverty rates (about 15 per cent). The poverty gap between immigrants and non-immigrants is widest in Norway, followed by Germany and the United Kingdom. It is the narrowest in Sweden (see Table 2.3). In Norway, immigrants are almost three times more likely to be poor than non-immigrants as measured by poverty ratios. Poverty can be caused, *inter alia*, by the lack of employment and long periods of persistent unemployment. However, unemployment benefits may reduce the incidence of poverty. In Table 2.3 we show how much poverty is reduced if unemployment benefits are included. Poverty incidence with unemployment benefits is about the same for immigrant and non-immigrant households in Norway, but not in other European countries. The ranking of the four European countries in the table changes when account is taken of these benefits. Now Germany ranks at the top instead of Norway.

Some studies indicate poverty gaps also within immigrant groups. For example, a disaggregated study by Berthoud (1998) shows that the first- and second-generation Indian immigrants to the UK have the same average market income as the white non-migrants. Average incomes are particularly low for immigrants from Bangladesh and Pakistan, which are the worst groups. Poverty rates for Indian and Chinese households were similar to those for the white population. Berthoud (1998, p. 47) concludes that 'these differences between the minority groups may be at least as important as any common factors which distinguish them all from the white majority'. In West Germany the average income for non-EU immigrants is about 70 per cent of that for the native-born German population (see Büchel and Frick, 2004).

The UNICEF Innocenti Research Centre (Florence) has underway a project on immigrant child poverty in eight industrialized countries, of which six are in Europe. It is working with eight country research teams in Australia, France, Germany, Italy, the Netherlands, Switzerland, the United Kingdom and the USA. The project is aimed at collecting relevant data from national censuses, population registers and surveys in order to undertake statistical analyses comparable across countries for both migrant and native families. It is concerned with such issues as health, education, cultural identity and social inclusion of immigrant children. Preliminary results show that immigrant children are more likely to follow vocational training than their native peers.

## Income poverty

There is little information on separate poverty rates for immigrant children in Western European countries. In Chapters 4 to 6 we provide whatever data we were able to collect on the poverty of immigrant and non-immigrant children in France and Switzerland. Information on these two countries suggests that generally immigrant children are much poorer than non-immigrant children in terms of both income and non-income criteria.

In the UK, Platt (2002, p. 1) notes that 'at the turn of the millennium nearly three-quarters of Bangladeshi children in the UK were living in families in the bottom fifth of the income distribution compared to a quarter of white children'. She further states: 'ethnic minority children experience excess poverty both compared to the rates in the poverty group as a whole and compared to children in the population as a whole' (*ibid.*, p. 59). The situation is particularly bad for Bangladeshi and Pakistani children: 90 per cent of these children fall into the bottom two-fifths of income distribution compared to 50 per cent for all children, and 73 per cent of these children live below the poverty line defined as 60 per cent of the median income. The corresponding ratios for other ethnic groups are: Caribbean, 40 per cent; Indian, 47 per cent; Black African, 63 per cent; and White, 29 per cent (*ibid.*, p. 60).

In Germany, Schluter (2001) compares child poverty in West and East Germany and among guest workers (immigrants). The study traces the child poverty situation from the early 1980s to the mid-1990s. It provides a dynamic picture of children (in the former East and West Germany as well as children of guest workers) entering and exiting poverty over a five-year period. More than one-sixth of all children in West Germany in the first half of the 1990s experienced poverty at least during one year out of the five-year period considered. Not surprisingly, child poverty was much higher in East Germany. An unusual conclusion of the study is that child poverty is not very different from that experienced by all persons in the population. The study concludes that 'children in guest worker households have a greater chance of being poor for at least one year in five than native West Germans do' (*ibid.*, p. 168). Children of guest workers have higher poverty rates, which may be partly due to higher unemployment rates among them.

In Spain, Cantó and Marcader-Prats (2001) study youth poverty of people from 18 to 29 years. Therefore, it is somewhat of a different nature from other studies discussed here which are concerned with children below 18 years. The Spanish study shows that youth poverty rates are relatively low because young people in Spain tend to stay at home with their parents who provide support (see below). Youth who leave home are much poorer than others who stay with parents. Families with employed young persons have a lower risk of poverty than those who have no employed youngster. On the one hand, dependence of young Spanish persons on their parents may reduce parents' economic well-being and that of their very young children. On the other hand, it may also raise their well-being since employed youth in low-income households act as a safety net.

Although there are few poverty estimates for immigrant children separately, a good number of quantitative estimates exist for both 'absolute' and 'relative' child poverty in Western European countries (17), Russia and Eastern Europe (5) and 'other developed countries' (5) (see Bradbury and Jäntti, 2001).[2] More recent estimates by the UNICEF Innocenti Research Centre (2005) show the highest child poverty rates in Italy, Ireland, Portugal, Spain and the UK. The ranking of countries does not change much whether one examines absolute or relative poverty estimates. However, in principle absolute poverty should decline with an increase in disposable incomes. But, as we discuss below, the overall level of development, which the per capita disposable income measures, is not the only determining factor.

In many cases (for example, Italy, the UK and the USA) there is no inverse correlation between per capita income and child poverty. First, while per capita incomes in these cases are high, so are child poverty rates. Second, there is greater child poverty in the USA, the wealthiest country, than in the worst cases among the European countries, namely, Italy, Ireland and the UK. Indeed, there may be some consolation for Europe in the fact that child poverty rates are as high if not higher in rich countries outside Europe, namely, Australia, New Zealand and the USA. Third, countries with the lowest child poverty rates (mainly Nordic countries and Luxembourg) are quite small (each with a population of less than 10 million) and have fairly high per capita incomes.

The European Commission (2008, pp. 18–19) shows that risk of child poverty has remained stable in France and Ireland, has increased in several countries such as Belgium, the Czech Republic, the Netherlands, Finland and Sweden, and has shown a declining trend in Austria, Hungary, Spain and the UK.

Why has child poverty increased in a number of OECD countries? The answer is to be found in a complex mixture of factors that are not necessarily monetary or economic. Incomes are an essential element but only one among many. Other factors may be the labour market situation (unemployment of parents), differences in social spending and income transfers to poor families (see below), demographic factors such as the age structure of heads of households, single or two-parent families (see below) in which the poor children live and government policies.

Bradbury and Jäntti (2001) come to a rather unexpected conclusion that single motherhood does not significantly explain variations in child poverty across countries, but government policy and social spending do. They decompose average incomes of the poorest fifth of children and find that cash transfers to poor families make an important contribution to the their well-being. Although this may well be true, we cannot downplay the importance of the single-parent factor. In order to examine this factor, in Table 2.4 we present Luxembourg Income Study (LIS) estimates for child poverty among two-parent and single-parent (single mother) families for six European countries: Ireland, Italy, Romania, Russia, Spain and the UK. The relative poverty rates for children in single-parent families are significantly higher in all the six countries. In some cases (for example, the UK) they are more than three times as high. In Romania and Russia, the single-parent child poverty rates are double those of two-parent families.

*Table 2.4*  Relative poverty among two-parent and single-parent families in selected European countries (%)

| Country | Year | All children | Two-parent families | Single mother families | % of children in single-parent families |
|---|---|---|---|---|---|
| Ireland | 1987 | 13.8 | 12.7 | 35.4 | 5.3 |
|  | 2000 | 17.2 | 11.8 | 52.7 | 13.5 |
| United | 1986 | 12.5 | 11.1 | 21.1 | 12.9 |
| Kingdom | 1999 | 15.3 | 9.9 | 33.8 | 21.7 |
| Spain | 1990 | 12.2 | 11.5 | 25.4 | 4.9 |
|  | 2000 | 16.1 | 14.7 | 32.8 | 6.9 |
| Italy | 1986 | 11.4 | 11.1 | 18.6 | 5.1 |
|  | 2000 | 16.6 | 16.5 | 19.2 | 4.9 |
| Russia | 1992 | 17.8 | 14.9 | 29.3 | 18.2 |
|  | 2000 | 22.2 | 20.6 | 32.9 | 14.5 |
| Romania | 1995 | 10.8 | 9.4 | 21.7 | 9.3 |
|  | 1997 | 10.0 | 8.8 | 17.4 | 10.0 |

*Note*: Figures represent poor children living in families with incomes less than 50 per cent of the median income (or below the poverty line).
*Source*: Luxembourg Income Study (LIS) database.

The share of children in single-parent families has increased significantly in Ireland (nearly three-fold), Spain, Romania and the UK. In the UK, between 1986 and 1999, the share increased from 13 per cent to nearly 22 per cent. Italy and Spain have rather low shares of children in single-parent families, which have declined in Italy but risen in Spain. Are low shares in these two countries to be explained by the Catholic religion, which may discourage divorce and family separations? Single-parent families and family separations are less common among immigrants, especially from the non-EU countries. For example, the shares of single-parent households among ex-Yugoslav, Portuguese and Turkish immigrants were similar and much lower than those for French, Swiss and Germans in Switzerland (Wanner, 2004, p.47; and Chapter 4). Therefore, the negative influence of this factor on immigrant child poverty is likely to be less serious.

Gabel and Kamerman (2006) use OECD time series data from 1980–2001 on social spending for 21 industrialized countries. They show that overall spending on social protection as a percentage of GDP was over 19 per cent in the 1980s and between 20 per cent and 23 per cent in the 1990s (*ibid.*, pp. 246–7). Trends in expenditure on families and children varied across countries: in 2001 Denmark spent 4 per cent of GDP on

*Table 2.5*   Impact of taxes and transfers on relative child poverty (%)

| Country | Child poverty before taxes and transfers | Child poverty after taxes and transfers |
|---|---|---|
| Denmark | 11.8 | 2.4 |
| Finland | 18.1 | 2.8 |
| Norway | 15.5 | 3.4 |
| Sweden | 18.0 | 4.2 |
| *Switzerland* | 7.8 | 6.8 |
| Czech Republic | 15.8 | 6.8 |
| *France* | 27.7 | 7.5 |
| Belgium | 16.7 | 7.7 |
| Hungary | 23.2 | 8.8 |
| Netherlands | 11.1 | 9.8 |
| Germany | 18.2 | 10.2 |
| Austria | 17.7 | 10.2 |
| Greece | 18.5 | 12.4 |
| Poland | 19.9 | 12.7 |
| United Kingdom | 25.4 | 15.4 |
| Portugal | 16.4 | 15.6 |
| Ireland | 24.9 | 15.7 |

*Notes*: 1. Data refer to household incomes. 2. Relative poverty is based on 50 per cent of the median income.
*Source*: UNICEF Innocenti Research Centre (2005).

family benefits whereas France spent 3 per cent, Germany 2 per cent and Switzerland 1 per cent. In 2001, family benefits as a percentage of public social expenditure varied from 2.5 per cent in Spain, 4 per cent in Italy, 5 per cent in Switzerland and 10 per cent in France and the UK. Low shares of family benefits in Italy and Spain may be owing to the fact that the family remains strong there as a provider of social safety net and protection to children. For example, a much larger number of children in these countries live with their parents even when they reach the age of 18. In Spain, in recent years the number of young people living with the parents has increased owing to high levels of youth unemployment and temporary employment.[3] As we discussed above, the incidence of poverty among young persons staying at home with parents is likely to be less severe than among those who leave home. This is because Spanish parents provide financial support to their children who may be students or young unemployed job-seekers (Cantó and Marcader-Prats, 2001, p. 216).[4]

The impact of taxes and transfers on relative child poverty is indicated in Table 2.5. With the exception of the Netherlands, Portugal and Switzerland, in all other countries, relative child poverty rates after taxes and transfers are considerably below those before transfers. This shows that income transfers have a positive cushioning effect on child poverty.

## Material deprivation

So far we have considered only income poverty of children, which is a rather restrictive view of poverty. While income is a *necessary* factor, it is not *sufficient* by itself. Thus non-income measures of child poverty need also to be examined. These may include per capita food consumption and calorie intake and other basic necessities to which poor immigrant children may not enjoy access. This takes us into the domain of such concepts as deprivation and destitution discussed in Chapter 1. Children whose basic needs are met but are living in low-income families are defined as 'poor'. Those whose basic needs are not met are defined as 'deprived'. Those children who permanently fail to achieve minimum basic needs considered critical for survival or 'decent living' may be considered 'destitute'.

Children in extreme poverty or destitution may be deprived of facilities for basic personal hygiene and health. Malnutrition may be the result of deficiency of proteins, vitamins and nutrients. Poor health can hinder proper schooling by encouraging truancy. Further, poor housing conditions and homelessness in which poor immigrant children live may also hinder them from receiving proper education (see Chapter 6 on the housing of immigrant children in France). Platt (2002, pp. 63–4) reports on housing deprivation in the UK by ethnic groups: Bangladeshis and their children live in the least desirable properties, and the other minority groups are not much better off. Parents may not be able to afford to send their children to school when they are desperately in need of food and access to health services to survive. The poorer the children the higher the illiteracy rate in the next generation and the greater the persistence of poverty, a vicious circle which cannot be broken by raising levels of income alone.

The Poverty and Social Exclusion (PSE) survey in the UK and Poverty and Social Exclusion in Northern Ireland (PSENI) define a child as deprived if he or she is lacking in one or more necessities because his or her parents did not have access to them. Table 2.6 shows that the degree of lack of access to goods and services considered 'essential' in the UK and Northern Ireland is quite significant.

*Table 2.6*   Children in the UK and Northern Ireland lacking basic necessities

| Essential item | PSE (1999) | | PSENI (2002/3) |
| --- | --- | --- | --- |
| | % lacking one item | % lacking two items | % who cannot afford item/ activity |
| *Food* | | | |
| Fresh fruit and vegetables daily | 5 | 9 | (4) |
| Three meals a day | (3) | (5) | 1 |
| Meat/fish/vegetables daily | 11 | 21 | (5) |
| *Clothing* | | | |
| New fitted shoes | 7 | 12 | (2) |
| Warm waterproof coat | 6 | 11 | (3) |
| School uniform | 6 | 18 | (1) |
| *Participation/activities* | | | |
| Celebrations | 10 | 20 | (1) |
| Hobby/leisure | 5 | (10) | 4 |
| Swimming once a month | 21 | 34 | – |
| Holiday away from home | 64 | 68 | 28 |
| Leisure equipment | 9 | 17 | 8 |
| Friends round for tea/snack | 11 | 21 | – |
| *Developmental* | | | |
| Books of own | 0 | (1) | (1) |
| Playgroup | (4) | (7) | (3) |
| Educational games | 12 | 21 | 5 |
| Toys | (1) | (3) | (0.4) |
| Construction toys | 10 | 19 | (4) |
| Bicycle (new/second hand) | 10 | 18 | 7 |
| *Environmental* | | | |
| Bed and bedding for self | (2) | (3) | (1) |
| Bedrooms for each child of different sex over age 10 | 10 | 10 | 7 |
| Bedroom carpet | (4) | (9) | – |
| Garden for play | 10 | 8 | 5 |

*Note*: Figures in brackets indicate less than 20 weighted cases.
–, indicates that these items were not on, or were different from the list of necessities in the PSE survey.
*Sources*: Gordon *et al.*(2000, p. 34); Hillyard *et al.* (2003, p. 30).

A pioneering study on the Republic of Ireland (Nolan, Maitre and Watson, 2001) examines poverty on the basis of non-monetary indicators of poverty, namely: (1) basic lifestyle deprivation (persons lacking food and clothing); (2) secondary lifestyle deprivation (lacking cars, telephones and holidays); and (3) housing deprivation (lacking indoor toilet, hot and running water). Although similar to the PSE and PSENI studies in terms of the basic concept, this Irish study undertakes a more sophisticated analysis to show how income and non-income measures of poverty can be correlated to obtain a more complete picture of child poverty. The direct non-monetary indicators offer a new dimension to social exclusion of children that may arise from lack of resources (whether current income or accumulated assets and financial savings).

Deprivation of basic goods and services noted in Table 2.6 may not necessarily mean severe income poverty. Even if parents of children have minimum incomes, they may not give the same priority to basic goods and services that an investigator of a survey does. Gordon *et al.* (2000, p.35) note that '45 per cent of children who lived in "income-poor" households (defined as below 60 per cent of the median household income) were not necessity-deprived' (according to the one-item threshold in Table 2.6). Of those who were deprived of two or more essential goods and services, '65 per cent were income poor but not necessities-deprived' (*ibid.*). Several studies (for example, Nolan and Whelan, 1996a, 1996b; Whelan, Layte and Maître, 2002) show a weak relationship between income poverty and deprivation of certain goods and services. This suggests that child deprivation is avoidable even in low-income families if parents take appropriate action and spend their incomes wisely. Clearly some needs are more basic than others and can be provided even at low incomes. However, if income poverty is severe and persistent it may not be possible for parents to protect their children from deprivation. Children living in low-income minority families in the UK, especially Bangladeshi children, belong to this group.

According to the 17 non-monetary indicators in the '1994 Living in Ireland survey', there is little housing deprivation. However, the rates of basic and secondary lifestyle deprivation in households with children are quite high. For example, over 50 per cent of the households with children could not afford holidays and 21 per cent could not afford a car. Twenty-six per cent of households could not afford having friends or family over for a drink. The levels of deprivation are influenced not only by current income but also by long-term income. The authors of the study conclude that 'sustained low income, as indicated by careful analysis of longitudinal data on income dynamics, is more likely to be a good indicator of need' (p. 212). However, one of the limitations of the study is that it has not gone far enough in linking directly income and deprivation dynamics. Still, it does make a methodological advance in searching for suitable empirical analyses to guide policy-makers to identify and target poor children.

Deprivation and destitution among minorities in the UK vary according to what their expectations are about their long-term income prospects rather than their current incomes. Housing deprivation is particularly noticeable, especially among Bangladeshis and Pakistanis. Moore (2000) has estimated a minimal deprivation index for children in the UK by ethnic groups. He shows once again that Bangladeshi children suffer from extreme deprivation in the most deprived group. Comparing ethnic minority children and white children, Moore (*ibid.*, p. 153) states that all minority children (Black Caribbean, Black African, Indian, Pakistani, Bangladeshi and Chinese) 'are more highly represented than white children in the highest level of deprivation'. He measures deprivation in terms of material indicators such as a lack or absence of access to a car, decent or non-crowded housing and employment of members of households in which minority children live.

Platt (2002, p. 62) notes that, in the UK, 'Caribbeans, Indians and East African Asians, and, especially Pakistanis and Bangladeshis were less likely to own consumer durables than even their income levels would suggest.' Their decisions may depend on their expectations and uncertainty about future income prospects rather than current incomes. These decisions may also depend on different perceptions about what is 'essential' or not. Cultural differences may, *inter alia*, partly explain a low priority to some consumer durables to which whites might give a high priority. Lower propensity among Asians than Caribbeans to borrow and incur debts for consumer spending is determined by different cultural orientation and attitudes.

The European Commission (2008, pp. 51–2) examines material deprivation in terms of economic strain (failure to afford to face unexpected expenses, to pay for mortgage or rent, to pay for a meal with meat every second day, to keep home adequately warm and to enjoy a one-week holiday away from home), lack of consumer durables and poor housing conditions. It estimates that about 10 per cent of the population in Denmark, Luxembourg, the Netherlands and Sweden suffer from at least two problems of economic strain out of the five noted above. For such countries as Greece, Portugal, Hungary and Poland, the share is over 40 per cent. The presence of children in a household cause financial strain and children have a higher probability of deprivation (*ibid.*).

A few points need to be made about the deprivation indicators used (see Table 2.6). The indicators are a combination of basic needs (for example, food and shelter) and secondary requirements such as holidays away from home or ownership of a car. It is matter of subjective judgement whether the deprivation (of individuals or households) of secondary requirements would necessarily qualify as 'poverty'. Second, none of the indicators mentioned in Table 2.6 relate specifically to children. Instead, they refer to households containing children. As Nolan, Maitre and Watson (2001, p. 200) note: 'we still do not have direct measures of living standards or deprivation for the children themselves'. Third, as they further note:

> Exactly as in using household income to measure poverty, the assumption is made that pooling of resources within the household equalizes living standards and poverty risks for all household members. The situation where children are in poverty because of insufficient sharing of resources within the household will not be captured, either with conventional income measures or with the deprivation indicators we have available. (*Ibid.*)

As we discussed above, resources are rarely distributed equally between adults and children within a household.

### Intergenerational transmission of poverty

So far we have discussed only a static aspect of child income poverty at a point of time. As we noted in Chapter 1, its dynamic aspects, especially its intergenerational transmission from poor children to adults is particularly relevant to immigrant children, who are generally much poorer than other children. These children are more likely to end up as poor adults after experiencing poverty in their childhood. A number of studies have been undertaken to analyze the relationship between parental income poverty in which children grew and their lifetime outcomes (see Jenkins and Siedler, 2007). A vast majority of these studies consider the impact of only income poverty without controlling for the impact of such other factors as family background, education of parents and natural ability of children, which are also correlated with childhood poverty.

There is no conclusive evidence that intergenerational persistence of poverty is necessarily attributed to the income poverty of parents of poor children. The results vary depending on the estimation techniques, as well as on the outcome variables such as education, health and access to the labour market. Taking account of such non-income factors as family background, parents' education and ability of a poor child tends to narrow the correlation between income and later outcomes but not eliminate them (*ibid.*).

Many studies (for example, Bonnie, Fulco and Liverman, 1999; Case, Lubotsky and Paxson, 2002) have shown that children from poor households suffer from greater health risks in terms of lower body weight, higher infant mortality and generally poorer health status. The consequences of poor health of children (which may result from low incomes of parents as well as their health) would be visible in frequent absences from school, lower chances of human capital accumulation, lower productivity in the job market and lower earnings leading to poverty.

Studies (for example, Haveman and Wolfe, 1995) show that poor children are less successful at school and in the labour market. Using British Youth Panel (BYP) data (part of the British Household Panel Survey, BHPS), Ermisch, Francesconi and Pevalin (2001) show that the experience of poverty by children aged 11 to 15, reduces their chances of educational attainment measured by a number of GCSEs with high grades. For France, Maurin (2002) shows the effects of parents' poverty on their children's educational performance are much larger than those of their sex or age within their class. Low family income is one of the main factors holding back children in primary school. He estimated that a 10 per cent increase in parental income is associated with a 6.5 per cent decrease in the probability of a child being held back in primary school. The probability of being held back 'is one and a half times greater for boys than for girls, or for children in large families than for children in small families' (*ibid.*, p. 316).

For the UK, Blanden and Gibbons (2006) show that children aged 16 who were poor are more likely to be poor as adults. They also show that the link between child poverty and adult poverty (later in life) has risen over time.

Within the framework of the European Union Survey of Income and Living Conditions (SILC)[5] a longitudinal study for the Republic of Ireland has empirically tested this notion on the basis of responses from adults about their teenage experiences (CSO, 2007). The study ends with the following conclusions:

(a) Those adults who suffered financial difficulty as teenagers have higher adult poverty rates than others who have not.
(b) The unemployed frequently experienced financial difficulty in teenage years.
(c) Adults who did not live with both parents during teenage years had a higher poverty risk than others.
(d) The risk of poverty was greater if during teenage years a person concerned lived in a household where neither of the two parents worked.
(e) Adults, who as teenagers lived in households where the highest level of education of parent(s) was primary or below, had a consistent

poverty rate double that of those who lived with parents with a university degree.

Very few studies mentioned above distinguished between immigrants and non-immigrants. Blanden and Gibbons (2006, p. 22) give family characteristics including a separate column 'non-white' (immigrants). They show that 'by the mid-1980s low education, parental non-employment and being non-white were more strongly linked to teenage poverty'; it is most likely that this group is at a greater disadvantage. As we discuss below and in Chapters 4 and 5, immigrants and their children suffer from a lack of educational and employment opportunities.

## Access to education and the labour market

Access to education and the labour market are two other aspects of non-income poverty. One may obtain some information about immigrant child poverty by examining these non-income variables. Immigrant children with lower level and quality of education on arrival in the host country concerned would be less likely to find jobs in the labour market; if they do, they would earn lower wages than those non-immigrants and other immigrant children/youth who have higher and better education. The issues of education and the labour market are discussed below.

### Education

Some immigrant children (for example, Turks and North Africans) are less educated than non-immigrant children at the time of their arrival in Europe. Turkish migrants in Europe are the largest migrant group approximating about 4 million people. Germany recruited the bulk of Turkish workers for its industry, starting in 1961. Besides Germany, second-generation children of these migrants are found in Austria, Belgium, France, the Netherlands, Sweden and Switzerland. There are great disparities in the educational situation of second-generation school children in these countries. Crul (2007) argues that the following three main factors: (1) age at which education begins; (2) number of face-to-face contact hours with teachers; and (3) school selection mechanisms, explain the disparities across countries. Turkish school children in Belgium and France have more years of schooling than in Austria and Germany, which puts them at linguistic and other advantages in the former two countries. However, the quality of education expressed in terms of drop-out rates is poorer in Belgium and France than in Austria and Germany.

Unemployment rates among Turkish children are much lower in Germany, which has a well-established apprenticeship system. This is not the case in France and the Netherlands. Thus, the apprenticeship system smoothes their transition to the labour market.

There are wide variations across European countries concerning the extent and type of support granted to immigrant children in and out of school. Several European countries have local, regional and national educational programmes and projects aimed specifically at immigrant children, particularly those with learning difficulties. While Belgium, France and the Netherlands are generous in their assistance to such children, Germany is less so (see Crul and Vermeulen, 2006, pp. 243–4).

Clear-cut guidelines do not exist on how best to provide second-language teaching. It forms part of the primary school curricula or the mainstream language programmes. A very large number of young immigrant children (birth to four and five to nine age groups) in most European countries (see Table 2.2) has implications for the early education (pre-school and primary school) of these children. Early education of immigrant and non-immigrant children takes place at home and in crèches and nurseries (kindergartens). Therefore, the parents' role in education is significant. Immigrant parents' education and literacy skills affect those of their young children. The quality of informal education imparted to these children will depend on the poverty situation of the parents, their social status and religious traditions and child-rearing beliefs (Leseman, 2007). Many traditional immigrant families tend to subordinate children's interests to those of (extended) family and local community. Leseman (2007, p. 3) notes that 'parents who immigrated from traditional non-schooled cultures often combine collectivist child-rearing beliefs with a strong, individualistic commitment to a successful school career for their children'. This situation may apply to parents with a rural background; educated urban parents are more likely to subscribe to more modern individualistic views.

In general, educational disadvantages of immigrant children may include socio-economic and psychological risks, lack of cognitive and language development in the family environment. As we discuss in Chapters 4 to 6, risks may arise from poverty of parents, problems of drug abuse and depression of parents, unemployment and job stress, and poor housing conditions.

**The labour market**

The lower level and quality of education among immigrant children will, *inter alia*, lower their access to the job market. Comparative research on the second-generation youth in Europe is still quite limited. One rare project on the subject, EFFNATIS (1998–2000), covered eight European countries, namely Finland, France, Germany, the Netherlands, Spain, Sweden, Switzerland and the UK. It studied the relationship between national integration policies and their outcomes for second-generation youth from different ethnic groups. A more recent study (Crul and Vermeulen, 2003) discusses the situation of one ethnic group, the Turks, in six European countries, namely, Austria, Belgium, France, Germany, the Netherlands and Sweden. The study examines the labour market transition of Turkish immigrants and concludes that differences in their employment situation in different countries depend on whether these countries have apprenticeship systems or not. Higher youth unemployment in France compared to Austria and Germany is explained by the absence of an apprenticeship system in the country.

Turkish youth with low vocational training are left out of the labour market. Employers tend to discriminate against Turkish youth. Crul and Vermeulen (2003) conclude that some countries (for example, Sweden and the Netherlands) have introduced integration policies to assist migrant youth to enter the labour market, whereas in other countries access to the labour market is restricted to national citizens. To quote: 'In all countries, immigrant youth unemployment is a policy concern and labour market discrimination is officially acknowledged, though policies to combat that discrimination vary widely' (*ibid.*, p. 976). In general, the situation of Turkish youth in different European countries is similar, considering that they generally come from the same regions in Turkey. The Turkish immigrants are generally from low socio-economic backgrounds, with a low level of education and traditional Muslim background.

The share of children in jobless households, regardless of whether they are male or female-headed, can influence the incidence of child poverty. In 2005, this share in households where no one worked was 12 per cent in Ireland, 16.5 per cent in the UK, 11 per cent in Germany, 6 per cent in Italy and 14 per cent in Hungary (EUROSTAT, 2005). These wide variations across Europe may partly explain the wide variations in child poverty rates. France, Germany, Ireland, Italy, Poland and the UK are countries with high rates of unemployment as well as high relative child poverty rates. As we shall discuss in Chapter 7, the unemployment rate is quite low in Switzerland compared to that in France and many other Western European countries, which may explain the relatively lower child poverty rates. Although the UK unemployment rate has declined considerably since 1995, its relative child poverty rate has remained high. On the other hand, in Belgium, Denmark and Sweden, relative child poverty is low despite high unemployment rates (Bradbury and Jäntti, 2001).

Although the overall unemployment rates may be low, those for immigrant youth are generally much higher, which explains greater risk of poverty among them (see Chapters 4, 5 and 7). In Switzerland, access of adult immigrants and youth to the job market is limited, *inter alia*, by the lack of long-term residence and work permits. It is also restricted by their low skills (see Chapter 4). In France, child poverty among immigrant households from within the EU-15 is much lower than that among households from outside the EU (see Chapter 5). Generally, the incidence of poverty is greater among immigrant households without work. These households suffer greater difficulties than non-immigrant ones, particularly when they are not eligible for unemployment insurance or receive less favourable treatment. Generally, newly arrived immigrants are either excluded from benefits or they receive much lower benefits. This is particularly so if they are non-permanent workers (see Chapters 4 and 5 on Switzerland and France). Morissens (2006, p. 189) notes that 'only in Sweden do immigrants in workless households have a similar poverty risk as their Swedish counterparts'. She shows that in Norway the poverty rate for workless immigrant households is 60 per cent compared to 30 per cent for workless non-immigrant households (*ibid.*, p. 190). Morissens concludes that 'poverty levels for the workless immigrant households are alarmingly high' (*ibid.*, p. 195).

## The EU approach to child poverty

Child poverty is an important element of the EU Social Policy to fight overall poverty and social exclusion. It was explicitly mentioned in the 2005 and 2006 EU Presidency Conclusions. In 2006, the European Council asked the member states to 'take necessary measures to rapidly and significantly reduce child poverty, giving all children equal opportunities regardless of their social background'. Furthermore, the need to invest in European youth is fully recognized in order to prepare them for their future adult responsibilities. However, there is no explicit mention or discussion of poverty among immigrant children in any of the EU documents. Related studies by scholars (for example, Marlier *et al.*, 2007) devote no more than one page to 'migrants and ethnic minorities' in a book of 300 pages on *The EU and Social Inclusion*. While the EU indicators of poverty and social exclusion (for example, employment rates), distinguish between 'immigrants and non-immigrants', one rarely comes across separate rates of child poverty for immigrants and non-immigrants by different age groups.

The recent emergence of the notion of 'children mainstreaming' is a welcome development for focusing on child poverty and well-being but it fails to capture the plight of immigrant children who, as we shall discuss in Chapters 4 to 6, generally suffer from worse poverty situations (multiple deprivation) and vulnerability. Marlier *et al.* note that 'children mainstreaming' involves viewing social inclusion from a child's perspective. It 'implies integrating a concern with the well-being and social inclusion of children into all areas of policy making' (*ibid.*, p. 11). The authors are not very explicit about what this perspective is and how it differs from that of adults. In passing, they present Ruxton and Bennett's (2002) argument and refer to such factors as the quality of neighbourhood services that may influence children's later development. Marlier *et al.* (2007) continue to mention that the notion of mainstreaming is not tantamount to identifying children as a 'target group'. They state that their 'purpose is not to single out a particular priority group; poverty and social exclusion are unacceptable for all groups in society' (*ibid.*, p. 11). But we cannot help feeling that under 'children mainstreaming' they are analyzing child poverty in the same way as one would considering children as a target group. The authors fail to convince the reader how poverty analysis would be fundamentally different from a child's perspective as distinct from that of his or her adult parents. Too much cannot be made of using children as one of the main sources of information about their poverty. Indeed, in essence the authors admit as much when they state that 'children mainly depend on their parents' decisions as to how family income is spent, and these can either favour or disadvantage children' (*ibid.*, p. 100). Their subjective perception of their parents' decisions, especially at a very young age, may not necessarily reflect their best interests.

However, one advantage of the notion of 'mainstreaming' is to highlight the need for developing specific poverty indicators for children of different age groups. The current EU Primary and Secondary Indicators are not particularly suitable for an analysis of child poverty and exclusion. The EU Laeken Indicators (that is, the first set of common indicators for social inclusion approved at the Laeken European Council meeting in December 2001) provide only two indicators with breakdown for children, namely: (1) the proportion of children in households with incomes below 60 per cent of the national median and (2) the proportion of children living in households without jobs. As we discuss in Chapters 4 to 6, these two indicators do not provide a comprehensive picture of child poverty. There are many more dimensions of child poverty that are left out. Similarly, such non-income dimensions of poverty as access to decent housing of children and their health status and education do not feature in the EU indicators. Chapters 4 and 5 show how difficult it is to analyze the conditions of housing for children (particularly of immigrants) because national or local data or longitudinal studies are rarely available by age groups. The same problem arises for analyzing the health status of immigrant or non-immigrant children. We were unable to find health data by age breakdown for either France, which is a member of the EU, or Switzerland, which is not. However, the data on education by age breakdown is sometimes available but mainly for older children (for example, over 16 or 17). Thus any rigorous analysis of the access of immigrant and non-immigrant children to education, health and decent housing remains hampered by the lack of data for all relevant age groups.

The EU member states are unlikely to collect data necessary for an analysis of child poverty, exclusion and well-being without clear directives from the EU. Marlier *et al.* (2007, pp. 187–8) rightly recommend that 'consideration should be given to child health and not just to mortality'. They also claim that, 'we need direct measures of early school attendance and performance, to supplement the attainment measures at age 15 and later', including school truancy or drop-out rates. They further recommend guidelines for countries on the range of indicators concerning child well-being. To our knowledge, at present such EU member countries as France have not developed any such indicators.

It is not clear whether the notion of mainstreaming has been formally accepted by the European Commission. However, in proposing this notion Marlier *et al.* (2007, p. 102) followed in the footsteps of the Social Protection Committee and its Indicators Sub-Group, which have agreed to give children and the older people a 'special focus' (see European Commission, 2004a, p. 6). In the 2006 Conclusions, the European Council asked the member states 'to take necessary measures to rapidly and significantly reduce child poverty, giving all children equal opportunity, regardless of their social background' (cited in Marlier *et al.*, 2007, p. 186). The Marlier Task Force on Child Poverty and Well-Being (European Commission, 2008, p. 68) recommended that the situation of migrant children, *inter alia*, should also be studied.

## Concluding remarks

In this chapter, we have provided empirical evidence on the basis of different interpretations of immigrant child poverty in Europe: (i) income or monetary poverty, (ii) non-income poverty defined as being deprived of basic goods (food, clothing and shelter) and services (education and health) and (iii) intergenerational transmission of poverty.

Empirical evidence on immigrant child poverty is very rarely presented in any systematic manner. Very few studies distinguish between immigrant and non-immigrant children. Those which do fail to provide any in-depth analysis of how poverty affects immigrant children. For example, it is not clear whether immigrant children suffer more from transitory or persistent poverty. Nevertheless, whatever evidence is available (for example, for the UK and Germany) suggests that immigrant children suffer more from monetary and non-monetary disadvantages than non-immigrant children.

In general, the effects of transitory poverty are temporary and can be mitigated through adjustment of financial means and by drawing on savings and financial assets. However, persistent poverty recurring year after year is more likely to leave scars on (immigrant) children's later development. One would expect that persistent poverty is more likely to be common among immigrant children than transitory poverty. This is because parents of such children have relatively low incomes and higher rates of persistent unemployment as we show in Chapters 4 and 5. They also tend to be less educated and low-skilled.

The data and estimates of absolute and relative child poverty in this chapter are based mainly on income poverty, which does not take account of the deprivation and destitution we discussed in Chapter 1. While attempts to look for non-monetary indicators of poverty are an improvement, they also suffer from a subjective bias. Perceptions of necessities vary across families and households.

But a fundamental conceptual problem is the failure to measure child poverty directly. All the measures noted above are based on economic and social conditions of the households and parents of children, not on children themselves. This indirect approach to measuring child poverty may fail to address many problems of children's health and schooling and other forms of social exclusion.

Having reviewed evidence of immigrant child poverty in Europe, in Chapters 4 and 5 we present two detailed case studies on Switzerland and France respectively. They should be considered in the context of the current European immigration debate summarized in Chapter 3.

# 3
# The European Immigration Debate

The debate on immigration in Europe, that is, whether immigration from both inside and outside Europe or from one or other country inside it should be increased, stabilized or decreased, is not new (see, for example, Niessen, 1999). But it has become ever more heated since the enlargement of the European Union to 25 countries and then 27 (in January 2007 Bulgaria and Romania became new EU members). One wonders whether the immigrant issue may not have played at least some part in the rejection of the European Constitution by the French and Dutch citizens in 2005.

Hardly any day passes in European countries without some press headlines concerning immigrant minorities. The challenge of European immigration has become more serious with the rising populations of immigrant workers, their spouses and children for whom schools, health care, housing and social benefits have to be provided.

The architects of the European Community had envisaged an economic union involving free flow of capital and labour within the Community. While free flow of capital was easy, that of labour raised eyebrows in the different member states. The EU-15 accounts for 15 million migrants (about 8 per cent of world's migrants) out of a population of 370 million inhabitants (Parsons and Smeeding, 2006, p. 5). According to the OECD, between 2004 and 2005 the general increase in immigration to Europe of a permanent nature amounted to 10.5 per cent (Garson, 2007).[1]

## The immigration debate

The challenge of European immigration has become more serious with the rising populations of immigrant workers, their spouses and children for whom schools, health care, housing and social benefits have to be provided. We discuss this challenge in some detail in this chapter at the European level before discussing it at the national for Switzerland and France in Chapters 4 to 7.

There are three types of immigration inflows into Europe, namely, (1) economic (immigrant workers), (2) humanitarian (refugees and asylum-seekers) and (3) illegal (clandestine immigrants).[2] Each of these continues to generate controversy, which has led to an EU-wide debate focusing on the various problems associated with how immigration takes place, either legally or illegally.[3]

Citing the French demographer, J. Cl. Chesnais, Severino (2007) claims that in the next 50 years the greatest demographic changes in world history will take place. He notes that 12 countries will see their populations triple; 51 will see their populations fall, notably in Europe. Moreover, many of these same European countries will see their populations age appreciably. The economic consequences for these countries will be dramatic. This is especially the case in Russia whose population will decrease by 17 million people in the next 20 years, while that of Eastern Europe is estimated to decrease by 22 million. One consequence of such significant declines in population will be the need to encourage European immigration, particularly of skilled workers whatever their origins.

The demand for unskilled and manual worker immigrants reached its peak during the 1960s and early 1970s when European economies were booming. However, after the first oil crisis in 1973 such demand ceased. The European host countries erected barriers against the inflow of immigrant workers. The composition of immigration started changing in favour of family reunification, asylum applications and illegal migration.

Since the early 1970s inflows of families (spouses and children) and asylum-seekers increased significantly, especially after the fall of the Berlin Wall in 1989 and the subsequent disintegration of former Yugoslavia. However, the number of asylum-seekers started declining in the early 1990s as countries such as France, Germany and the UK tightened the conditions of their entry and reduced the social benefits to them and to other humanitarian migrants. In these countries an active policy was implemented to encourage refugees to return home voluntarily. As we discuss in Chapter 5, in France ANAEM pays a stipend to each migrant to return home.

The magnitude of illegal immigration into Europe is not known, although Europol estimates their inflow at about 500,000 per annum (Boeri, Hanson and McCormick, 2002, p. 19). The stricter immigration rules against migrant workers, family members and asylum-seekers in recent years may have swelled the ranks of illegal immigrants. If immigrants cannot stay in the host countries legally they tend to go underground and find illegal employment. As we discuss in Chapters 4 and 5, children of illegal migrants are in a particularly precarious situation with respect to access to education, health care and housing.

## Anti-immigration arguments

The critics of immigration into Europe often argue that immigrants from both within Europe and outside take away jobs from the nationals. In the receiving countries, there is a fear among the general population that migration would lower wages and raise unemployment. These fears are particularly widespread during periods of economic recession and slow growth. When average levels of unemployment are high as in many European countries, it is easy to blame immigrants for loss of jobs. As we discuss in Chapter 7, these fears have been particularly pronounced in Switzerland and France. However, there is no empirical evidence in support of this argument (*ibid.*, p.122). A recent study (Brücker, Frick and Wagner, 2006, p. 140) notes that 'the impact of migration on the unemployment rates and displacement risks of natives is small... fears that international migration affects the wages and employment opportunities of natives are largely exaggerated'.

On the contrary, immigrants make a positive contribution to the national economies of Europe in several ways. First, many migrants take up jobs in which the natives are not interested. In other words, they may be working in non-competing segments of the labour market. Furthermore, they may be complementary to native workers if they are working in sectors and activities with excess demand. Third, highly skilled immigrants help overcome serious labour shortages in most European economies with rapidly ageing populations. Acceptance of immigrants can make a positive contribution also in another way. They can help host countries to manage the transition to stricter regimes of immigration control, and mitigate the costs of population ageing.

A second argument against accepting immigrants into Europe hinges on the claim that they put a heavy burden on the already shrinking welfare states of Europe. On this point there is 'some evidence that migrants are indeed receiving proportionally more social transfers than the native population in Europe' (Boeri, Hanson and McCormick, 2002, p. x). Boeri, Hanson and McCormick (2002, pp. 89–90) also accept that the most generous countries in Europe may have been acting as welfare magnets for immigrants.

However, the composition of migrants and their welfare dependence vary considerably across Europe. Highly qualified and young legal immigrants not only benefit from social welfare but they also make payments to national schemes in support of the ageing native populations. They may be welcome for another reason also: more immigrants may lower production costs through lower wages.

Third, there may be uneasiness about accepting immigrants owing to cultural differences. This is particularly true for those coming from outside Europe, as we discuss in Chapter 4 on Switzerland. Such cultural differences may also affect migration from the former Eastern European countries such as Poland, Bulgaria and Romania. Their presence has become particularly marked in such Western European countries as the UK. Many elites in the Western European states have been keenly aware of the very different ways in which people from Eastern Europe lived through the postwar years.

Notwithstanding temporary restrictions, all the EU members are bound by law to accept nationals of member countries. However, empirical evidence, particularly from EUROSTAT, has suggested that movement of nationals of one member country to another is not nearly so great as many might have expected. This may be due partly to language and cultural barriers. For example, Boeri, Hanson and McCormick (2002, p. 40) note that 'no more than 1.5 per cent of the EU's population reside in other member countries', which is quite a low proportion. The majority of foreigners are non-citizens from outside the EU, mostly from developing countries of Asia and Africa.

Boeri, Hanson and McCormick (2002, p. 122) conclude that racial factors and ethnic hostility prevalent in Europe are far more important than the above factors militating against migration inflow. They state: 'there are social tensions caused by ethnic rivalry and other negative social externalities such as crime. It will be hard to fight racial feelings although education may be useful as a long-term measure'. As we discuss in Chapter 4, in Switzerland the general public especially, with rightist political leanings, tends to blame foreigners for all crimes and thefts. The racist and xenophobic tendencies there and elsewhere are also related to economic concerns. Many Europeans feel that migrants would aggravate unemployment in Europe and depress wages leading to economic hardships for them.

While it is true that generally more foreigners (especially immigrant youth) are known to commit crimes than native people, this may be because the local population tends to report more crimes by foreigners. Crimes by the local people may remain unreported. Furthermore, immigrant youth are generally over-represented in the economically and socially disadvantaged people. Thus their crime may be more a consequence of social disadvantage and extreme poverty than of ethnicity per se (see Chapter 4).

Finally, those who oppose immigration blame immigrants and their families for failing to integrate into the host societies. While some immigrants from non-EU countries are well integrated, others are not. The European populations (for example, in Switzerland, France, Denmark and the UK) are particularly hostile to the Muslim minorities, seen as terrorists since the events of 11 September 2001 in the USA. Terrorism and security concerns increasingly explain anti-immigrant sentiments.


## Protagonists of immigration

Protagonists of European immigration point to the ageing populations and very low fertility rates in European countries. Fertility rates are declining further, which is leading to stagnating and even declining populations. Combined with this, the rapidly ageing populations reduce the ratio of working-age population to total population.[4] The protagonists argue that the acceptance of immigrants is justified to compensate for the loss of working-age populations in Europe. The loss of such populations is creating serious labour shortages of both skilled and unskilled labour. The European economies will fail to grow if excessive controls are introduced on labour immigration. However, the demographic shifts are so large that even a substantial increase in the number of immigrants is unlikely to restore age balances. This point refers to immigrant workers, not to their dependent spouses and children (Day, 2007).

Another argument presented by the protagonists is that, on average, migrants, who are often young, contribute significantly to public finances and social security systems. Brücker, Frick and Wagner (2006, p. 141) conclude that 'increasing the population through migration increases the number of future taxpayers who will contribute to the financing of public goods'.

Progressive people in Europe may be prepared to accept immigrants (especially refugees and spouses and children) on humanitarian grounds. They may not be in favour of expelling refugees and asylum-seekers who have escaped from civil strifes and wars in the countries of their origin. Equally they may not like to see families being torn apart. Human dignity, sanctity of family life and community spirit are factors which underlie the arguments of pro-immigrant people in Europe.

**The Schengen agreements**

The Schengen Agreement was signed in June 1985. The Agreement provided for a single external border and the harmonization of policies and rules regarding visas and asylum applications, and policies concerning customs. It emphasized police and judicial cooperation among participating countries, thus implicitly associating immigration with crime and terrorism. The Agreement also provided for the establishment of a common information system, the Schengen Information System (SIS), which is a data bank concerned mainly with wanted persons.

The fall of the Berlin Wall in 1989 and the collapse of the communist regimes that followed created a fear among Western European countries of a massive inflow of immigrants from the former Soviet Union territory. The Schengen Agreement was a political response to this potential threat. Thus migration became an important issue which was discussed at many international forums.[5] The European debate has recently reached new heights of national concern with the extension of the so-called 'Schengen Space' on 21 December 2007.[6]

Much of the current concern has arisen out of the extension of the Schengen zone in the context of a widespread misunderstanding. For many Europeans continue to mistake the Schengen agreements as authorizing the free circulation of *workers* (a completely separate matter governed by completely different agreements) for the free circulation of *persons* within the EU. If non-EU foreigners are residents of a member country, they are allowed to travel within the Schengen area but not to reside or work in other EU countries. Generally, refugees and asylum-seekers are not allowed to leave their country of residence.

With the dramatic expansion not only of the European Union but also of the Schengen Space, opportunities for illegal immigration have greatly expanded, for example, on the mountainous frontiers between Ukraine and Slovenia. Understandably, the duties of states with respect to immigrants has become an increasingly contentious matter (see below).

**Attitudes towards immigrants**

The European attitudes to migration and migrants vary a great deal across European countries. There are anti-migrant people as well as protagonists of migration, as we discuss below. Public opposition to migration is motivated by economic, social, cultural and racial factors.

The European Social Survey (ESS), an ongoing research project funded by the European Commission, is designed to collect data on the attitudes and behaviour of European populations (persons aged 15 years and older) towards immigrants and asylum-seekers. On the basis of ESS data for 2002–3, Citrin and Sides (2006) analyze immigration attitudes in European countries (both EU and non-EU) such as France, Germany, Norway, Switzerland and the UK. They show that negative attitudes to immigration are much more common than positive ones. The public perception is that immigration leads to greater crime and that it undermines a nation's culture and national identity. European people are more negative about asylum-seekers than immigrants as a whole.

In a survey published in November 2007 in response to the question as to whether the person surveyed believed immigration represented more of an opportunity or more of a threat to his or her country, 40 per cent of those surveyed in Spain, 33 per cent in Italy, 32 per cent in the UK, 27 per cent in Germany and only 25 per cent in France saw immigration as an opportunity (TNS Sofres, 2007). In the UK 37 per cent saw immigration as a threat. Corresponding figures for some other countries were: 29 per cent for Italy, 23 per cent for both Spain and Germany and 24 per cent for France. Those who saw immigration as neither an opportunity nor a threat were 43 per cent in Germany, 32 per cent in Spain, 27 per cent in Italy, 24 per cent in the UK and 44 per cent in France. If neither an opportunity nor a threat, then exactly how these people in France actually saw immigration was not noted in the survey.

In France, the European Centre for Strategic Analysis reported in 2006 that 33 per cent of French persons surveyed believed that the presence of immigrants increased insecurity, whereas 42 per cent of those surveyed in the EU believed that to be the case. Similarly, 38 per cent in France believed that the presence of immigrants worsened unemployment, whereas 46 per cent in the EU believed so. By contrast, 62 per cent in France believed that some economic sectors needed immigrants, whereas only 48 per cent in the EU believed that to be the case. And 66 per cent in France believed that the presence of immigrants enriched the culture of France, whereas only 54 per cent believed so in the EU (Eurobarometer, 2006).

In summary, the key elements of the European immigration debate include restrictions on labour immigration of unskilled and semi-skilled labour from outside Europe, curbing of the reunification of families with immigrants already in Europe, regulation of humanitarian immigration relating to asylum-seekers and refugees, and restrictions on payment of social welfare benefits to non-European immigrants. Increasingly, immigrants and their children and spouses are considered a heavy burden on the welfare systems. Responding to the public sentiment against immigrants the European national governments have attempted to control immigration, especially of unskilled workers. These increasing restrictions have gradually created 'a system of inequalities' that has progressively involved more and more of the EU's expanding immigrant population (Bihr and Pfefferkorn, 2008, pp. 55–77).

## Family reunification

Given the changing economic climate in many European countries such as France and Switzerland and the tightening of laws governing future immigration, immigrant families are even less welcome now than they were before the new immigration laws came into effect. Whereas earlier a significant number of immigrants were being allowed into such countries on the grounds of family reunification, in virtually all European countries today family reunification is being subordinated to such concerns as professional skills for their economies. Many prospective immigrants to Europe are not only skilled workers but entire families with children who are bound to suffer. Free flow of labour from nationals of the EU within EU boundaries has involved increasing restrictions on immigration from non-EU countries, particularly the developing countries of Asia and Africa. Barriers against immigrants from these countries were imposed by most Western European countries in the wake of the oil crisis in 1973. The increasing difficulty of immigrants to gain entry to Europe on the grounds of family reunification has large negative impacts, especially on the children of such families (Marlier *et al.*, 2007, pp. 186–8).

However, even when barriers to worker immigration from non-EU countries were high, the EU member states continued to allow family reunification. These high barriers to worker entry may have increased the inflow of spouses and children of workers. This may have changed the age composition of immigrants in favour of the young and low skilled. Some observers argue that the barrier to worker immigration 'has increased the importance of the channels of family reunification, humanitarian migration, and presumably illegal migration from there' (third countries) (Boeri, Hanson and McCormick, 2002, pp. 50–1).

Since 2005, family reunification has become much more difficult with the introduction of new barriers. Increased restrictions have made it more difficult for families of immigrants (children and spouses) to join their husbands/parents. As we note in Chapter 4, in Switzerland the new law regulating foreigners restricts immigration to highly skilled and professional people who cannot be found within the country. France has adopted similar restrictive measures concerning the reunification of families with immigrant workers in France (see Chapter 5).

Between 2000 and 2005, family reunification was the most important single factor in France, accounting for the inflow of immigrants (see Chapter 5). Over time this factor is likely to affect the age composition of migrants whose dependants are more likely to be outside the labour market and of school-going age, a factor which will have an impact on school systems, payment of child benefits and the economic and social situation of immigrant children (see Chapters 4 to 6). But as we point out in Chapter 7, the November 2007 changes in French immigration law are partly motivated by a pronounced political will to decrease the share of those immigrants allowed entry into France on the grounds of family reunification in favour of a much more important share of those with professional qualifications.

In the past, particularly the 1990s, family reunification accounted for a significant proportion of immigration inflows into Europe: 50 per cent of the inflows in 1992 and 70 per cent in 1998. However, this channel and category of entry (compared to workers and asylum-seekers) varies a great deal across Europe. In 1998, in Sweden family reunification accounted for 55 per cent of the total number of immigrants compared to only 2 per cent of workers. For France, the figures were 55 per cent and 21 per cent; for the UK, 50 per cent and 45 per cent; and for Italy, 34 per cent and 55 per cent (OECD, 2000). However, in France the importance of family reunification has been declining since 1988 (see Chapter 5).

In the 1960s, Germany and Switzerland, with their 'guest worker' programmes considered immigrant workers as temporary residents with limited rights and opportunities to bring their families with them. On the other hand, countries such as Belgium and Sweden were much more liberal and allowed full worker rights, including the right to bring their families, which explains why families and children constitute the bulk of the total number of immigrants in these countries.

Between 1974 and the mid-1980s family reunions with migrants already in Western Europe grew rapidly. Inflows of spouses, children and other relations of migrants led to an unprecedented demand for housing, schools and other public services such as health care.

The national legislations in most European countries recognized the right of immigrants to invite their families. However, in general only permanent migrant workers are entitled to family reunions, not temporary or seasonal workers (Palier, 2007). The clauses relating to family reunions generally allowed in only minor children who are below 16 or 18 years of age and are dependent on parents for financial support. As noted above and in Chapters 4 and 5, the national and EU legislation concerning the reunification of immigrant children with their parents has increasingly become more restrictive.

At the EU level, rules have been enacted which cover such issues as entry, residence, economic rights of immigrants and family reunification (see Table 3.1). Concerning children the legislation most relevant is that on family reunification, which turned out to be quite controversial. In September 2000, the European Parliament voted on a number of amendments to the legislation and the EU Commission accepted most of these amendments. However, the Council failed to reach an agreement on the bill, which was dropped. Another bill on the subject was introduced with two modifications to the original bill, namely, (1) a clause restricting national discretion in the application of the terms of the legislation and (2) a clause proposing 'a deadline of two years after the legislation for the initiation of a more fully harmonized law on family reunification'. The Council adopted this law in September 2003 (Hix and Noury, 2007, p. 190).

The above situation presents a paradox and a contradiction between the EU policies and programmes (for example, EU social policy and anti-discrimination policy) and the national policies of members states. For example, the EU social policy promotes child welfare through protection of the rights of children whereas national policies of member states discourage family reunification, discriminate against children from outside the EU and reduce child and other welfare benefits. The new laws concerning immigrants (see Chapter 7) are in direct violation of the sanctity of family life and family cohesion and the rights of the child. They are also inconsistent with humanitarian values, which would oppose the deportation of refugees and their children.

The EU legislation on family reunification does not include any clauses concerning the access of family members to social welfare benefits in the host country. However, it does recommend 'fair treatment' of workers and their families including children from non-EU countries. Does this mean that the rules governing the participation of immigrant workers from within the EU in social security schemes also apply to those from outside the EU? This does not seem to be the case as individual member states are free to deny or reduce social benefits to non-EU immigrants. They are equally free to withdraw their residence permits if they continue to depend on these benefits.

## A common immigration policy for Europe?

Despite the Schengen agreements governing the free circulation of persons discussed above, the nation states of Europe, especially those

*Table 3.1* Migration legislation in the Fifth European Parliament

| Legislation | Date initiated | Date passed | No. of RCVs in EP | Date of EP votes |
| --- | --- | --- | --- | --- |
| Equal treatment between persons without racial and ethnic discrimination | 25 November 1999 | 29 June 2000 | 8 | 18 May 2000 |
| Third-country nationals' right to family reunification | 1 December 1999 | (dropped) | 9 | 6 September 2000 |
| Equal treatment between persons-general non-discrimination | 25 November 1999 | 27 November 2000 | 2 | 5 October 2000 |
| Third-country nationals' long-term resident status | 13 March 2001 | 25 November 2003 | 18 | 5 February 2002 |
| Entry and residence of third-country nationals for the purpose of employment | 11 July 2001 | (awaiting Council approval) | 15 | 12 February 2003 |
| Third-country nationals' right to family reunification | 2 May 2002 | 22 September 2003 | 9 | 9 April 2003 |

*Note*: EP – European Parliament. RCVs – roll call votes.
*Source*: Hix and Noury (2007), p. 189.

comprising the present 27 members of the EU, have not yet been able to agree on a common immigration policy. This is partly owing to social, political and language differences among the member countries.

However, all countries have agreed that the problems of immigration cannot be properly resolved by individual states alone and that a common policy is necessary. Some steps towards this goal have already been taken. For example, on 18 June 2008 the EU law-makers in the European Parliament (Strasbourg) allowed the EU member countries to hold undocumented or illegal migrants in detention centres for up to 18 months and ban them from the EU territory for five years.[7] Amnesty International has described this law as 'severely flawed', reflecting an erosion of human rights standards (Brothers, 2008). Under the French presidency of the EU that began in July 2008 a strong campaign got underway to mobilize support for a fully unified EU-wide immigration policy.

A common policy at the EU level is required not only for external border controls but also for equal treatment of workers, the eligibility to welfare benefits and refugees and asylum-seekers. Such a common policy may also help overcome discrimination against immigrants and their families (spouses and children), who are often exploited inhumanely.

At present there is no common asylum policy in Europe.[8] National policies of member states continue to vary widely with the result that refugees and asylum-seekers are very unevenly distributed. These policies towards them have been tightened in countries such as Germany, France and Switzerland (see Chapters 4 and 5 for the latter two).

It may be useful to make a distinction between an immigration policy (for example, policy towards refugees, border controls and equal treatment of workers) and policy towards immigrants. The former refers to human movements, whereas the latter deals with the living conditions of immigrants covering such issues as their schooling, health care, housing, welfare benefits, political participation and national integration (Hammar, 1985; Martiniello, 2006, pp. 307–8). These latter issues are very much in the national domain and the responsibility for them is unlikely to be shifted to a supranational body such as the EU. Many member states see a common European immigration policy as an attack on their national sovereignty. Concerns of national security and identity are bound to override any considerations of a common policy.

In recent years, both economic (labour) and humanitarian immigration in the form of asylum-seekers from developing countries have been restricted in Switzerland and France, as well as in other European countries. As we discuss in Chapters 4 and 5, restrictions include rejection of work permits, shortening the duration of stay and reducing the eligibility for and payment of social welfare benefits. These short-term benefits to the host countries have been achieved at the expense of curbing the legal and political human rights of immigrants and ethnic minorities. Another adverse side effect of the tightening of immigration controls in Europe has been an increase in illegal immigration. Many prospective immigrants, often disguised as tourists, are increasingly prolonging their three-month legal stay to illegal stay for indefinite periods.

It is a paradox that economic and demographic considerations require more immigration whereas political considerations and popular opinion call for a more restrictive immigration policy. European employers continue to hire labour from the non-EU countries to meet growing demands in the labour market. Apart from economic motivation (wide wage differentials between developing countries and the European countries), immigration is a response to demographic needs in Europe. The populations in most European countries are ageing with a concomitant decline in numbers in the active population.

## Rights of immigrants, duties of states

One controversial question that continues to arise in ongoing discussions about developing a general European approach to immigration is whether the basic human rights of so-called 'economic immigrants' and their families originating from developing countries include the freedom to migrate to European states where they have better chances of achieving greater well-being. A related question is whether affluent European states today, say at least the European members of the OECD, have basic legal and moral obligations to welcome such immigrants and their families to the degree that their societies can reasonably share with them the well-being they themselves already abundantly enjoy.

We recognize that these questions are difficult to answer; they remain matters of active debate among specialists (Hinsch, 2001). For example, the determination of a precise relationship between natural rights and human rights still eludes professional consensus (Pogge, 2002, pp. 52–70). Furthermore, the central issues surrounding what constitutes the basic principles of distributive justice at the level of nation states are still not sorted out (Rawls, 1999). Moreover, the fundamental nature of the responsibilities of nation states with respect to international justice is unclear (O'Neill, 2004). Even the quite basic question as to whether there are general moral principles as opposed to intermediate ethical norms is still the subject of continuing debate among moral philosophers (Audi vs Lance and Little, both 2006).

Still, we remain persuaded that immigrants and their families do have the basic human right to try to improve their well-being, and that the European states do have the legal and moral obligations to welcome such immigrants to the degree that they reasonably can (Dummett, 2001).

Many immigrants into Switzerland are from within the European Union (EU). So the EU has been successful in exerting political pressure to improve their nationals' social and legal conditions in Switzerland (Afonso, 2005, p. 658).[9] The rights of EU immigrants and their children received a boost after EU pressures led to the abolition of the 'seasonal worker' category of immigrants into Switzerland in 2002 (see Chapter 4). Seasonal workers were not entitled to any social benefits: they were asked to leave Switzerland for three months out of a year and re-enter with new permits.

However, non-EU immigrants are less fortunate since they are considered 'culturally distant', as we discuss in Chapter 4. Furthermore, as we discuss in Chapter 7, the rights of immigrant children and youth are now denied after a rejection in a referendum of the Swiss Federal government proposal to grant accelerated citizenship to second- and third-generation children.

Similarly in France both internal and external pressures have recently improved the situation of EU immigrants. The French Constitutional Court has been examining details in the new French legislation laying down conditions that prospective EU immigrants must fulfil. The Court has ruled against the proposed DNA testing requirement for some prospective immigrants from countries where valid birth certificates are difficult to obtain.

One way to move towards a satisfactory articulation of the relationship between these individual rights of relatively poor immigrants and corresponding duties of affluent nation states is in terms of the notion of 'first-class citizenship'. Sir Michael Dummett (2001, p. 10), the English philosopher, argues:

> Thus, the truth within the principle of national self-determination is that everyone has the right to live in a country in which he and others of a group to which he belongs are not persecuted, oppressed or discriminated against, in which his religion, language, race and culture are not reviled or held up to contempt and in which he can fully identify himself with the state under whose sovereignty that country falls. Whether that holds good of where he is living depends in part upon the conduct of that state, and in part on the behaviour

of its people: it is ultimately decided by whether that individual feels that he belongs. This may be called the right to be a first-class citizen.

However, by itself, the notion of first-class citizenship does not go far enough. While it encompasses the situations of those who seek asylum in another country from an intolerable situation in their own, it does not provide sufficient justification for those simply seeking a better economic life. However, where the country of origin may well involve not active discrimination but fundamental inequalities between human beings with respect to economic capacities and capabilities, a case can be made in favour of families seeking equality of basic economic well-being in another country.

As to the question of what legal and moral obligations such affluent European nation states may have with respect not just to immigrants seeking asylum but also to relatively impoverished immigrant families seeking a more just level of economic well-being, one may argue that states have the duty to give such immigrants 'their due'. Dummett asks: '[W]hat duties and what rights does a state have towards individuals seeking to enter the land over which it rules?' And he answers: 'The initial answer has to be that it must deal with them justly: it must give them their due' (2001, p. 27).

But this 'initial answer', while surely correct, remains too general. In fact, Dummett himself goes on to offer a much stronger version of this answer to his own question when he writes later on: 'To refuse help to others suffering from or threatened by injustice [including those economic injustices of what he qualifies earlier as 'savage inequalities of wealth and opportunity', 2001, p. 12] is to collaborate with that injustice, and so incur part of the responsibility for it' (2001, p. 34).

Behind Dummett's strong remarks lies the general recognition that all human beings have a major moral obligation to alleviate suffering. The general problem is how to give priority to such an obligation with the apparently equal major moral obligation of nation states and societies to shoulder the extensive burdens of creating and sustaining just social institutions for their own citizens. This is the beneficence problem, the problem of 'the grounds, scope, and stringency of the duty of beneficence', the duty of contributing to the good or well-being of other people (Audi, 2004, pp. 94–101).

Strong philosophical claims such as these underlie an important move from individual to communal concerns. Whether such a basic move is always justifiable may be questioned. But our concern here is the granting of entry to immigrant children for the purposes either of maintaining the unity of the immigrant family presently seeking entry or to achieve family reunification of immigrant children with their already admitted parents. Affluent European states have a legal and moral obligation to assist such persons to the degree that they are threatened by persisting economic injustice in their countries of origin. We argue (and much of the evidence in subsequent chapters demonstrates) that at least such European states as France and Switzerland are at present failing in the fulfilment of these obligations. This failure is not just a very serious legal, political and social error. As a persisting failure to fulfil a fundamental duty of justice with respect to others, it is a very serious moral failure as well.

Roberts (2008, p. 12) notes: 'The moral case for migration is incontrovertible.' Summarizing a wealth of relevant empirical material, he insists on the humanitarian as well as cultural benefits of migration. However, he points out that the economic benefits of migration, including meeting the demand for larger workforces, greater job growth and wealth creation, need to be communicated widely.

In short, we believe that the move from the individual level to the level of nation states is justified. That is, 'If an individual has a duty to give help to those in need when they ask him for it, he also has a duty not to deny them the opportunity to ask. The same applies to states. 'They have an internationally recognised duty towards refugees: they therefore have a duty to do nothing to prevent refugees from reaching their borders. This duty is currently violated by almost all "developed states"' (Dummett, 2001, pp. 42–3). We agree with Dummett that the same argument holds with respect not just to refugees but also to immigrant families.

After these reflections on the general immigration debate in Europe, we need now to turn to particular cases of Switzerland and France in Chapters 4 and 5.

# 4
# Immigrant Child Poverty in Switzerland[1]

In this chapter, we undertake an in-depth case study of poor immigrant children in Switzerland. Poverty is defined here in terms of both income (percentage of the population below a defined poverty line) and non-income aspects (access to education, health services and housing).

Our analysis is handicapped by the fact that few statistics or studies exist of child poverty in Switzerland. Therefore, we have resorted to both official and unofficial statistical and other information sources to obtain a picture of the magnitude and nature of child poverty among Swiss children in general and immigrant children in particular.

## The magnitude of immigrant population

According to the Swiss Federal Statistical Office (OFS), in 2004 there were 1.6 million foreign inhabitants in Switzerland accounting for 21.8 per cent of the total population (OFS, 2005). This figure does not include immigrants who obtained Swiss nationality. According to the 2000 Population Census, the proportion of immigrants would rise to 28 per cent if they were included.

More than half of the foreign residents in Switzerland without Swiss citizenship have either been living in the country for more than 15 years or were born here. In 2005, 2.5 per cent of foreigners acquired Swiss citizenship. During the 1990s, the growth of population with Swiss nationality was due almost exclusively to naturalizations (OFS, 2007, p. 24). The bulk of the foreign population is quite young.

The majority of foreigners living in Switzerland originate from within Europe although the number from Asia and Africa has been rising in recent years. The number of immigrants from Asia rose from 22,000 in 1980 to 62,000 in 1990 and 108,000 in 2004. The corresponding number of immigrants from Africa for the same years were: 11,000, 25,000 and 65,000 (see below a discussion of refugees from Somalia who total about 5,000).[2] From within Europe, the most significant immigrant communities are Italians, Serbs, Montenegrins (and other communities from former Yugoslavia, for example, Croats and Bosnians) and Portuguese (OFS, 2005).

The number of immigrants from former Yugoslavia increased substantially, from 173,000 in 1990 to 364,000 in 2004. In 2004, of the total number of immigrants from former Yugoslavia, over 28 per cent were children under 15 years and 9 per cent between 15 and 19 years. After Italians, the Serbs constitute the second most important group of immigrants. This community is dominated by children under 15 years of age who account for 31 per cent of the total immigrant population of this group. The number of children and young adults in this ethnic group grew seven-fold between 1985 and 1997 (see Rosenberg *et al.*, 2003).

Information on immigration into selected European countries by eligibility category shows that family reunification became much less important a criterion than skills for seeking immigration into Switzerland. This contrasts with the situation in France, Sweden and the UK where until recently immigration for family reasons had increased significantly.[3]

The shares of children in the total immigrant population hide wide variations across different regions and countries of origin. For example, young children (0–14 years) predominate among the immigrant populations of Serbs and other former Yugoslavs (over 28 per cent), from Turkey (about 24 per cent) and Portugal (about 22 per cent). These shares are much higher than those of German, Italian and Spanish immigrant children (Table 4.1).

If we take the regions, shares of young children (0–14 years) are high for Africa (about 21 per cent) and Asia (22 per cent) but relatively low for the Americas and Australia/Oceania. The share for Europe as a whole, though higher at 18 per cent, is well below that for ex-Yugoslavia, Portugal and Turkey. As we shall discuss below, this situation may well account for the relatively greater deprivation of children among these communities than among the European children in Switzerland.

We do not know of any systematic country data on the age structure of immigrants from poor developing countries of Asia and Africa comparable to that for ex-Yugoslavia, Portugal and Turkey. Yet, some information on Somalian asylum-seekers suggests that the share of young children among developing-country immigrants is also very high if not higher than among those from the former Yugoslavia. In 2003, nearly half the

*Table 4.1*   Immigrant population in Switzerland by nationality and age (2004)

| Country of origin | Total no. of immigrants (thousands) | Children 0–14 years (thousands) | Children 0-14 years (%) | Children between 14 and 19 years (thousands) | Children between 14 and 19 (%) |
|---|---|---|---|---|---|
| Europe | 1,397.8 | 251.6 | 18.0 | 76.1 | 5.4 |
| Americas | 61.7 | 9.3 | 15.0 | 4.2 | 6.8 |
| Asia | 108.5 | 24.6 | 22.2 | 5.7 | 5.5 |
| Africa | 65.1 | 13.5 | 20.8 | 4.9 | 7.6 |
| Australia/ Oceania | 3.4 | 0.5 | 14.4 | 0.2 | 4.8 |
| Italy | 307.7 | 37.7 | 12.2 | 12.3 | 4.0 |
| Germany | 163.9 | 15.6 | 9.5 | 3.6 | 2.2 |
| Former Yugoslavia | 363.8 | 102.5 | 28.2 | 32.3 | 8.9 |
| Spain | 76.1 | 9.7 | 12.7 | 3.6 | 4.8 |
| Portugal | 173.3 | 38.0 | 21.9 | 9.8 | 5.7 |
| Turkey | 80.5 | 19.2 | 23.8 | 6.1 | 7.6 |

*Source*: Swiss Federal Statistical Office (OFS) (2005).

Somali population of about 5,000 persons in Switzerland was under 19 years of age and 36 per cent were between 20 and 39 years (Moret, 2006).

## Residence status of foreigners

Before we examine in detail the socio-economic situation of immigrant children and their parents, we need to understand the nature of the legal categories under which foreigners from within Europe and developing countries outside Europe are allowed into Switzerland. This discussion is important because the legal status (and the nature of a permit an immigrant holds) can influence his or her poverty situation. Often it determines the stability or precariousness of his or her residence, the scope for obtaining employment, the level of earnings and so on.

While the Swiss bilateral arrangements with the EU for free labour movement (which came into force in June 2002) have improved the residence status of Europeans in Switzerland, they have made the status of immigrants from outside Europe relatively more difficult. Table 4.2 describes different categories of permits granted to foreigners in the ascending order of their precariousness of stay. As the table shows, there were, until June 2002, six types of such permits.[4] Below we discuss how these different categories affect the employability of immigrant parents and the schooling of their children.

*Table 4.2*  Residence status of foreigners in Switzerland, including asylum-seekers and refugees

| Residence status/permit | 2002 (no.) | 2004 (no.) | Family reunification? | Social benefits? | Other remarks |
|---|---|---|---|---|---|
| Permit C | 4,799 | 3,400 | Yes | Yes; entitlement to social welfare benefits such as unemployment insurance | Granted after five to ten years of stay in the country; entitles holders all rights and privileges except the right to vote; permit valid for three (non-Europeans) to five (Europeans) years and renewable |
| Permit B | 79,017 | 62,651 | Yes, if immigrants have a job contract; spouse and unmarried children under 18 are allowed after a waiting period of one year | Yes | An annual permit for a specific purpose or economic activity (e.g. study and research), which may not be changed without prior permission; requires a work contract; possibility of renewal |
| Permit L | 3,784[a] 97,086[b] | 98[a] 106,901[b] | No | Yes? | Short-term residence, generally for less than a year (generally four months) depending on the nature of the job contract. This replaced permit A (see below) abolished in 2002) |

| | a | b | | | |
|---|---|---|---|---|---|
| Permit N | 25,988 | 14,434 | No. Family members may arrive illegally | Social welfare benefits are much lower than those granted to recognized refugees or Swiss nationals | For asylum-seekers for the period required for processing application; restrictions of employment and school attendance, and freedom of movement outside Switzerland |
| Permit F | 340 | 393 | No. Family members may arrive illegally | Social welfare benefits are lower and more restricted (even after many years of residence) than those of recognized refugees | A provisional admission granted to asylum-seekers; also for tourists who have overstayed; renewable every year. It is mainly for asylum-seekers and refugees |
| Permit A | 32,272 | 0 | No | No; no entitlement to any social welfare benefits | For seasonal workers for jobs not suitable for the Swiss; generally for nine months after which the workers must leave Switzerland and re-enter with a new permit. Possibility of a B permit after four years. Abolished in June 2002 |

*Notes*: [a] More than one-year validity. [b] Less than one-year validity.
There is also a Permit G for workers living in neighbouring border villages of France, valid for one year and renewable. The person working in Switzerland is required to return to his or her domicile in France every day.
*Sources*: Based on Swiss Federal Statistical Office (OFS) (2005); Moret (2006); Wanner (2004).

One can draw a number of conclusions from the information provided in Table 4.2.[5] First, immigrants' countries of origin can be divided into two categories: (a) European Union and North America and (b) poor developing countries. The former receive better treatment in terms of a more stable and longer-term residence and work permits and easier access to employment and schooling. Second, with the exception of permits B and C, other permits do not entitle the holder to any social welfare benefits such as unemployment insurance. Third, the three categories of foreigners in Switzerland, namely, asylum-seekers, recognized refugees and persons with a provisional admission status (permit F), suffer from various types of restrictions. Most of these foreigners are from former Yugoslavia and such poor developing countries as Somalia and Sri Lanka.

The rights and benefits of people with provisional status are more restricted than those of recognized refugees. They have restricted access to employment and higher education. They also suffer from a lack of freedom of movement as they are not entitled to any travel documents. While they are insured against sickness, their other social benefits 'are 40–60% lower than those granted to Swiss nationals or to recognized refugees' (*ibid.*, p. 25). Giugni and Passy (2006a, p. 65) note that migrants with short-term permits do not enjoy access to credit, mortgage or real estate. They cannot establish a private enterprise in Switzerland.

The above restrictions tend to encourage many short-term migrants and asylum-seekers (for example, Somalians) to attempt to move to an EU country. Indeed, the number of applications for asylum from most countries (except Bulgaria and Somalia) declined between 2003 and 2004. This decline may be due to the introduction of new measures, which exclude social welfare benefits for those asylum-seekers whose applications are rejected.[6]

The Swiss Federal Office of Migration (OFM) undertook an interview survey of Somali refugees between June 2004 and March 2005.This survey (see Moret, 2006) noted that many Somalians interviewed complained of the restrictions deriving from their F permits, which prevented them from visiting families and children in other countries, and which denied their children access to higher education or the job market. (A new federal law on asylum-seekers passed in December 2005 was intended to improve some of these conditions; see Chapter 7.)

## Poverty among immigrant children

Not much is written on child poverty in Switzerland, much less on poor immigrant children (however, see Falter, 2005; Macculi, 2005). The rate of poverty (determined by a poverty line below which a person is considered to be poor) among immigrants in 2003 was more than twice as high (21.4 per cent) as among Swiss nationals (10.4 per cent). However, the above average figures conceal wide variations. The rate of poverty among North and West Europeans is the lowest (7 per cent), lower than that of the Swiss. Immigrants from Southern Europe suffer from the most acute poverty (over 19 per cent). Within this group, the ex-Yugoslav Balkans record the highest rate of over 33 per cent, followed by new EU candidate countries (for example, Turkey, Romania and Bulgaria) (see Figure 4.1) (OFS, 2005).

The OFS study on the immigrant population employs the concept of 'the working poor', which is defined as persons working in an economic activity offering part-time (as against full-time) employment that offers incomes that are below the poverty line. Thus the nature of the labour

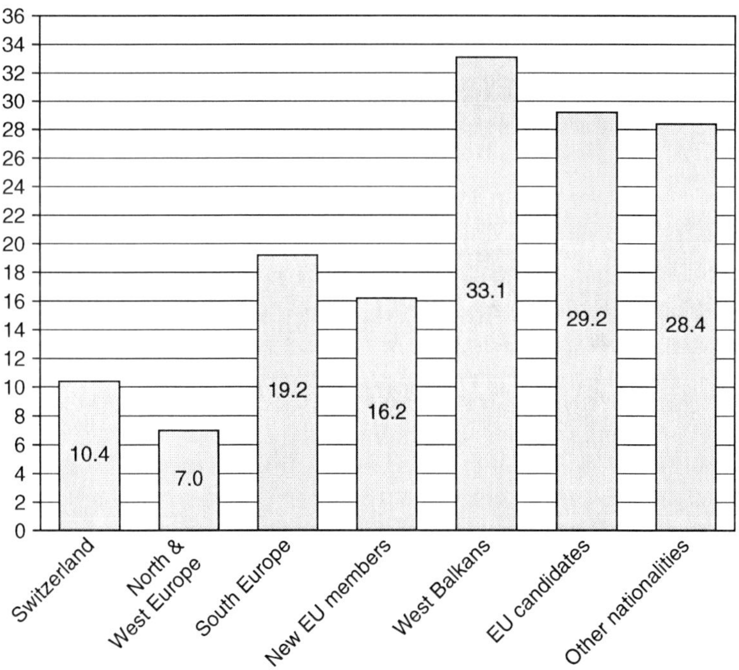


*Figure 4.1*   Poverty rates for persons aged 20–59 by country groups/nationalities (2003) (%) Switzerland, North and West Europe, South Europe, New EU members, West Balkans, EU candidates, Other nationalities
*Source*: OFS (2005), p. 67.

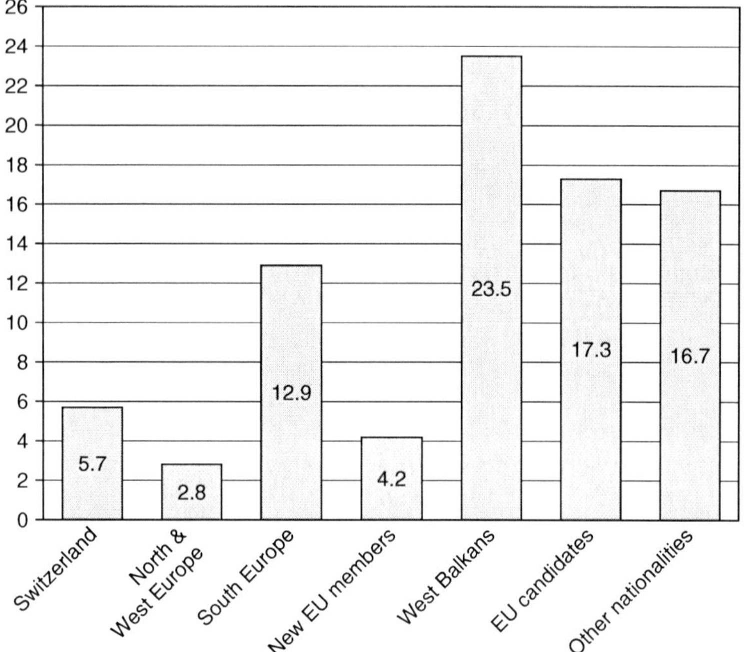


*Figure 4.2* Proportions of the working poor aged 20–59 by country groups/ nationalities (2003)
Switzerland, North and West Europe, South Europe, New EU members, West Balkans, EU candidates, Other nationalities
*Source*: OFS (2005), p. 67.

market and economic activities (including discrimination and higher rates of unemployment among immigrants) explain a much higher proportion of the working poor (over 13 per cent) among immigrants compared to Swiss nationals (only 7 per cent). There are wide variations in the proportions of the working poor by nationality (see Figure 4.2). As in the case of overall poverty rates (Figure 4.1), the highest proportion of the working poor are among ex-Yugoslavs (23.5 per cent) followed by the new EU candidates (17.3 per cent).

Over 6 per cent of Swiss children suffer from relative poverty (1.6 per cent are estimated to be absolute poor – see Chapter 2) compared to 9.8 per cent in France, 11.8 per cent in Germany and 21.3 per cent in the UK. While relative child poverty in Switzerland is lower, it is growing. The OFS estimated that in 2003 there were 233,000 children (birth to 15 years,

*Table 4.3* Incidence of child poverty in Switzerland by headcount ratio (1999–2003)

|  | 1999 | 2000 | 2001 | 2002 | 2003 |
| --- | --- | --- | --- | --- | --- |
| HCR for: | | | | | |
| (a) Swiss children | 7.45 | 5.42 | 5.41 | 6.56 | 8.88 |
| (b) Foreign children | 9.48 | 9.82 | 9.47 | 12.82 | 13.14 |

*Source*: Macculi (2005).

living with one or two parents in a household, and children between 16 and 24 still training or at school) whose parents were 'working poor'. The number of working poor (between 20 and 59 years) is about 231,000 living in 137,000 households.

According to a staff member of OFS, 'unfortunately, we do not have similar figures for children who have poor parents but the amount of work within households is lower than full-time employment (90 per cent to be precise) or members of these households do not work at all' (personal communication, 31 August 2006).

Macculi (2005) estimates child poverty among Swiss and foreign children on the basis of the Swiss Household Panel data for 1999–2003. She measures the incidence of poverty by the headcount ratio (HCR) (that is, the number of children below a poverty line of 50 per cent of the median income divided by the total population of children) as shown in Table 4.3.

The above estimates show that (i) poverty among Swiss children declined between 1999 and 2001 before rising again; (ii) poverty among foreign children has a rising trend although there was a slight dip from 2000–1; and (iii) the incidence of poverty was higher among immigrant children.

Macculi (2005) also estimates for 1999 the FGT poverty ratio and the poverty gap ratio reflecting the intensity of poverty rather than just its incidence. These indicators show how poor the poor are below the poverty line.[7] She comes to a rather unexpected and surprising conclusion that 'the poverty gap and the FGT-index are both lower for foreign children than for natives ones, and also lower than the overall child population' (*ibid.*, p. 27). A priori, one would expect higher intensity of poverty among foreign children whose parents have lower incomes, are less educated and include many single-parent and large families. Macculi does not go on to explain the above. Does a small sample size of foreign children account for this unexpected result? Or is 1999 a special year?

One cannot give much credence to the results, which are presented here mainly for illustrative purposes.

Macculi (2005, p. 45) concludes that 'immigrant children have a higher probability of being poor than Swiss children and that "persistent poverty" (remaining poor for 4–5 years) was found highest among children in single-parent and large families as well as non-native children'. Swiss children suffer mainly from 'transitory poverty', which is defined as being poor once.

A meaningful quantitative analysis of child poverty among immigrant children in Switzerland is difficult for lack of appropriate data. Available statistical series do not sufficiently disaggregate data for Swiss citizens, foreigners and immigrant children. Furthermore, how does one define immigrant children? Are they children who were not born in Switzerland; that is, those who came to the country after their birth abroad? Or are they children of foreign nationals who were not born in Switzerland? Studies discussed above do not make such distinction. Failure to distinguish between such factors as legal status of immigrant children, length of their stay in Switzerland, their ethnic origin and linguistic knowledge often make it difficult to compare results of different studies.[8] Another problem is the sample size. The Falter (2005) study on child poverty in Switzerland, which uses the Swiss Income and Expenditure Survey (SIES), contained only 300 foreign children in a sample of 2,300 (personal communication, 1 September 2006). The Swiss Household Panel data used by Macculi (2005) are also inadequate as foreigners are under-represented and the statistics on household income are less accurate than those of the SIES. The third set of data is that of the Labour Force Survey, which is also not very useful since it covers data only on individuals over 15 years of age.

One is obliged to resort to unofficial estimates to obtain an idea of the magnitude of child poverty in Switzerland. The Swiss Labour Assistance (*Oeuvre Suisse d'entraide Ouvrière* (OSEO)), a charity organization, which launched a campaign to tackle rising child poverty in Switzerland in 2003, estimates that there are between 250,000 and 300,000 poor children in the country (*Swissinfo*, 2003a).[9] This suggests that one child in ten is poor. However, the Director of OSEO (Brigitte Steiman) told *Swissinfo* that this figure was based on the number of families claiming social welfare benefits. Considering that nearly half the families fail to claim benefits (ignorant about their entitlement), the figure may be closer to one in five children living below the poverty line (*Swissinfo*, 2003b). The Swiss Agency for Child Protection (ASPE) estimates that between 200,000 and 250,000 minors in Switzerland need social welfare assistance.

The poverty problem among immigrant children in Switzerland needs to be examined by countries of origin and levels of income. A priori, the situation of Asian and African young children in Switzerland is likely to be relatively more precarious considering that generally parents of these children tend to be less skilled than European immigrants. Children from outside Europe will be even poorer than those from ex-Yugoslavia with higher levels of income and skills.

The poverty situation is particularly acute among Roma children who live on the fringes of society. Single-parent families in Switzerland account for 5 per cent of the total population, 13.4 per cent of which benefit from social welfare assistance. Among immigrant households with children on social welfare, 55 per cent have only a single parent (Kehrli and Knöpfel, 2007, p. 92). Single-parent immigrant families, which suffer from a greater risk of poverty, generally come from Africa, France and the USA. As we noted in Chapter 2, these families are less common among Muslims or Roman Catholics from ex-Yugoslavia, Italy and Portugal.

The Roma suffer from racial and ethnic discrimination in their countries of origin as well as in the host countries. Roma children and their parents and families are much larger in number in France than in Switzerland (see Chapters 5 and 6). However, there is a growing influx of Roma in Geneva (see Box 4.1).

**Deprivation**

In Chapter 1 we discussed the concept of deprivation and in Chapter 2 we provided some empirical evidence of child deprivation in a selected number of EU countries on the basis of selected indicators. In the case of Switzerland there is no systematic study of child deprivation. However, some anecdotal evidence suggests that poor children lack basic consumption goods and social/leisure activities. For example, social participation of children is limited: one out of four immigrants is a member of any social group. Poor immigrants are left out of social clubs for lack of income to pay for membership (Kehrli and Knöpfel, 2007, p. 139).

Leu and Burri (1999, pp. 322–4) examine the standard of living and welfare of poor people in Switzerland by using objective (living in a crowded apartment, unemployed or suffering from bad health) and subjective (depression, anxiety and loneliness) indicators. For 1992 they show that poor immigrants lived in crowded housing, were unemployed and suffered from loneliness more than all poor people. They also conclude that 'children are by far the largest single population group affected by poverty' (*ibid.*, p. 324).

### Box 4.1   Roma children in Geneva

Roma children have been arriving in Geneva since 2004, mainly from the small town of Aiud in Transylvania in Romania. Many arrive via other European countries (for example, Italy) when they or their parents fail to find any income-earning opportunities there. Racial discrimination against Roma people in Romania largely explains their exodus to Switzerland and France, among other European countries. They come to Switzerland as they have been able to enter the country without a visa since 2007, when Romania and Bulgaria joined the European Union.

The number of Roma families and children in Geneva has been rapidly growing since September 2007. This influx is causing the cantonal and city authorities serious concern, especially since the local social service agencies are ill-equipped to cope with the reception and board and lodging for these people. Noel Constant, the director of Carrefour-Rue (an association to help the destitute and homeless), states that there is no political will to solve the problem of Roma people in Geneva.

Roma children eke out a meagre living by begging in the streets, theft and petty crime. The Geneva police spokesman noted that sometimes Roma children as young as ten to 12 years old are arrested for crime or theft. They steal money and jewellery and are generally well equipped like professionals, and rarely leave any evidence (*Tribune de Genève*, 31 October 2007). They and their parents live in appalling conditions without any hygienic or sanitary facilities. Many are homeless and sleep on the pavements and under bridges.

Quite a few Roma children interviewed by journalists stated that they preferred begging to stealing. A 17-year-old girl outside a supermarket in Carouge in Geneva made about 15 francs daily by begging, which is a very low amount. Herzog (2007a) notes that the Roma can expect to make between 10 and 30 francs a day. He met Marcel who came to Switzerland several times. Marcel believes that he can raise about 3,000 Swiss francs in a few months by begging.

Some people believe that quasi-impunity of minors before the law encourages their parents to send them to rich countries to make money through hook or crook. Many Roma parents based in France send their children to Geneva to beg, steal and raise money. This strategy is effective thanks to the numerous porous borders with France that surround Geneva. Children and their families steal and return to France, escaping arrest by the Geneva authorities.

Very few Roma children go to school. Since the Roma come to Geneva on a short-term visa of three months, their children are not entitled to schooling even if they were interested. Many families do not like the idea of Roma children attending school classes along with their children.

Many observers in Geneva, including the local police, associate the presence of Roma with crime, delinquency and drug addiction. The local population and the town and cantonal authorities are divided in their attitudes towards the growing Roma population. An increase in begging associated with Roma has led the conservative local government to ban begging in the canton (Faas, 2007). On 1 November 2007, the Judicial and Police Commission of the Cantonal Parliament of Geneva (*Grand Conseil*) approved by a substantial majority draft legislation to make begging illegal. In May 2008, the Federal Tribunal in Lausanne upheld this ban on begging, noting the possible harassment of people by beggars and the risk of exploitation of minors and children. It is not clear whether Roma are being forcibly expelled from Geneva, as in France and other European countries.[10] At the end of November 2007, it was reported that Roma were asked to leave Geneva. A few (including several children ranging from two to 15 years of age) had already left for Spain and other neighbouring countries (Herzog, 2007c).

It is difficult to determine the number of Roma and their children in Geneva since they are nomadic people without any fixed residence. Many travel frequently between their villages of origin in Romania and Geneva, which makes their enumeration problematic. According to a rough estimate, there are over 100 Roma people in Geneva, many of whom are children. A police survey shows that three-quarters of beggars in Geneva come from Romania; others are from Slovenia, Hungary, France and Switzerland (*Tribune de Genève*, 21 October 2007).

## Social welfare benefits

Welfare benefits generally tend to reduce the rate of poverty as we discussed in Chapter 2. However, only 3 per cent of the population (or 237,500 persons) in Switzerland in 2005 benefited from welfare payments (Drilling, 2007a, p. 37). This is a rather small figure. Most of the benefits go to unemployed workers, single parents and youth. A Report of the Federal Commission for Children and Youth (2007) notes that in 2005 nearly 45 per cent of the beneficiaries were below 25 years of age.

Drug- and alcohol-related assistance is provided mainly to Swiss youth. Such assistance is much less common among immigrant youth. This is also true of welfare payments to single mothers, who are much less common among immigrants. Foreigners represent nearly 44 per cent of the welfare beneficiaries. The rate of welfare payments is the highest for children below ten years of age, followed by the adolescent group (ten to 17 years) (Drilling, 2007a, p. 37).

Child benefits in Switzerland are very low: in 2002 they amounted to only 5 per cent of the total welfare benefits compared to a much larger proportion in neighbouring countries such as France and Germany (see Chapter 2). Although all the 26 Swiss cantons pay child benefits, the amounts of benefits vary enormously between cantons: from 150 Swiss francs per month in Zurich to 200–50 Swiss francs in Zug and 210–94 Swiss francs in Valais (Mäder, Kutzner and Knöpfel, 2003; *Swissinfo*, 2005). In a national referendum held on 26 November 2006 the Swiss population voted in favour (68 per cent) of the Federal government proposal to harmonize child benefits throughout Switzerland with a uniform allowance of 200 Swiss francs per month for a child up to the age of 16 and up to 250 Swiss francs per month for a student till the age of 25 (the referendum was significant in that all the cantons except Appenzell AI voted in favour).

The amount of child benefit is small compared to the cost of child rearing. On average the total cost of a child till the 20th year is 43 per cent of the income of a household with a couple and one child, 61 per cent for two children and 75 per cent for three children. In the case of a single-parent household, the cost rises to 118 per cent with one child. Rearing a child also involves indirect costs in terms of extra workload and even withdrawal of a mother from the labour market.[11] In absolute terms, the cost of a child is translated into 1.2 million francs (40 per cent direct cost and 60 per cent indirect cost), which amounts to 2,500 francs per month. The data refer to 1990; since then the cost has been steadily rising (Kehrli and Knöpfel, 2007, pp. 90–1).

A survey of young adults (18 to 25 years) in Basle city receiving welfare benefits shows that the largest number of recipients of long-term assistance are Turkish youth, followed by Italian and Swiss youth (Drilling, 2005). Welfare assistance for training is more significant for Swiss youth than for immigrant youth. This is also true of the total subsidiary assistance.[12] Drilling (2007b) argues that economic (income and savings), social (contact with parents) and cultural (for example, migration to Basle, education and occupation of children and their parents) poverty of urban youth (including immigrants) started in their childhood, long before they enrolled for social welfare benefits. Once these urban youth exit from the welfare system to join the labour market, they join the corps of urban working poor, a situation that is inherited from generation to generation. This information supplements the evidence on intergenerational transmission of poverty presented in Chapter 2.

## Access of immigrant children to education and employment

Income poverty is closely related to other indicators such as access to education, health and housing. A poor child may be unable to afford to go to school and university, especially if he or she belongs to a large household with many children. In 1998, a Bureau of Labour Policy and Social Studies (*Bureau d'études de politique du travail et de politique social*) (BASS) survey estimated that it would cost 340,000 Swiss francs to educate a child during the first 20 years of his/her life. This amounts to a sum of 1,400 Swiss francs per month, which is beyond the capacity of many poor immigrant parents to pay.

As we shall discuss below, poor parents with limited education may attach low priority to giving their children much formal education. Similarly, children in poor families are less likely to consult a doctor frequently than children in rich families. Access to housing is also restricted by low incomes and high rents. As we note below, immigrants tend to live in very small apartments because they cannot afford anything bigger.

### Education

The composition and share of immigrant children in Swiss schools has changed dramatically since the 1980s, when one out of two immigrant children were from Italy. Today one out of three immigrant children originate in ex-Yugoslavia. In 1980, only 16 per cent of these children were receiving compulsory education (for nine years starting at age six or seven); this share went up to nearly 24 per cent in 2004 (OFM, 2006).

The Swiss Federal Office of Migration (OFM) (*ibid.*) notes that 14 per cent of immigrant children are not born in Switzerland, and 7 per cent among them did not do all their schooling there. Language difficulties and poorer quality of schooling in their countries of origin may handicap these children.

There are fewer immigrant children in *crèches* and day care centres (*garderies*) (50 per cent) than Swiss children (70 per cent). This may explain the difficulties faced by the immigrant children in learning languages; they are less exposed to the external environment and contact with Swiss children at an early age. Half of the immigrant children whose parents were born abroad have reading difficulties (*ibid.*).

Another discriminatory practice in some Swiss cantons during 1997–2001 (now discontinued) was to provide segregated classes for immigrant children at the request of parents of Swiss children. Such a practice clearly smacked of racism and was declared illegal and unconstitutional (ECRI, 2004).

A study shows that immigrant children in Switzerland are increasingly assigned to special classes for pupils with learning difficulties (see Kronig, 2003). Their number in these classes has more than trebled since the early 1980s, whereas places (quota) for immigrant children in regular classes have increased only by 35 per cent. This discrimination may partly explain the low educational attainment of such children.

An OECD study (2006a) covering 17 countries/territories (including France and Switzerland) with large immigrant populations concludes that 'in the majority of countries there are significant differences (in student performance) between immigrant students and their counterparts (p. 54). It notes that 'immigrant students fail to reach baseline performance levels defined by PISA' (p. 55). The study also notes that educational performance sometimes depends on the geographical and ethnic origin of immigrants. For example, children of Turkish immigrant families in many countries show below-average performance, but they perform better in Switzerland and France than in Germany. It is not clear why this is so. Differences in the nature and content of the educational systems in these countries may be a factor in explaining this situation.

Some recent evidence suggests that early tracking of children increases educational inequality. Early tracking takes place throughout Germany, whereas it occurs only in some places in Switzerland, which may partly explain lower educational achievement of Turkish immigrant children. Crul (2007) argues that tracking in Germany and Austria at the age of ten offers little time to Turkish second-generation pupils 'to overcome their disadvantaged starting position'.

Another factor may be differences in language instruction. Swiss schools in different cantons (Geneva, Berne and Zurich) offer special language instruction to immigrant children (OECD, 2006a), which children in Germany may not enjoy. For example, in the canton of Geneva, the emphasis is on systematic language support to immigrant children who have limited proficiency in French. Fully trained schoolteachers are involved in offering additional language instruction (three to 20 hours per week) in elementary and lower secondary schools. The

Swiss experience suggests that an appropriate public education policy for immigrant children can make a difference.

Access of immigrant children of refugees and asylum-seekers to higher education and professional/vocational training is restricted. It is restricted partly because of the limited financial means of the parents with low incomes, who cannot bear the cost. Another restriction arises when educational qualifications and certificates of immigrant children (especially from developing countries) are not formally recognized by the Swiss institutions. Third, access to vocational education in polytechnics is generally in the form of part-time apprenticeships lasting for three to four years.

In Switzerland the majority of Turkish children enter an apprenticeship system under which they study and work at the same time. Since, during apprenticeships, pupils work part-time, immigrant children with short-term permits are discriminated against by Swiss employers who, other things being equal, prefer applicants with longer-term (C) permits generally held by Western Europeans. The Swiss legislation encourages employers to give priority to longer-term residents rather than to holders of N, F, or L permits (Moret, 2006, p. 25).

The Swiss educational system is relatively inegalitarian as is indicated by the results of PISA 2000. Immigrants naturally suffer from this inequality since they are generally at the lower end of the social distribution.

The scholastic achievement of immigrant children depends, *inter alia*, on the educational background of parents. Children of ex-Yugoslavs, Portuguese and Turks tend to have less education than those from other Western European countries. Table 4.4 shows that children from these countries have far fewer numbers and proportions with tertiary education (university and advanced professional training). They form less than 4 per cent of the total number of children in each of these countries compared to 35.3 per cent of children from Austria, France and Germany.

It is rather surprising that the proportion of Swiss children with tertiary education (13.9 per cent), though much higher than children from ex-Yugoslavia, Portugal and Turkey, is substantially lower than that for children from Austria, France and Germany (see Table 4.4). This may be explained by the fact that the Swiss educational system places heavier emphasis on apprenticeship rather than on university education in order to keep unemployment low. Poor immigrants rarely encourage their children to acquire tertiary education, which they may not be able to afford. They may also perceive that their children's opportunities in the labour market would be limited owing to their foreign origin.

*Table 4.4* Educational attainment of Swiss and immigrant children (2003–4) (% given in parentheses)

| Educational level | Swiss | Immigrants | | | | | | | Others |
| --- | --- | --- | --- | --- | --- | --- | --- | --- | --- |
| | | Western Europe | | | | Southern Europe | | | |
| | | Austria, France, Germany | Italy | Spain | Portugal | Ex-Yugoslavia | Turkey | | |
| Total | 1,151,790 | 34,111 | 46,713 | 13,047 | 33,072 | 94,411 | 22,250 | 88,551 |
| Kindergarten | 111,976 (9.7) | 3,187 (8.8) | 5,321 (10.9) | 1,451 (7.7) | 5,218 (15.1) | 12,267 (12.8) | 2,944 (13.6) | 11,416 (12.5) |
| Primary | 359,160 (31.2) | 7,598 (20.6) | 14,277 (30.4) | 3,451 (23.1) | 12,715 (39.4) | 36,907 (39.3) | 7,668 (36.4) | 24,001 (27.3) |
| Secondary | 257,199 (22.3) | 5,110 (14.7) | 9,937 (21.7) | 3,055 (23.1) | 5,475 (15.1) | 13,954 (13.8) | 3,428 (13.6) | 12,484 (13.6) |
| Tertiary | 160,494 (13.9) | 12,248 (35.3) | 4,540 (9.7) | 1,662 (12.7) | 707 (2.1) | 1,356 (1.4) | 714 (3.2) | 14,718 (16.6) |
| – Advanced professional training | 37,648 (3.2) | 1,234 (3.6) | 1,108 (2.4) | 300 (2.3) | 156 (0.5) | 413 (0.4) | 152 (0.7) | 2,514 (2.8) |
| – University | 85,947 (7.5) | 8,467 (23.5) | 2,501 (4.3) | 1,018 (7.7) | 348 (1.1) | 692 (0.1) | 412 (1.8) | 9,949 (11.4) |

*Source*: OFS (2005).

Immigrants from Portugal, ex-Yugoslavia and Turkey tend to have larger families, which may handicap their children more severely in terms of educational access than those from Western and Northern Europe. Statistics show that in these countries the size of a household is much larger than, say, in Switzerland or Germany. According to the Swiss Census of Population 2000, there are 1.81 children on average per household in Switzerland compared to 2.33 for immigrants from ex-Yugoslavia, 2.01 for those from Turkey and 2.0 for those from Africa.

To conclude, one notices a hierarchy of educational achievements among immigrant children, which corresponds roughly to the levels or rates of poverty of their parents. At the top of the ladder are Northern and Western Europeans (for example, Austrians, French and Germans). At the next rung of the ladder are Southern Europeans (for example, Italians and Spaniards). At the bottom are ex-Yugoslavs, Portuguese and Turks.

## Enrolment of clandestine immigrant children in Geneva public schools

Clandestine children of seasonal workers and refugees with short-term permits are, in principle, eligible for attending a public school. In 11 Swiss cantons, these children are accepted in compulsory schools without any attestation from the police. In the past, three cantons, namely, Basle-City, Tessin and Grison, prohibited schooling of such children. A more recent policy allows such children to go to school if the police authorities provide an authorization (see Forster, 1993). However, discussions with Mr Boillat (responsible for registering clandestine children in public schools) of the Centre for Contact between Swiss and Immigrants (CCSI) (Geneva) suggest that, in practice, only in the Canton of Geneva has there been an official regulation since 1990 to accept clandestine children of four to 12 years of age (at the primary school level) in public schools where they are offered free education. Other Swiss cantons have no such official policy, although they make claims, which are unfounded. Besides accepting clandestine children in public schools, the Canton of Geneva subsidizes health insurance of these children through a subsidy granted to the CCSI. Most of the children benefiting from this insurance come from very poor families.

Estimates of clandestine immigrants in the Geneva canton vary. The Geneva Professional Workers Trade Union (SIT) estimates 6,000 such immigrants, whereas Mr Boillat of the CCSI believes that they number between 8,000 and 12,000.[13] The number of clandestine children is not known. These children generally live with their families or parents, who

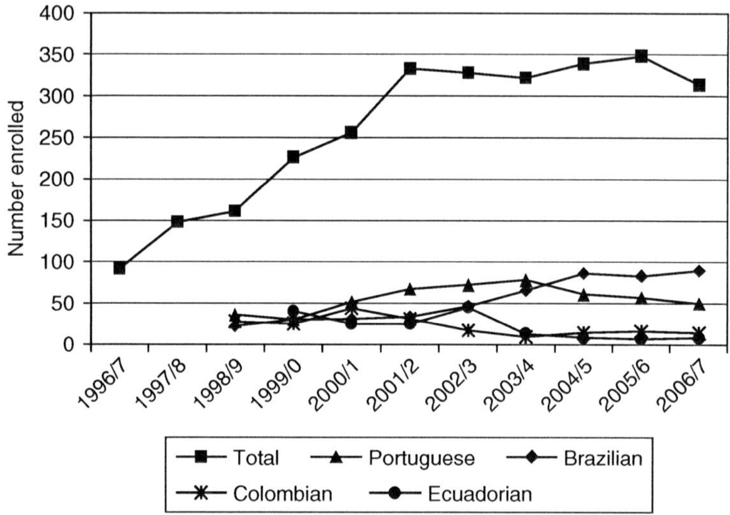


*Figure 4.3*   Annual enrolment of clandestine children (4–12 years) in Geneva public schools, by nationality
*Source*: Based on data provided by Mr Jean-Pierre Boillat of CCSI, Geneva.

came to Switzerland because they had some initial contacts in the canton. Most children are studying at a public school, although a few may be delinquents or working in the black market. Most come from Latin American countries, notably Colombia and Ecuador. Some Portuguese children (about 20 per cent of the total) also opt to become 'clandestine' temporarily while awaiting work permits which they eventually obtain, unlike other Latin American children.

There is less police control of clandestine immigrants and their children today than a few years ago.[14] Despite this relaxation of control, new enrolment of clandestine children for public schools has been declining due partly to the introduction of visa requirements for nationals of Colombia and Ecuador (see Figure 4.3). Annual enrolment increased rapidly from 1996/7 till 2001/2. Since then it has stabilized; it started declining in 2005/6. A forecast of annual enrolment for 2007/8 suggests that it will be at the level for 1999/2000, which was much lower.

## Employment

Immigrant children are less prepared for employment than Swiss nationals. Their access to the labour market is restricted for several reasons.

First, as we noted above they often receive education with children suffering from learning difficulties, which puts them at a disadvantage. Second, language difficulties faced by immigrant children is a barrier despite the fact that some Swiss cantons offer special language classes. Third, immigrant children (particularly, the first generation), especially from developing countries, have lower educational qualifications, which contributes to higher school drop-outs. At higher levels of education, foreign educational qualifications (except from other European countries) are not recognized by Swiss educational institutions and universities.

While schooling and higher education may be important determinants of earnings in the labour market, other non-economic factors may also be relevant. A comparative study on the earnings of foreigners and Swiss nationals in the labour market concludes that nationals have a significant advantage in earnings over foreigners – 16 per cent for males and about 14 per cent for females. The study concludes that 'the discrimination effect plays a more important role than the endowment effect (human capital formation, schooling and experience) for males as well as females' (see Golder and Straubhaar, 1999a).

The results of a Swiss study (de Coulon *et al.*, 2003) shows that, other things being equal, there is no earnings penalty for Western European immigrants but that there is one of 40 per cent for African immigrants. Differences between Swiss nationals and foreigners in returns to education (education acquired outside Switzerland is valued less in the labour market) was the main source of discrimination. Second, there is no discrimination against second-generation immigrants born in Switzerland. Here different endowment explains earnings differential.

Many observers, including such NGOs as CARITAS, have noted discrimination against immigrant children seeking jobs or vocational training and apprenticeship (Zeugin, 2007). A precarious legal status restricts their occupational mobility. A study undertaken by the Institute of Education at the University of Fribourg shows that Swiss nationals are given preference over foreigners. Over a three-year period, the authors of the study interviewed those responsible for recruitment in 80 SMEs covering petty trade, woodwork, motor mechanics and painting of cars (cited in *Le Temps*, 13 March 2007). They came to the conclusion that the selection process was not based on merit or competence. Discrimination was particularly marked against immigrants from ex-Yugoslavia and Turkey. SME managers were afraid that these immigrants would make trouble on the shop floor. However, a very small sample does not allow any generalizations.

Unemployment among immigrant youth (between 15 and 24 years) is significant, which may be explained by a prolonged economic recession. In 2004, the unemployment rate for immigrants was more than twice as high as that for Swiss citizens (OFS, 2005).

In Switzerland, about 10 per cent of all employment (or 400,000 persons) is estimated to be 'precarious', which is defined in terms of the following criteria: lack of stability, uncertainty due to the short-term nature of contract, lack of legal protection against dismissal, economic vulnerability caused by low wage/salary, and lack of means to avoid social exclusion.

There are no separate data on the magnitude of precarious employment among immigrant youth in Switzerland. However, their proportion is likely to be significant. As we noted above, they suffer from uncertainty and discrimination because of, *inter alia*, their precarious legal status. Kehrli and Knöpfel (2007, p. 113) note that in cases of retrenchments, it is often immigrants who lose jobs through rationalization. Retrenchments drive them into the informal labour market, thus worsening their poverty situation. Studying young urban poor in the city of Basel (Switzerland), Drilling (2007a, p. 13) concludes: 'Even those young people who have had schooling and training, are usually not working within their occupations but have taken temporary jobs and occasional work.' Referring to young immigrants from Turkey and former Yugoslavia, he notes that they are particularly handicapped because 'they are endowed with so little economic and cultural capital' that 'it seemed safe to posit that at the very start of entry into the welfare system they stood very close to social exclusion' (*ibid.*, p. 14).

Immigrant children in Switzerland are caught up in a vicious circle. They are initially handicapped because their parents are poor and low skilled. This is particularly true of children from Southern Europe. They become poor in later life because they find it hard to get well-paid jobs. If they are poor because they find jobs in occupations requiring low skills, they will tend to give a low priority to education of their children.

## Access to health services

Very little information is available on immigrants' access to health services and their actual utilization. What information is available is rather old, dating back to the 1990s. A recent study by Kaya (2006) notes that the state of immigrants' health is likely to vary depending on the nature of their legal status determined by the type of permits they hold (see above).

In general, holders of short-term permits and asylum-seekers/refugees are likely to suffer from greater health risks than Swiss citizens. According to a Swiss Health Survey (ESS) undertaken in 1992–3, immigrants have a higher rate of doctor consultation than Swiss citizens, which is somewhat surprising. It would be more logical to expect immigrants to utilize health services less frequently than the local population, owing partly to poverty and a lack of information about availability of health services. Winkelman (2002) compared immigrant and local population for frequency of medical consultations by using data on the number of visits to a physician over a 12-month period. His empirical findings show that (1) immigrant women, but not men, have a higher health utilization; (2) married women have a lower utilization rate than unmarried ones; (3) women in full-time employment have fewer visits to a doctor than unemployed ones.

Some studies (for example, OFSP, 2002; Holly and Benkassmi, 2003) show that the disease rate among immigrants is higher than that among the native population. To take the particular example of tuberculosis, immigrants (excluding asylum-seekers) are three times as vulnerable as Swiss citizens (Bischoff, 1995). It is mainly young immigrants who are affected by this disease, in contrast to Swiss citizens who are affected by it mainly in old age. This particular disease is linked to poverty and precarious living conditions, which explains why it is more common among foreigners (Kaya, 2006). The life expectancy of the poor is known to be shorter than that of the rich. Since immigrants and their children tend to be poorer, they are more likely to live for fewer years.

There is another way in which the poverty situation of immigrant parents may adversely affect their children's health and physical development. It is reported that poor families tend to spend less on food and nutrition (Hoffmann, Nadai and Sommerfield, 2001). Furthermore, living in poor households can have psychological and social consequences for children, who may suffer from psychological problems on account of several factors, for example, risk of marital conflicts among parents, strained parent–child relations and possible family breakdown leading to separation and divorce.

The legal status of immigrants can also have an indirect effect on their health condition. Precarious legal status determined by the short-term nature of residence permits may limit access to health services and insurance, and result in poor living conditions and risk at work. Social welfare benefits for asylum-seekers are limited or non-existent (see Table 4.4). The situation of illegal immigrants regarding access to health services is even worse.

Turning to immigrant children, let us consider two indicators affecting them: (1) infant mortality, defined as death during the first year of birth, and (2) peri-natal mortality, defined as death of an infant from the sixth month of pregnancy up to seventh day of its life. There are gaps between infant mortality rates of immigrants and Swiss citizens. Wanner (2001, cited in Chimienti and Cattacin, 2001) gives infant mortality rates for the period 1969–97. During 1994–7, these rates were 5.3 per cent for Swiss boys and 4.4 per cent for Swiss girls; corresponding rates for foreigners were 6 per cent for boys and 5 per cent for girls. For the Turkish immigrant children, these rates were 8.6 per cent for boys and 9.6 per cent for girls.

More detailed information is available on peri-natal mortality. Here too there are wide gaps between immigrant mothers and Swiss mothers (Table 4.5). Between 1979 and 1981 children of Turkish mothers had mortality rates 50 per cent higher than those for Swiss mothers. Bischoff (1995) argues that one reason for this result may be the recent arrival of Turkish mothers and their failure to integrate. He is led to this conclusion by the fact that the second- and third-generation Spanish mothers had rates very similar to those for Swiss mothers. This suggests that the results are influenced not only by the country of origin and nationality of immigrants but also by their living conditions in the adopted country and the degree of their integration with the local population. Greater peri-natal mortality rates among immigrants may be caused, *inter alia*, by a lack of proper health care during pregnancy, inadequate knowledge of local languages and limited availability of health facilities. Precarious living conditions and poor legal status of seasonal workers with short-term permits (see above) may be partly responsible for a lack of proper health

*Table 4.5*   Peri-natal mortality rates in Switzerland, Northern Europe and the USA

| Country/nationality | Peri-natal rate of mortality (%) |
| --- | --- |
| Swiss mother | 9.4 |
| Turkish mother | 17.5 |
| Italian mother | 11.3 |
| Spanish mother | 9.3 |
| Northern European mother | 6.5 |
| US mother | 6.5 |

*Source*: Kaya (2006).

care facilities for immigrant mothers whose access to these facilities is also limited by the nature of their husbands' work.

## Other indicators

Other direct indicators of poverty among immigrant children include: homelessness (or poor housing conditions), factors such as nutrition affecting child development, child protection and child abuse, teenage pregnancy and youth crime and delinquency. Information on these variables is rather scant for immigrant children in Switzerland, but we report below whatever information is available.

**Housing** for immigrants is often cited as one indicator of their poor living conditions. The Swiss Population Census 2000 collected some data on this indicator. However, one needs to be careful in interpreting the census data. Since the status of migrants varies according to the permits they hold, it is difficult to determine whether their modest housing is due more to their short-term permits than to their poverty situation (low incomes) as such. Wanner (2004, p. 50) notes that immigrants' lack of access to adequate and decent housing may also be due to discrimination against them, about which not much is known. Ownership of a house or apartment is particularly limited among ex-Yugoslavs, Turks and Portuguese immigrants: only 5–7 per cent of households with children reported as being property owners. These low figures contrast with 59.5 per cent of Swiss ownership of residential property. For such Western European households as French and German with children, corresponding figures are 42 per cent and 30 per cent respectively (Wanner, 2004). Uncertainty and risk involved in holding short-term (renewable every year) residence permits discourages foreigners in Switzerland from investing in decent housing.[15]

We believe that **teenage pregnancy** is a good indicator of a young girl's current and future socio-economic condition. This hypothesis is based on the premise that being a child and mother at the same time occurs as a result of poor and precarious family backgrounds of parents and their lack of education and employment. It is reported that in 12 out of 13 EU countries teenage mothers were much worse off in terms of such indicators of ill-being or disadvantage as poverty, unemployment and educational underachievement (UNICEF Innocenti Research Centre, 2001). In Belgium, France, Germany and the UK, teenage mothers are twice as likely to be living in poverty (the poorest 20 per cent by income) and in Denmark and the Netherlands thrice as likely.

*Table 4.6*  Teenage pregnancy in Switzerland and selected European countries

| Country | Pregnancy rate (birth to women below 20 years per 1,000 women aged 15 to 19 years) | | Income inequality index (Gini based on per capita household income) (%) | 15–19-year old not at school (%) |
|---|---|---|---|---|
| | 1970 | 1998 | | |
| Switzerland | 22.6 | 5.5 | 35.5 | 15.9 |
| France | 36.8 | 9.3 | 32.4 | 12.2 |
| Spain | 14.1 | 7.9 | 32.4 | 23.5 |
| Italy | 27.4 | 6.6 | 35.9 | 30.2 |
| Germany | 55.5 | 13.1 | 30.0 | 11.7 |
| Portugal | 29.4 | 21.2 | 38.2 | 23.8 |
| UK | 49.4 | 30.8 | 36.6 | 30.5 |

*Source*: UNICEF (2001).

Switzerland has the lowest rate of teenage pregnancy in Western Europe, and the third lowest in the world after South Korea and Japan (see Table 4.6). This is explained by several factors, namely, long-established sex education at school, programmes to promote condom use in the campaigns against AIDS and easy access to abortion services (Narring, Michaud and Sharma, 1996). In Switzerland, an accurate assessment of the pregnancy rate is difficult because of unreliable national data on legal abortions: there are wide variations in the application of the law in different cantons.

In the last 30 years, Switzerland, France, Germany, Sweden and Italy have succeeded in reducing the teenage birth rate by three-quarters. As we noted above, Switzerland has compulsory education till the age of 15, when children generally go to a vocational school. However, as Table 4.6 shows, nearly 16 per cent children chose not to continue schooling after 15. Teenage pregnancy occurs among women who are generally out of school.

We do not know of any separate estimates of teenage pregnancy among immigrant children, but the rate is likely to be higher among immigrants than Swiss citizens. According to the 1990 Census, the proportion of 15–19 years old girls who dropped out of school was much higher among immigrant children (27 per cent) than among the native population (14 per cent). Furthermore, more foreign-born immigrant girls marry at 18 or 19 years of age (only 1.5 per cent of Swiss women married at that age). The fertility rate among immigrant girls is five to ten times the rate for native girls (*ibid.*). These factors would suggest that the pregnancy rate among immigrant girls is much higher.

Is teenage pregnancy a cause or consequence of poverty and destitution? One cannot be categorical about answering such a question on account of a multiplicity of factors. It is safe to assume that it is a consequence of prior economic and social disadvantage, which leads to future disadvantage and poverty. An Expert Working Group in the UK (Wellings, 1999) reviewed evidence that women who grew up in poverty during the 1960s and 1970s almost doubled their chances of still living in poverty today by having had a baby during their teens. Such evidence led the Working Group to conclude:

> Whatever the extent to which teenage birth results from hardship and deprivation, it also contributes to such outcomes. After taking into account the effects of education and social class, women who give birth in their teens are more likely to live in a poor area of the country, are less likely to own their own home, and are less likely to be in paid work, than those who did not. (*Ibid.*)

**Youth crime and delinquency** are more prevalent among immigrants than among Swiss. About 37 per cent of those convicted in Switzerland are minors. In 2005, about 0.7 per cent of Swiss adults and nearly 3 per cent of foreigners were convicted of a crime (Zeugin, 2007, p. 91). Surveys have shown that the local population is more inclined to lodge complaints against foreigners, which may partly explain their over-representation in the crime statistics. As we shall discuss in Chapter 7, the right-wing Swiss People's Party associates crime with immigrant population in order to build a case against them. The statistics on crime and drug addiction are classified by sex, age and nationality but not by the social class to which criminals and drug addicts belong. Crime, physical violence and drug addiction are generally a consequence of social disadvantage, extreme poverty and long-term unemployment prevalent among immigrant youth. It is not their nationality per se or ethnic origin that is to blame.

The high **divorce rate** in Switzerland is considered an important factor in explaining child poverty. According to the Swiss Federal Office of Statistics (OFS) (2005, p. 87), two couples divorce out of five marrying today. The risk of divorce increases with each successive year of marriage. The number of 'children of divorce' is increasing rapidly even though about 50 per cent of couples concerned do not have minor children.

During the past few years, more than 12,000 minor children have been added each year to the total number of children of divorce (Kehrli and Knöpfel, 2007, p. 95). Separate data on divorce rates for immigrants and Swiss people are not available. One cannot be certain that divorces among immigrants are equally high. We believe that for religious reasons divorces are less common among immigrants from non-EU countries and Catholic EU countries. To that extent, the problem of children of divorce may be less acute among these categories of immigrants.

## A comparative study of immigrant children from former Yugoslavia, Turkey and Portugal

Ex-Yugoslavs, Turks and Portuguese constitute a sizeable number and proportion of permanent residents in Switzerland. In 1950, these foreigners were insignificant, no more than 0.1–0.3 per cent of all foreigners (permanent residents). However, their number rose significantly during the 1990s.[16]

A spectacular growth in the number of ex-Yugoslavs was caused not so much by the break-up of Yugoslavia (which had some role to play) as by the grant of long-term resident permits by the Swiss authorities to workers and their families. In 2003, family reunifications accounted for nearly 75 per cent of the migrant inflows from ex-Yugoslavia (Gross, 2006). This factor may partly explain a large proportion of young migrants. The Turkish immigrants are smaller in number than those from ex-Yugoslavia and Portugal; also a greater proportion of these immigrants are unemployed (see Table 4.7).

A large proportion of young immigrant children have parents from ex-Yugoslavia, Turkey and Portugal. These countries, especially the former two, form the lowest rung of the economic and social ladder. Therefore, it is interesting to examine their cases on a comparative basis using the Population Census data for 2000. Table 4.7 presents the socio-economic characteristics of these three nationalities: working-age population, employment, unemployment, occupational skills and educational attainment of parents, the nature and size of households, the magnitude of very young children and their educational attainment. Unfortunately, we do not have any information on the economic characteristics and earnings of immigrants from these countries. However, judging by the fact that immigrants (20–59 years) from the three countries are preponderantly employed as unskilled workers (over 50 per cent in each case) with low levels of education (over 80 per cent in each case have only primary education), they are bound to earn very low incomes

*Table 4.7* Social characteristics of immigrants from ex-Yugoslavia, Turkey and Portugal (2000) (% in parentheses)

| | Ex-Yugoslavia | Turkey | Portugal |
|---|---|---|---|
| Total no. of immigrants | 213,524 | 83,312 | 142,415 |
| **Population and employment** | | | |
| Working-age population (unemployed + employed + inactive) | 144,672 (100.0) | 60,548 (100.0) | 108,892 (100.0) |
| Unemployed | 13,877 (9.6) | 6,696 (11.0) | 4,153 (3.8) |
| Employed | 96,202 (66.5) | 38,339 (63.3) | 89,085 (81.8) |
| **Occupation and education** | | | |
| *Occupation* | | | |
| Total no. of respondents | 47,615 (100.0) | 19,232 (100.0) | 56,224 (100.0) |
| Unskilled workers | 24,645 (51.7)* | 10,348 (53.8)* | 37,694 (67.0)* |
| Skilled workers | 7,885 (16.5)* | 2,189 (11.4)* | 5,824 (10.3)* |
| Management cadres | 580 (1.2)* | 402 (2.1)* | 484 (0.9)* |
| *Education* | | | |
| Total no. of respondents | 55,213 (100.0) | 20,396 (100.0) | 27,534 (100.0) |
| Primary | 48,187 (87.3) | 16,557 (81.2) | 22,172 (80.5) |
| Secondary | 6,248 (11.3) | 3,101 (15.2) | 4,511 (16.4) |
| Tertiary | 778 (1.4) | 738 (3.6) | 851 (3.1) |
| **Immigrants in households** | | | |
| Single households | 9,308 (4.5) | 4,580 (5.7) | 12,888 (9.5) |
| Unmarried couples with children | 3,122 (1.5) | 1,071 (1.3) | 2,307 (1.7) |
| Married couples with children | 161,215 (78.5) | 60,854 (75.6) | 94,026 (69.0) |
| Single-parent households | 8,685 (6.3) | 5,084 (4.2) | 6,760 (5.0) |
| Total no. of households | 39,274 (100.0) | 17,250 (100.0) | 28,984 (100.0) |
| *No. of households with* | | | |
| 4 or more children | 6,203 (15.8) | 1,139 (6.6) | 250 (0.9) |
| 3 children | 8,488 (21.6) | 3,368 (19.5) | 1,792 ( (6.1) |
| Average no. of children per household | 2.33 | 2.02 | 1.60 |
| **Children's education** | | | |
| *– 15-year-old* | | | |
| Total no. | 3,581 (100.0) | 1,345 (100.0) | 1,647 (100.0) |
| Out of school | 870 (24.3) | 269 (20.0) | 287 (17.4) |
| Primary | 2,552 (71.3) | 991 (73.7) | 1,118 ( 67.9) |
| Secondary | 159 (4.4) | 85 (6.3) | 242 (14.7) |
| *– 18-year-old* | | | |
| Total no. | 3,533 (100.0) | 1,481 (100.0) | 1,721 (100.0) |
| Out of school | 1,728 (48.9) | 626 (42.3) | 702 (40.8) |
| Primary | 381 (10.8) | 160 (10.8) | 120 (7.0) |
| Secondary | 1,401 (39.6) | 673 (45.4) | 874 (50.8) |
| Tertiary | 23 (0.7) | 22 (1.5) | 25 (1.4) |

*Table 4.7*  Continued

|  | Ex-Yugoslavia | Turkey | Portugal |
|---|---|---|---|
| *– 24-year-old* |  |  |  |
| Total no. | 4,085 (100.0) | 1,581 (100.0) | 2,636 (100.0) |
| Out of school | 3,912 (95.7) | 1,472 (93.1) | 2,492 (94.5) |
| Primary | 13 (0.3) | 8 (0.5) | 17 (0.7) |
| Secondary | 87 (2.1) | 37 (2.3) | 53 (2.0) |
| Tertiary | 73 (1.8) | 64 (4.1) | 74 (2.8) |

*Note*: * percentage of total respondents who indicated their occupational status.
*Source*: Swiss Population Census 2000.

working in such low-skilled fields as hotels, restaurants and the construction industry. As we noted above, ex-Yugoslavs have the highest rates of poverty (see Figures 4.1 and 4.2). This is consistent with high rates of unemployment among them (nearly 10 per cent). Although we do not have poverty rates for the Turks, their high unemployment rates (11 per cent) would suggest poverty conditions.

Added to this, the size of households (number of children per household) is quite large, particularly in the case of ex-Yugoslavs: nearly 16 per cent of households had four children and over 21 per cent had three children. The size of Turkish households also tended to be larger than that of Portuguese households though smaller than ex-Yugoslav households. There were 6.6 per cent of Turkish households with four or more children and 19.5 per cent of households with three children. This high dependency rate would further add to poverty and economic disadvantage. As we noted above, the rearing of a child is expensive and child benefits in Switzerland are relatively low.

The number of young children (birth to 14 years) from Portugal remained steady between 1995 and 2000 but started rising thereafter. That of Turkish children steadily declined during this period. The number of these children from ex-Yugoslavia (namely, Bosnia and Herzegovina, Croatia, Macedonia, Serbia and Montenegro and Slovenia) peaked in 1999 and started declining steadily thereafter (see Figure 4.4). Children in the age group 15–19 years are not reported, as their number is relatively quite small. However, the change pattern for 15–19-year-old children was very similar. This change in pattern fits in with the 'three-circles immigration policy' under which immigrants from within the EU countries (e.g. Portugal) were more easily accepted as they had

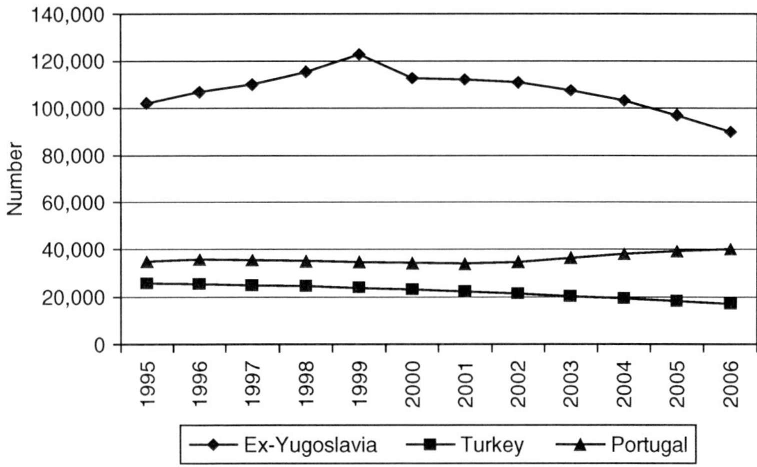


*Figure 4.4*  Number of young children (0–14 years) from ex-Yugoslavia, Turkey and Portugal
*Source*: Based on data from the Swiss Federal Statistical Office (OFS).

cultural affinity with the Swiss population. The first circle consisted of immigrants from the EU and EFTA. The second circle included Eastern Europe, Canada and the USA. The third circle consisted of all other countries (mostly developing countries), whose immigrants were to be accepted only under exceptional circumstances because they were culturally very different and would find it difficult to integrate into the Swiss society (Zeugin, 2007, p. 63). Turkey is a non-EU Muslim country; therefore Turks are less welcome because they are considered 'culturally distant'. However, the case of ex-Yugoslavia, in Eastern Europe, is surprising, especially since ex-Yugoslavs have been traditional immigrants into Switzerland.

The situation of Portuguese households is quite different from that of the Balkan households and, to a lesser extent, Turkish households. Less than 1 per cent of Portuguese households had four or more children; only 6 per cent had three children. Most of the households had only one or two children, as in Swiss households.

There are other differences between the Portuguese immigrant children and those from ex-Yugoslavia. While two out of three Portuguese children are born in Switzerland, only one in six ex-Yugoslav children are born there (Fibbi and Lerch, 2006). The parents of Portuguese children arrived in Switzerland much earlier, in the 1970s, as seasonal workers (often working as clandestine workers) compared to ex-Yugoslavs, who arrived two decades later in the 1990s. Very young children (birth to nine years) account for a significant proportion (22 per cent) of the total number of immigrants from ex-Yugoslavia. This proportion is smaller for Turks and Portuguese. That for older children (ten to 19 years) is also large: 19 per cent for ex-Yugoslavs, 18 per cent for Turks and 13 per cent for Portuguese (Table 4.7).

Between 1993 and 1996, the Centre for Contact between Swiss and Immigrants (CCSI) and the University of Geneva undertook a joint study on young Portuguese children's access to vocational training (see Cattafi-Maurer *et al.*, 1998). It notes that the Portuguese students in Geneva constituted the largest share (8 per cent). The study sample of 31 students included ten Portuguese (five boys and five girls) and 15 students from ex-Yugoslavia. Although not a representative sample, the study presents some interesting findings. Eight out of ten Portuguese families had broken up (separation or divorce) before migration to Switzerland, which shows the precarious family situation of Portuguese students. The marital problems of parents are bound to interfere with the scholastic performance of their children.

In the case of ex-Yugoslavs, their legal status was more stable and less precarious than that of Portuguese children, but many did not enjoy any access to vocational training. This may be due to the fact that, unlike Portuguese immigrants, ex-Yugoslavs did not bring their families with them. The able-bodied men came alone as *'saisonniers'* in the 1970s (*ibid.*).

Single-parent households are less common among ex-Yugoslavs and Turks. They represent no more than 4 to 6 per cent of the households. This proportion is much smaller than those for Swiss, Africans and Americans owing to cultural and religious factors. Other differences are also worth noting. Unlike Swiss single-parent households, those of ex-Yugoslavs have a married parent, low rate of labour force participation and a short-term permit, leading to precariousness and uncertainty (Wanner, 2004). Studies have shown that single-parent households with children and with only one breadwinner suffer from more acute poverty, economic hardships and precariousness than two-parent households with children (see Chapter 6 for a similar situation in France).

There are differences between the Portuguese households on the one hand, and ex-Yugoslav and Turkish households on the other. While in the former households both husband and wife often work, in the latter it is generally the husband. Is it because women in the two latter cases find it more difficult to find employment (discrimination or a lack of education may be explanatory factors)? Another plausible reason is that the Portuguese (who have a much larger proportion of unskilled workers) find it harder to make ends meet with only one salary. A relatively low rate of unemployment (3.8 per cent) among the Portuguese also distinguishes them from the Turks and the ex-Yugoslavs.

Why do Portuguese immigrants enjoy better access to the labour market given the fact that they are equally unskilled with equally low education? Is it because they came into Switzerland much earlier, had ample time to learn the local language, find information about job opportunities and assimilate into the local society? Or is it because they are less discriminated against than immigrants from the Balkans (mostly Serbo-Croat Muslims)?

Children's poverty among ex-Yugoslavs, Turks and Portuguese is mainly explained by low levels of education and schooling. Over 24 per cent of ex-Yugoslav children, 20 per cent of Turkish children and over 17 per cent of Portuguese children at age 15 are out of school. At the same age, Swiss, French and Italian children have much greater access to secondary-school education. Furthermore, ex-Yugoslavs represent a multi-lingual and multi-ethnic group of immigrant children whose lack of knowledge of a local language accounts for educational under-achievement. The Swiss PISA 2000 study (Moser, 2002) shows that children from the Balkans lag behind other children at school in reading, writing and mathematics. These children are handicapped because they arrived more recently in Switzerland and had earlier schooling in their country of origin, compared to those from Italy, Spain or Portugal who were most probably born in Switzerland and were thus better integrated. Portuguese and Italian children arrived in Switzerland before the age of schooling (at the age of, perhaps, four or five), whereas those from ex-Yugoslavia arrived at a much higher age.

## Concluding remarks

In this chapter we analyzed both income and non-income indicators of poverty among immigrant children in Switzerland. We noted that a rigorous comparative analysis of immigrant and non-immigrant children was not possible for lack of requisite data by different age groups. But the fact that the rate of income poverty among immigrants is more than twice as high as among non-immigrants would suggest that immigrant children in Switzerland are generally much poorer than non-immigrant children. The situation of special categories of immigrant children (for example, clandestine children and Roma children) is likely to be much worse. They would fall into the categories of deprived and destitute, as discussed in Chapter 1. As child benefits in Switzerland are a very small proportion of total welfare benefits, the incidence of poverty is not reduced by social welfare assistance. In any case, illegal immigrant children do not qualify for such assistance.

It is surprising that hardly any meaningful studies exist of child poverty in Switzerland (Falter, 2005, and Macculi, 2005, are exceptions), not to speak of poverty among immigrant children. This may be due to the fact that Switzerland remains a very affluent country despite a prolonged economic recession. However, it is encouraging to note that the problem of child poverty has finally started receiving the attention it deserves from policy-makers, NGOs and scholars.

The problem of immigrant children's poverty is one of income disparities (or relative poverty) rather than absolute poverty or deprivation. It is also one of lack of access to goods and services (for example, education, health, jobs and decent housing). We presented a comparative picture of immigrant children from ex-Yugoslavia, Portugal and Turkey, who account for a significant proportion of the population of immigrant children in the country. Low levels of education, high rates of unemployment and high dependency rates account for their poverty and economic and social disadvantage.

We described how legal status (the nature and duration of residence permits) of immigrants, including asylum-seekers, influences their economic and social conditions as well as their access to education, health services and the job market. Their legal status is often uncertain and marred by short-term and restrictive resident and work permits, which worsens their poverty situation. Schools shy away from them because they have short-term permits. Employers discriminate against them in the job market because of their uncertain legal situation. They are often denied decent housing because of this precarious legal status. Their political status is weak because they are often non-citizens and are thus denied many human rights and political and social participation.

The situation of immigrant children has become worse since Swiss citizens rejected the Federal government's proposal to change the law to facilitate the naturalization of second-generation children. We noted that in a nationwide referendum Swiss citizens rejected the two laws proposed by the Federal government and the Parliament that would have facilitated the naturalization of young foreigners. The voters also said no to the proposal that would have granted automatic citizenship to third-generation children.

It is not yet clear how these recent developments affect social justice and respect for the human dignity of immigrant children in a wealthy country such as Switzerland. Part of this lack of clarity derives, as we have noted, from the continuing lack of reliable data and longitudinal studies on immigrant child poverty. Nevertheless, based on the evidence discussed in this chapter, we can say that there is some discrimination against immigrant children in housing, education and the job market. Such discrimination violates their human rights and personal dignity.

We recognize that instituting more effective federal legal and social policies in Switzerland is especially difficult since different cantons enjoy a very large degree of local political autonomy, markedly different mentalities and languages, and divergence between cantonal and national concerns which give rise to an unusual number of referendums. However, it is heartening to note that, in a referendum held on 1 June 2008, both the cantons and people rejected a discriminatory and arbitrary proposal (see Chapter 7) of the Swiss conservative political party for 'democratic naturalizations' in secret ballot.

# 5
## Immigrant Child Poverty in France

Following Chapter 4 on the situation of immigrant children in Switzerland, we now examine their situation in France, another rich country in Western Europe. In 2004, the French Council on Employment, Incomes and Social Cohesion (CERC) estimated that roughly 1 million children in France were living below the French poverty rate of 50 per cent of the median income. Roughly 74 per cent of these children were in families headed by persons of French nationality. Roughly 26 per cent were living in families headed by persons of recent and not so recent immigration. The actual number of poor children, immigrant and non-immigrant, is probably higher today given the recent demographic trends (Martin, 2007, pp. 43–9).

In 2008, the French definition of the poverty threshold was brought into accord with that of the European Union, that is, the poverty threshold of 60 per cent of the median income instead of 50 per cent. According to this new definition, over 12 per cent of the French population in 2005 lived below the poverty line compared to 6 per cent under the old definition. The child poverty rate (for children under 18) in 2005 was 15.5 per cent instead of 8 per cent under the old definition (ONPES, 2008, p. 54).[1]

Although the numbers of poor people in France have remained relatively stable over several years, their material and non-material situations have substantially worsened. Between 2003 and 2005 alone the number of the 'working poor' has increased by 21 per cent (ONPES Travaux, 2008, p. 41). In France they are defined as persons living below 40 per cent of the median income. While individuals living alone are clearly at risk of poverty, households and especially single-parent households with children are even more severely affected.

Before discussing the plight of immigrant children in France, we first need to discuss briefly the magnitude and trends of overall immigration.

## Immigration: magnitude and trends

Immigration to France is not new. France has been an important destination for immigration from within and outside Europe since the late 19th century and early 20th century. A low fertility rate, an enormous number of deaths during the First World War, the rapid economic expansion during the 1920s and reconstruction following the Second World War; all these factors generated a massive demand for foreign labour (Barou, 2007; INSEE, 2007a). However, since the end of the Second World War successive French governments have struggled to regulate immigration by revising complicated immigration policies (van Eeckhout, 2007, pp. 36–8). The fundamental fairness of these policies regarding respect for human dignity and rights of prospective immigrants to France discussed in Chapter 1 is now being called into question.

The statistics compiled by the French National Statistical Office (INSEE) distinguish between 'foreigners' and 'immigrants'. The definition of foreigners is based on the nationality criterion; all those living in France without French nationality are considered foreigners. They include those who are born abroad and others who are born in France but of foreign parents. According to the INSEE annual survey for 2004, there were 3.51 million foreigners. Immigrants are defined in terms of a double criterion of nationality and place of birth. They include foreigners born abroad (about 3 million in 2004) and others who were born abroad but acquired French citizenship (about 2 million in 2004). Thus the total number of immigrants in 2004 was about 5 million, or 8.1 per cent of the French population (van Eeckhout, 2007, p. 14; INSEE, 2005, p. 34).

A child born in France of two foreign parents is considered a 'foreigner' except when both his/her parents themselves were also born in France. In the census population many children were erroneously counted as French when they should have been counted as foreigners. Thus there are problems with the statistics of immigrant children in France. According to the 1999 Census, about 410,000 minors born in France of foreign parents were erroneously classified as French by birth. INSEE has made adjustments to correct this bias. The adjusted figures show that the number of minors increases from 3.26 million to 3.67 million (INSEE, 2005, p. 34).

In early Spring 2007 the French Interministerial Committee for Fight Against Illegal Immigration (*Comité interministeriel de lutte contre l'immigration clandestine*) estimated that at least 90,000 persons who settle in France each year do so illegally.

Trends in immigration from 1988–2006 of the total number of workers, their family members (spouses and children) and children show that from 1992–9 the total number of immigrant workers continued to decline before rising again till 2006. The trend for family members and children is very similar.

A regular decline in the number of immigrant children reflects a more restrictive immigration policy regarding family reunification, which was a significant source of immigration in France. However, the importance of family reunification is now declining. The new immigration laws tend to favour professional and highly skilled workers (as against unskilled workers) whose number has been rising since 1998, while those of their families and children have been declining.

**Age-composition of immigrant children**

Only 13 per cent of immigrants were under 25 years of age. Two-thirds of immigrants were between the ages of 25 and 64. Most of the immigrant children in France in 1999 were from the Maghreb, Portugal and Turkey. More recent immigrants, namely, those from Turkey and sub-Saharan Africa, have more young children (ranging from 22–9 per cent of immigrant population) than the early immigrants such as Spaniards and Italians. In 1999, immigrant children between birth and 14 years formed 4.1 per cent of Moroccans, 5.6 per cent of Turks and 3.9 per cent of Algerians. Older children and youth (15–24 years of age) formed a greater proportion: 14.5 per cent of Moroccans, 17.6 per cent of Turks and 7 per cent of Algerians. With the exception of America and Oceania, the share of young children (birth to 14 years) is lower than that of youth (15–24 years) for all regions and nationalities. However, in the total population the share of younger children is larger (18 per cent) than that of older children (13 per cent) (see Table 5.1).

The number of immigrant children in France was much larger in the early 1990s. It declined to its lowest level in 1998 before rising again. But we notice a consistently declining trend since 2003. A similar trend occurred for four nationalities, namely, Algerians, Moroccans, Tunisians and Turks. Moroccan children formed the largest number throughout the 1990–2006 period, followed by Algerian children.

Children in the 15–19 age group represent the largest number of Algerians, Moroccans and Tunisians. The number of immigrant children over 20 is extremely small. In 2006 the total number of immigrant children was quite insignificant. This may be due to the new stricter immigration laws concerning family reunification.

*Table 5.1*   France: share of immigrant children by age and country of origin (%)

| Country of origin | Age of children | |
|---|---|---|
| | 0–14 years | 15–24 years |
| *Europe* | | |
| Spain | 0.9 | 1.6 |
| Italy | 0.8 | 1.1 |
| Portugal | 2.2 | 3.7 |
| Other countries of EU-15 | 5.9 | 7.8 |
| Other European countries | 5.9 | 7.3 |
| *Africa* | | |
| Algeria | 3.9 | 7.0 |
| Morocco | 4.1 | 14.5 |
| Tunisia | 2.6 | 5.8 |
| *Asia* | | |
| Cambodia, Laos, Vietnam | 4.5 | 8.9 |
| Other Asian countries | 7.7 | 15.3 |
| *Other* | | |
| Turkey | 5.6 | 17.6 |
| America, Oceania | 14.8 | 14.6 |
| *All immigrants* | 4.3 | 8.4 |
| *Total population* | 17.9 | 13.1 |

*Source*: INSEE (2005), p. 43. Based on the 1999 Population Census.

In his first interim report (June 2008) on the new French immigration policy, the Minister of Immigration and National Identity reported that between 1 June 2007 and 31 May 2008 the number of those migrating to France under the reunification clause (which concerned mainly immigrant children) had substantially declined. By contrast, the number of economic immigrants had increased from 6 per cent in 2007 to 36 per cent in 2008. The Minister further reported that the number of expulsions had increased by 31 per cent and that those seeking health benefits had decreased by a little over 6 per cent. The report concluded that these figures showed signs that the new 'dissuasive' immigration policies 'were beginning to bear fruit' (see Chapter 7).

The age structure of immigrant children is relevant not only for demographic reasons but also for social, cultural and educational ones. A much larger number of young children (below nine years or below four years) means that they will go to school in France and will thus have a better chance of integration into French society than older children. Their entire education will be in France, giving them a better chance to learn French language, culture and values. Finally, their education in France (unlike older children who started schooling in their home countries) will prepare them much better for the job market.

## The status of immigrants and their children

The status of immigrants in France is determined by the type of visas and resident permits they hold. Many are eligible to apply for French citizenship. To stay in France a prospective immigrant must receive a residence permit. As in the case of Switzerland (see Chapter 4), the number, type and conditions governing such residence permits are manifold. There are three basic kinds of residence permits in France – temporary, permanent and for retired persons. Temporary permits are of seven different 'categories': visitor, student, scientist, artistic or cultural professional, other active professional, personal or family, and 'exceptional' (*Code*, 2007, pp. 95–100). The conditions governing any immigrant's stay in France mainly centre on work possibilities: very strict regulations must be observed in exercising either one's own profession or in performing in any other kind of professional activity (*ibid.*, pp. 101–4).

In October 2007, the French Parliament changed the above *Code* substantially. Excluding questions of asylum, the changes fall under the following headings (a) language, (b) DNA tests, (c) consent, (d) family requirements, (e) work, (f) residence permit and (g) statistics (van Eeckhout, 2007).[2] Before entering France, prospective immigrants must now pass both language tests and tests based on 'the values of the Republic' (as in the Swiss case of 'success-orientation' of immigrant families, 'the values of the Republic' remain vague).[3]

The Cachan incident discussed below (see Box 5.1) involving the expulsion of immigrant children suggests that prospects for immigrant children to obtain French citizenship remain quite uncertain.[4] Among other things, the Cachan incident shows the serious difficulties faced by immigrant children in France in seeking naturalization and eventual citizenship. The incident also underlines a less often noted problem affecting such children, that is, their uncertain legal status and the consequences of such uncertainty on their access to proper education and health care, and, later, their access to proper housing and employment and income-earning opportunities.

**Box 5.1   The Cachan incident**

On 17 August 2006, several weeks before the resumption of school classes for children and the return to work for many people after the long summer vacations, France's Ministry of the Interior gave the orders to the French riot police (CRS) to physically evict 500 persons, including many poor immigrant children, from an unused former university building in which they had squatted for several years in Cachan, one of the poorer Paris suburbs. The Ministry cited issues of safety and hygiene as reasons for the evictions; it gave no reasons for the particularly problematic timing of the evictions or their brutality. The evictions did not go smoothly.

Public opinion was at first quite firmly against these untimely and brutal evictions. When school classes reconvened on 4 September 2006 about 40 children whose families lacked residence permits returned to class without incident. Their untroubled return was in partial fulfilment of the earlier promises made by the then Interior Minister, Nicholas Sarkozy, on 13 June 2006 (the 'Second Sarkozy Circular') not to expel such school children during the current school year, if born in France, if one parent had been in France legally for at least one year and if already enrolled.

Yet public opinion remained quite volatile, hesitating between sympathy for the expelled, especially the children, and support for firmly controlling illegal immigration. INSEE estimated that at the time there were 4.9 million legal immigrants and between 200,000 and 400,000 illegal immigrants.[5] According to an IFOP survey between 31 August and 1 September 2006, public opinion shifted quickly in favour of the evictions (*Le Figaro*, 5 September 2006).

The Prefecture had first offered one month's free accommodation in several selected hotels for all those evicted. However, since the hotels were situated in other suburbs quite far from their regular schools and workplaces, roughly 200 persons, including 76 children, refused the offer. Instead, they asked for appropriate alternative housing in or very close to the neighbourhood where they had lived and worked for several years. The Prefecture refused this request: instead it offered them access to regular public housing (the infamous multi-storeyed apartment blocks or HLMs). The persons concerned preferred to stay in a nearby school gymnasium, first offered by the socialist mayor of Cachan who had initially protested against the evictions.

During the last week of summer (with the Cachan housing emergency still unresolved), when the gymnasium was required for regular classes with the reopening of schools, the mayor of the municipal-ity concerned requested the Ministry to evict the families camping in the gymnasium. Mr Sarkozy then complained on prime-time evening national television of the unscrupulous socialist political exploitation of the event. But, according to pollsters and commentators the next day, his complaint moved few viewers.

Meanwhile, the Public Prosecutor had separated one of the Cachan children, a two-year-old, from its parents and placed it in a subur-ban social centre for children. He had the child's parents arrested and interned at an Orly Airport hotel, where they were still being kept tem-porarily two weeks after their eviction from Cachan. Together with their second child, an infant, he then sent the family to a detention centre in another suburb to await the results of procedures for expul-sion to Mali, the country of their birth.[6]

Most of these immigrant families figure statistically among the rel-atively new French category of the 'working poor'.[7] Benefiting from generous French social welfare programmes, most Cachan parents actually held modest jobs and succeeded in schooling their children despite their difficult housing situation.

The number of immigrant children involved in the Cachan incident who lived with their parents illegally was not known at the time. Although some of the parents had legal residence and work permits, the legal status of other parents was not known.

After the media attention paid to the Cachan incident the French immigration authorities were quick to realize the general importance of gathering data on the precise legal status of immigrants and their chil-dren. By the summer of 2008, the French Ministry of the Interior had succeeded in including in the new reforms regarding police information policies a new decree, which became effective 1 July 2008. For the first time it authorized the establishment of a new database dedicated solely to information on all minors (including immigrant children), 13 years and above, who were deemed 'to be susceptible to disturbing public order'. Thanks to the efforts of the National Commission on Information Tech-nology and Freedom (CNIL) and the League for the Defence of Human Rights, the Ministry's attempts to keep secret the decree authorizing the creation of such databases were frustrated. The existence and contents of the decrees became public in hearings held by CNIL in May 2008.

The vagueness of the criteria for including minors in police records may now make it probable that any minor found at the scene of any incident or crime, whether directly involved or not in the so-called 'disturbances of the public order', will have his or her personal details (legal status, immigration status, health situation and even sexual orientation) entered into the police computers. There is some evidence to show that any young person, 16 years and above, immigrant or not, whose personal details are registered in the older police computer system for 'violent behaviour' is discriminated against when seeking first-time employment.

Discrimination against young immigrants has been noted by HALDE (2008). Precarious legal status (short-term residence and work permit, for example) can limit the access of immigrant youth to housing and job market opportunities. ONPES (2008, pp. 141–82) notes that the short-term nature of residence of immigrant youth in France precludes their regular long-term access to normal social services and job market opportunities. However, we have no direct evidence to show that the actual legal status of immigrant minor children contributes to their suffering from discrimination regarding access to educational and health opportunities.

## Poverty among immigrant children

Poverty among immigrant children needs to be studied in the context of overall child poverty in France (Chauvel, 2007). In 2004, CERC (2004, p. 41) estimated that 28 per cent of children from six to ten years of age had a poverty rate of nearly 8 per cent, and 32 per cent of children between 11 and 15 years had a poverty rate of a little over 8 per cent (under the poverty threshold of 50 per cent of the median income). The poverty rate was the highest (10.5 per cent) for children between 16 and 17 years. The most important factor contributing to the poverty of households in which these children lived was the difficulty for the household members to find employment. Single-parent households were particularly hard hit (CERC, 2004). In principle, an increase in the share of full-time employment should improve the poverty situation of single-parent families, most of which are from within the EU where the institution of family and married couples is gradually weakening. Single-parent families are much less common among those from outside the EU, who are mostly immigrants from developing countries.

In France, there are wide regional variations in child poverty (a child is considered poor if he lives in a household, which is below the poverty line defined in terms of a threshold of 50 per cent of the median income). In the Nord-Pas-de-Calais and Languedoc-Roussillon one out of four children is below the poverty line, that is, a child (birth to 17 years) poverty rate of 25 per cent (which is the highest rate of all the regions). The child poverty rate is also very high in Corsica and Provence, 22 per cent and 21 per cent respectively. In Ile-de-France the child poverty rate is lower, 14 per cent. Although in Paris the poverty rate is equal to the average, it is highest for the youngest workers (see Auzet, Février and Lapinte, 2007).

### Income poverty

Income levels of and poverty rates for immigrants vary with the country of origin. Immigrant households from Europe (Italy, Portugal and Spain) were less poor than those from the Maghreb and other countries such as Turkey. The shares of poor households and persons were the highest for the Maghreb: nearly 23 per cent and over 27 per cent respectively (INSEE, 2005, p. 137). This may be explained partly by the large size of these households. Sixty-one per cent of couples with children among the Maghreb immigrants lived in poor households compared to only 19 per cent of European immigrants. INSEE (*Ibid.*) notes that seven out of ten poor immigrant households consist of couples with children.

As we noted in Chapter 2, the poverty rates are lower when one takes account of taxes and transfers. As Table 2.5 in that Chapter shows, in France child poverty was nearly 28 per cent before taxes and transfers and only 7.5 per cent after taxes and transfers. Social transfers (child and housing benefits) form an important part of the household incomes of immigrants: 14 per cent against 5 per cent for non-immigrant households.

French social welfare benefits (as in other EU countries) generally involve a number of elements. Thus, as of 1 January 2007, social welfare programmes provide assistance under several disparate headings such as employment, family, health, housing, retirement, savings, 'social minima' and French 'social security' (ONPES, 2008, pp. 60–1). However, these programmes are becoming increasingly restrictive under the growing financial constraints of the French economy in 2008 (ONPES Travaux, 2008).

The level of monthly family allowances depends on the number of children concerned. As of 1 July 2008, this allocation was 120 euros per month for two children and 274.5 euros for three children; and for each subsequent child, an additional 154 euros. Further, there are other family allocations, including a birth allowance for every child, special considerations for single mothers, adoption previsions and so on. Each

*Table 5.2* France: child poverty by nationality of household head (%)

| | Total | Parent from within the EU | | Parent from outside the EU |
| --- | --- | --- | --- | --- |
| | | **Country of birth within the EU** | **Country of birth outside the EU** | |
| Total | 7.8 | 5.9 | 11.3 | 25.9 |
| *No. of children under 18 years of age* | | | | |
| 1 child | 6.8 | 5.6 | 11.0 | 25.8 |
| 2 children | 6.4 | 5.2 | 9.2 | 25.4 |
| 3 children | 7.8 | 5.9 | 10.8 | 21.3 |
| 4 or more children | 17.1 | 11.9 | 19.2 | 31.2 |
| *Type of household and employment situation* | | | | |
| Single-parent with job | 7.2 | 6.3 | 7.0 | 23.4 |
| Single-parent without job | 27.8 | 25.8 | 35.6 | 36.5 |
| Couple with two jobs | 1.9 | 1.7 | 3.0 | 7.8 |
| Couple with one job | 8.3 | 6.4 | 10.4 | 20.3 |
| Couple without job | 44.1 | 40.0 | 49.6 | 50.2 |
| *Education of household head* | | | | |
| Without a degree or diploma? | 16.7 | 13.4 | 18.5 | 28.6 |
| +BEPC, CAP, BEP | 5.4 | 4.8 | 11.8 | 17.6 |
| Secondary school and higher | 3.1 | 2.0 | 6.2 | 20.9 |

*Note*: EU = 15.
+ = lower secondary school certificates.
*Source*: CERC (2004), p. 47.

of these elements influences the situation of poor immigrant children in France. Each is subject to growing budgetary pressures.

Table 5.2 provides data on child poverty by the nationality of household head. It shows that child poverty rates are much higher in larger households, especially those with four or more children. Child poverty is even higher in households with parents originating from outside the EU (31 per cent compared to 12 per cent).

The poverty rate for children of immigrant families headed by a person who came from one of the 15 EU countries was 5.9 per cent, the lowest compared to that for immigrant families headed by a person who migrated to France a long time ago, 11.3 per cent, and that of families headed by a person who migrated much more recently, nearly 26 per cent.

Four points stand out. The first concerns the relative weight of the recent nationality of the household head in the probability of the household's children being poor. The qualification 'recent' is necessary since some household heads with immigrant children acquire French nationality over time, whereas our main concern is with those heads who themselves are still immigrants and have not yet acquired French citizenship. The weight of the recent nationality factor is important, along with others such as degrees or diplomas of the household head, the number of children in the household, the type of family structure and the employment situation of the head and other members of the household. But it is shown to be less important than both the type of household and the employment situation in determining the probability of the household's poverty.[8]

A related point is that poor children in France who live in households headed by someone who migrated some time ago and who has already achieved French nationality have a lower risk of falling below the poverty line than those who live in households headed by someone who migrated recently. Third, child poverty in immigrant households is influenced by the relative difficulty encountered by adults in overcoming both unemployment and under-employment (see below).

Finally, the legality of the parents' stay in France and their employment are important factors influencing the poverty rates of immigrant children. For example, if both parents lack the requisite legal authorizations for their continuing stay in France, their children will most likely lack access to proper health care, education and housing. Here a distinction needs to be made between immigrant household heads who are legal residents and others who are not. Data presented above do not include illegal immigration and its many consequences for immigrant child poverty. This factor contributes to an underestimation of the numbers of immigrant children in France, which, according to the Ministry's official report of 19 June 2008, are based on the numbers of those benefiting from state medical aid (AME) programmes, those expelled from France or refused legal entry and those whose requests for asylum have been denied.

### Deprivation

Children's deprivation can be examined in either of two ways: in terms of deprivation of a single major indicator, for example, poor housing situation, or in terms of a whole series of connected indicators. As we noted in Chapter 2, Table 2.6, studies in the UK and Northern Ireland defined such poverty in terms of a lack of such basic necessities as food, clothing, shelter, leisure and so on. For France, CERC (2004) notes such additional indicators as the household's capacity to deal with current expenses without going into debt. CERC (2004, p. 45) notes that roughly 10 per cent of poor families with children suffered from non-income poverty, or, strikingly, about 1.4 million children. Most at risk were poor single-parent families and those with four or more children (*ibid.*, pp. 57–8).

In France, SILC surveys for 2004–6 (cited in ONPES, 2008) provide information for some of the above deprivations caused by limited financial means at the disposal of households. This information relates to a lack of adequate food, shelter, clothing and leisure and social activities. It is striking that a substantial proportion of households are unable to afford new clothes or an annual holiday, and a large proportion have very small lodgings. Using the EU-SILC data for 2005, the European Commission (2008, pp. 53–4) estimates rates of deprivation for total population and for children from birth to 17 years for EU-25 including France (see Table 5.3).

Table 5.3 shows that the French children and population in general suffer more from economic and financial strain than from lack of consumer durables. Poor housing conditions in terms of leaking roofs and damp walls are also an important factor. We do not have separate data for immigrants and their children. However, it is likely that immigrants with relatively lower incomes are more deprived of these necessities than French citizens. Some recent ONPES data would support this supposition, especially the data on poor families without fixed residence (ONPES, 2008, pp. 131–42).

## Access to education and employment

Non-income poverty discussed above can be explained, *inter alia*, by such factors as access to education, employment and health services. These issues are discussed in this and the following section.

### Education

Immigrant children in France find themselves in a paradoxical situation. On the one hand, their parents have great aspirations of giving them higher education. On the other hand, these children belong to a lower economic and social class, which makes them vulnerable in

*Table 5.3*   France: shares of total population and of children affected by material deprivation (2005) (%)

| Indicator of deprivation | Total population | Children (0–17 years) |
|---|---|---|
| *I. Economic strain* | | |
| Could not afford: | | |
| – to face unexpected expenses | 18.1 | 18.7 |
| – one-week annual holiday away from home | 15.7 | 16.6 |
| – to pay for mortgage or rent | 7.9 | 10.4 |
| – a meal with meat or chicken every second day | 2.9 | 3.3 |
| – to keep home adequately warm | 0.72 | 0.99 |
| *II. Consumer durables* | | |
| Enforced lack of: | | |
| – washing machine | 4.3 | 4.5 |
| – colour TV | 0.6 | 0.4 |
| – telephone | 0.1 | 0 |
| – personal car | 0.03 | 0 |
| *III. Poor housing conditions* | | |
| – leaking roof, damp wall, etc. | 14.5 | 15.5 |
| – accommodation too dark | 3.1 | 3.2 |
| – no bath or shower | 0.3 | 0.2 |
| – no indoor toilet for sole use of household | 0.04 | 0 |

*Source*: European Commission (2008), p. 53.

the educational system. For example, many drop out before completing secondary education. INSEE (2005, p. 98) reports that almost twice as many immigrant children leave the secondary school system without any qualifications as non-immigrant children. One out of four immigrant children obtains a BA degree (roughly equivalent to the *baccalauréat général*) without repeating.

During 2003–4, 35,600 non-francophone pupils (mostly immigrants) entered French primary and secondary schools: 16,000 in primary schools, 17,100 in secondary schools, (mostly vocational) (61 per cent). Another 4,000 children over 16 years of age received specialized training within the framework of two programmes, namely, the programme for the promotion of national education (*mission générale a l'insertion de l'éducation nationale* (MGIEN)) and institutional networks for adult training (*les groupements des établissements pour la formation continue* (GRETA)).

Only 27 per cent pupils from immigrant families were in general secondary schools in May 2002 compared to 40 per cent from native

*Table 5.4*   France: family environment of pupils entering sixth form in 1995 (%)

| Type of family situation | Non-immigrant families | | Mixed families | Immigrant families | | |
|---|---|---|---|---|---|---|
| | Total | of which workers' children | | Total | of which children born in France | Children born abroad |
| Share of pupils living in a family of: | | | | | | |
| Workers | 31.7 | – | 36.1 | 68.5 | 71.0 | 55.4 |
| Illiterate father | 12.1 | 24.5 | 16.6 | 58.3 | 61.8 | 39.3 |
| Illiterate mother | 14.0 | 25.6 | 22.3 | 62.6 | 65.8 | 44.3 |
| A working mother | 74.4 | 68.5 | 69.9 | 44.0 | 42.4 | 52.4 |
| Four or more children | 19.5 | 23.0 | 24.0 | 63.2 | 65.4 | 51.7 |

*Source*: INSEE (2005), p. 99. Based on data from the National Ministry of Education.

families and 48 per cent from mixed families. However, it is interesting to note that the proportions of pupils in technical and vocational schools are similar. Pupils from immigrant families, particularly from the Maghreb and sub-Saharan Africa, mostly go to vocational schools (Caille, 2005a, p. 12).

Some information on the influence of family environment on the education of immigrant children is presented in Table 5.4. Seventy-one per cent of these children born in France belong to working-class families compared to only 32 per cent from non-immigrant families and 36 per cent from mixed families. Also a very large proportion of immigrant pupils born in France have either uneducated fathers (62 per cent) or uneducated mothers (66 per cent). Many born abroad come from large families with four or more children. These factors are likely to explain poorer educational performance and higher drop-out rates among immigrant children.

Young immigrant children are exposed to serious deficiencies in the French educational system, especially in the primary school system. Despite new measures announced by the Education Ministry for 2006–7 school year and more extensive ones for 2007–8 and 2008, debates concerning several issues have continued among school principals, teachers, parents' associations and unions. The two biggest problems concern the extraordinary increase in school violence,[9] and entrenched retrograde practices in many elementary schools of the teaching of reading by the scientifically discredited 'global method' and its equally deleterious variants, instead of by the 'syllable method'.[10] Widespread illiteracy continues among many school children.

School violence and illiteracy threaten the present and future well-being of many French children in almost all milieus. However, immigrant children are especially affected. They are subject both to repeated discrimination and to special difficulties in learning how to read because of their frequent struggles with bilingualism.

There are numerous other obstacles limiting the access of immigrant children to primary and secondary education. Many instructors are reluctant to accept these children with poor or no knowledge of French. Second, the additional cost of special requirements of immigrant children with learning difficulties discourages teachers from accepting them (Schiff, 2004). Third, there are traditional prejudices against these children (particularly against Roma children; see below).

A major problem arising from these concerns is that of the human rights of the child discussed in Chapter 1. Does the persistence of widespread poverty among immigrant children in such an affluent country as France constitute a continuing violation of their human rights as defined in the United Nations and EU documents? We argue that it does. Moreover, as we have suggested earlier, as a signatory country of these major documents, France has persistently violated several of their most important articles. France is also a signatory country to the European Union 2000 Charter of Fundamental Rights. Here too some French policies regarding restrictions on immigration and the treatment of new arrivals in France seem to be in violation of the Charter.

## Employment

Lower and poorer quality of education of immigrant children may mean that they are less prepared for the job market. However, INSEE (2005, p. 110) argues that the level of education is not an adequate explanation because even those immigrant males who pursued studies beyond 19 years of age suffer from high rates of unemployment (15.4 per cent) compared to non-immigrant males (5.5 per cent).

Access of immigrant youth (15–24 years) to the labour market is more restricted than that of non-immigrant youth. In general, in 2002 the rate of unemployment among immigrants (16.4 per cent) was twice as high as that among non-immigrants (*ibid.*). One-quarter of male immigrant youth and one-third of female were unemployed. The participation rates for young immigrants (15–24 years) declined between 1992 and 2002 compared to those of other young persons.

Unemployment is less prevalent among those immigrants who have acquired French nationality, which suggests some discrimination in the labour market. The level of discrimination varies according to the country of origin. Very low unemployment rates for such Western European nationals as Italians, Portuguese and Spaniards suggest low discrimination. However, it is high against immigrants from the Maghreb, sub-Saharan Africa and Turkey, who suffer from a much higher risk of unemployment. Between 1992 and 2002 the unemployment rate for young male immigrants (15–24) increased; it was much higher than that for the older age group (50–9) for both years. The situation for female immigrants was very similar (*ibid.*, p. 111).

It is difficult to assess the importance of discrimination against immigrant youth in the job market. It is even more problematic to measure it accurately. Many cases of discrimination are never reported for fear of penalty or further discrimination. However, some figures for complaints have been registered since the creation in 2005 of the High Commission for the Fight Against Discrimination and for Equality (*Haute Autorité de lutte contre les discriminations et pour l'égalité* (HALDE)). Of the first 2,000 complaints HALDE received, over 43 per cent were concerned with discrimination in employment and a little over 18 per cent with access to public services. In June 2008, HALDE published the results of its latest controversial experiments designed to determine how many of and to what degree France's top companies practice regular discrimination in their current employment practices. The results show that the policy of 'name and shame' was not a success, given some demonstrated methodological problems. Nonetheless, HALDE plans to improve the design of its experiments and enquiries so as to provide substantial empirical evidence of discriminatory practices, which raise issues of justice and basic human rights. Discrimination concerning access to education and housing was much less marked, each accounting for only a little over 5 per cent of all complaints (van Eeckhout, 2007, pp. 88–9).

There is no one single factor explaining high rates of unemployment among immigrant youth in France. Immigrants face high unemployment at both ends of the occupational ladder: in unskilled and semi-skilled occupations requiring low education as well as in professional and managerial occupations. Their relatively lower social and economic position, or income inequalities are only partly to blame for this situation. A combination of factors, namely, social status, level of education, age, sex and country of origin, explain the high level of unemployment among immigrant youth.

## Access to health care

French immigrant children's access to proper health care is another important issue relating to their non-income poverty. In general, data on the health situation of poor children in France is fragmentary and incomplete. The basic information is to be found in the documentation of various investigations of the French government's group on Health and Social Protection (ESPS). These investigations cover such topics as the types of health insurance of poor families, the extent to which they use prescription medicines and the types of health care to which they enjoy access in the case of serious illness. But few of these enquiries give an appropriate account of the actual health situation of immigrant families and children.

Immigrant children between the ages of two and 16 show a higher risk of obesity than other children. Besides obesity, which afflicts both poor parents and their children, specific information on different kinds of medical problems among immigrant children in particular is lacking. Still, for poor children two particular problems are especially important. The first is asthma and the second, lead poisoning. Both problems are closely linked to sub-standard housing which is often humid and involves the use of flaking lead-based paint (see Chapter 6). Poor children with asthma are twice as frequent patients as non-poor children. A significant number of children were known to be living in sub-standard housing with problems relating to lead poisoning.

There are more children from low-income households than those from other households who did not consult a general practitioner in the previous 12 months. This gap widens when one considers visits to a specialist medical doctor (de Saint Pol, 2007).

Moreover, access to the French social security system as well as to the government's nine major welfare programmes (the so-called 'minimal social programmes') became more and more constrained by the cost-cutting measures (ONPES, 2008, pp. 60–1). Reforms such as those being discussed in Germany, the Hartz I-IV programmes, seem unthinkable in France. Despite the government's October 2006 draft legislation to Parliament for refinancing the social security system, reform measures for poor families' access to public health services were either delayed or rejected. Throughout 2007 and 2008 the situation remained roughly the same. However, in spring 2008 the government announced a thorough overhaul of the French health care system. It is not evident that such a massive 'reform', one more in a series of promised social 'reforms', can be implemented given the obstinacy of the French unions.

Immigrants benefit much less from the health insurance system with regard to its covering their health expenditures: only 62 per cent of immigrants as against 87 per cent of non-immigrants. There are many more immigrants (22 per cent) than non-immigrants (6 per cent) whose health expenditures are not reimbursed at all or are covered only by social security (INSEE, 2005, p. 152). In particular, health care provisions have declined. To underline this problem general practitioners, as well as specialists such as obstetricians, considered new strike actions after the earlier ones in summer 2006 (*Le Monde*, 4–18 August 2006).

Health care deficiencies were acute in at least the 4,422 communes that the government classified as 'under-medicalized' in January 2006 (*Le Monde*, 26 January 2006). Many medicines were no longer reimbursed as the social security system struggled in 2006 with an expected shortfall of 10.3 billion euros (*Le Monde*, 2 June and 9–10 June 2006).

## The plight of minor children

Having discussed issues of poverty of immigrant children and their access to education, employment and health, we now review the emerging phenomenon of 'minor children', often separated from their parents (*mineurs isolés*). In France this phenomenon can be traced back to the late 1990s. However, there is no definitive information on the number of these children and the magnitude of their problems. One reason for this is a lack of consensus on the precise definition of 'minors' or separated children. In fact, all these children are not separated from their parents and some may have come to France to join their parents or other family members.

A vast majority of minor children (over 55 per cent) are concentrated in the Paris region, although many are dispersed throughout France. Many can be seen around two major railway stations of Paris, the Gare Saint Lazare and the Gare du Nord. These children make up a heterogeneous group from different regions and countries. Also there are different reasons explaining their separation from their parents.

The French institutions recognize the following five categories of these children:

1. *Asylum-seekers* who have escaped from civil wars or ethnic strifes in their countries of origin. Children from Angola, Congo and Sri Lanka would fall under this category.
2. *Mandatés* are street children who are sent by their parents to make a living in rich countries and to send back remittances. Many poor Romanian children may fall under this category.
3. *Exploited* children who often fall prey to drug-traffickers, pimps and paedophiles. Most such children are forced to act as conduits for transporting drugs and to indulge in other underground and illegal activities.
4. *Runaway* children who leave home because they are abused or maltreated.
5. *Errants* (idle or wandering children) who may have indulged in begging and pilfering in their home countries before coming to France to do the same.

The above categories are not watertight. Children in one category can often slip into others. There may also be overlaps between categories. For example, delinquents may have run away from home because of abuse and maltreatment.

The first official statistics on minor children in France were provided by the Border Police (PAF), the Directorate of Civil Liberties and Legal Affairs (*La direction de libertés publiques et des affaires juridiques* (DLPAJ)) and the French Office for the Protection of Refugees and Stateless Persons (*Office français de protection des refugiés et des apatrides* (OFPRA)). These institutions estimate that over 1,400 minors were kept in the Retention Centre of Roissy (where Charles de Gaulle airport is located) in 2001. Out of these, 1,100 applied for asylum on entry into France. In the same year another 200 minors applied to OFPRA for asylum (Etiemble, 2002). But these figures were probably incomplete considering that all minor children were not detained in the Retention Centre only.[11] Many minors are under the supervision of the French Welfare agency, Children's Social Assistance (*Aide Sociale à l'Enfance* (ASE)).[12]

In 2001, Europe (for example, Romania and Albania) accounted for 35 per cent of the total number of minor children in France. Africa (Angola and Congo) and Asia (for example, China and Afghanistan) accounted for 26 per cent and 21 per cent of minor children respectively. The shares of other countries from the Americas, for example, were insignificant (*Migrations Etudes*, September–October, 2002).

The majority of minors (40 per cent) are in the 15–16 age–group, followed by those in the groups 17–18 years (34 per cent) and 13–14 years (16 per cent). Most of these immigrant children (eight out of ten) are boys. However, girls come from some countries, such as Angola, Romania and Zaire. This is not the case with Albanian and Moroccan children, who hardly include any girls.

More restrictive requirements for obtaining French citizenship discussed above (for example, raising the eligibility age to 18) may prolong the precarious situation of minor immigrant children and prevent their social integration. The new restrictions and the harsher expulsion policy are also likely to prolong their clandestine existence and activities.

The French welfare agencies (responsible for minor immigrant children) vary across the country in administrative structures and the amounts of resources available. This results in a general failure to guarantee equal treatment to all immigrant minors. Some departments and regions have better facilities for taking care of these children than others. The growing number of these children frequently overburdens the weak structures and limited resources (for example, emergency shelters) to cope with the problem.

In 2007 the General Inspectorate for Social Affairs (IGAS) made several recommendations to the French government (better reception, accommodation and education and training) to improve the situation of minor immigrant children. Two institutions already exist to undertake responsibility for these children, namely, (1) The Reception and Orientation Centre for Separated Children seeking Asylum (CAOMIDA) and (2) The Reception and Orientation Centre (LAO). These centres are weakly organized and suffer from serious financial difficulties. They need to be strengthened and the resources for education and training of children need to be raised.[13]


## Romanian street children

Nearly 17 per cent of minor children in France come from Romania. Many end up roaming the streets of Paris. A French NGO, Off the Streets Association (*Association Hors La Rue*), has as its main objective taking these children off the streets, where they indulge in violence, theft, petty crime and even prostitution. It traced 418 minor immigrants (between the ages of 15 and 18) between March 2002 and August 2005, mostly from Romania. Thirty-three out of 100 minors interviewed admitted to having committed thefts; 27 sold newspapers in the street; 13 begged; eight worked illegally; and two indulged in prostitution. Two social workers' organizations, viz. Child Welfare Agency (ASE) and the Legal Protection of Youth (PJJ), took charge of most of these marginalized children. Thanks to the efforts of these organizations, nearly 200 children escaped from the precarious situation of street squatters in the Paris region. Their lives improved after the social workers' organizations started taking care of them. They are known to have abandoned their clandestine existences as well as violence and petty crime (Bigot, 2006).

The Association has undertaken a first phase of a two-phase study of Romanian street children. The results of the first phase are briefly discussed below. The second phase will be concerned with interviews of 30 street children and the tracing of their lives. While the first-phase study is based on information collected from social workers, the second phase is based on the views of children themselves. One has to recognize the subjective nature of the study, which relies on the judgements and opinions of the social workers and children interviewed. For example, some social workers admitted that they were less than candid in offering information on such sensitive subjects as prostitution on the part of some children in the sample. Thus, cases of prostitution may be much more numerous than reported. Similarly, cases of theft and crime may not be included in the files on children in order not to expose them to the police and judicial authorities.

Many children from Romania and Bulgaria in the streets of Marseille continue to band together in small groups, and literally forage to stay alive. Properly speaking, they have no housing since they live in the streets. Many have run away from the few centres that exist in France for helping such children. For example, in 2000 the Paris suburb of Seine Saint-Denis reported that roughly 40 per cent of unaccompanied immigrant children who were given appropriate shelter had run away, thus becoming easy prey to prostitution, child labour exploitation and stealing (IOM, 2002, p. 53).

Many Romanian street children are Roma[14] who have been forced by their parents/guardians to go abroad in search of better living conditions. Some of them may be stolen children (some Roma have been known to steal children) who are used as slaves or servants. The Romanian government does not have adequate resources to undertake searches for these kidnapped children. However, some serious crimes during the first half of 2008 in Italy,[15] which involved the Roma, encouraged the Romanian government to deal with the problems of Romanian citizens abroad, including the Roma in Paris. For example, in 2008, new bilateral agreements between France and Romania, and Italy and Romania, were negotiated.

The new agreement between Romania and France focuses on repatriating isolated Romanian children.[16] It will substantially update a series of previous agreements going back to 2002. The new accord (unlike the earlier requirements that a judge of the children's courts pronounce on the suitability of each repatriation) will substantially raise the number of repatriated Romanian children. This consequence has already disquieted many NGOs concerned about the fate of these unusually vulnerable children.

Between 1998 and 2006, 726 Romanian children were granted the right of residence in France to join their parents or other family members under the 'family reunification' clause. Of these 349 were boys and 377 girls. The reunification of children with their parents and families reached a peak in 2004. From 2004 onwards their number started declining but it stabilized between 2005 and 2006. In late 2007 the French Parliament approved new immigration laws according to which fewer people would be able to migrate to France on the grounds of family unification. In 2008 the French government added still more restrictions to the reunification.

Three major factors explain the motivation of Romanian street children to migrate to France (mainly Paris): (1) economic and financial reasons, since most of the children come from families in which parents have no jobs back in Romania; (2) desire to go to school in France; and (3) family problems or breakdown (divorce, separation or child abuse at home). However, these explanations are given by the children themselves. Therefore, their credibility cannot be established.

Romania is one of the poorest countries in the European Union, in which children tend to be neglected. It is quite plausible that poor parents with limited incomes encourage their children to move to richer countries to earn some livelihood. This was the major reason given by children interviewed. The next in importance was the desire to study in France. However, it is not clear why they came to France in particular and not another affluent country in Western Europe. Is it because Romania is a Latin country and hence close to France? It is difficult to determine what motivates Romanian children to want to study in France.

In the survey, Romanian children gave much less importance to the third factor, namely, problems with their families such as child abuse and maltreatment. Is it because they were less forthcoming about criticizing their families or because this factor is genuinely less important? Finally, it is rather surprising that very few children (only 16) mentioned lack of a future in Romania as a reason for migrating to France.

A vast majority of children from Romania had high-school education at the time of their arrival in France, which is surprising and unexpected of street children. This would suggest that they were not really street children of the type one associates with crime and delinquency. Many children noted higher studies in France as a reason for moving there. The majority of these children had interrupted their studies in Romania before coming to France. Out of 100 children in the study sample, 57 were actually under training, the cost of their training being borne by the French welfare agency (ASE). Eleven were in college, 13 were taught in a family home (*foyer*), ten were in a vocational school and seven were in apprenticeship training (Bigot, 2006). Over 90 per cent of those in the care of social workers were in apprenticeship/training in construction and public works, hotel and restaurant industry, and office work.

The education and training of Romanian street children is likely to be hindered by the lack of available places in schools and the shortage of funds allocated to the responsible agencies. Besides, preference is most likely to be given to other immigrant and French children, especially when places are limited.

Before concluding this chapter, we discuss in more detail below the situation of Roma children in France.

## Roma children

Roma or 'gypsy children' are different from other Romanian children discussed above. They are generally much younger than 15 or 16 years, and have had much less education in their countries of origin before coming to France.[17]

Most Roma children in France live in poor immigrant families who most often have not yet achieved either French citizenship or settled into decent housing (see Chapter 6). In fact, many Roma families, especially those coming from the former Yugoslavia, continue to suffer from social ostracism. The result is their understandable withdrawal into their own community ('*repli communautaire*'). They live together in small and segregated groups. Hence their integration becomes more difficult.

The consequences of this lifestyle on Roma children are generally very negative. Most children in such families are not enrolled in any school programmes since they do not remain in any one place for very long. (A few exceptions are children whose parents enrol them in correspondence courses.)

In France the Roma suffer from serious discrimination with respect to education, health care and employment because of a variety of traditional prejudices. For example, with respect to education, many French schools tend to relegate Roma children to special classes for children with learning handicaps or 'gypsy classes' in ordinary schools (European Commission, 2004, p. 19). A European Commission Report on Roma (2004b, p. 2) notes: 'Where Roma children are included within mainstream schools, these are often poorly provided for, or become "ghettoised".' Moreover, since their families often lack any general medical coverage, these children do not have any regular medical or dental care, except in the case of emergencies. Their poor health condition results from their poverty, poor housing and discrimination against them in the provision of health services. Cases of such communicable diseases as tuberculosis and hepatitis are common.

In France (as in Belgium, Germany, Italy, the Netherlands and Spain), many Roma children fall partly under the provisions of a convention on the 'Trafficking of Unaccompanied Minors in the European Union' (IOM, 2002). This convention focuses on the situations of children under 18 years who are not living with their families. The provisions are numerous and complicated, but the intentions behind the convention are transparent. The main intent is to protect such children from exploitation. Further improvements in the convention are expected to be made at the time of the adoption of the new European Social Agenda in 2010, which is to reinforce children's rights generally.

As any brief subway transit in Paris or almost any visit to a prominent Parisian historical monument demonstrates, many (but not all) mothers of small Roma children accustom their children from an early age to public begging and, occasionally, to pick-pocketing and petty theft. Their fathers very often enrol young Roma adolescents into well-organized gangs involved in break-ins, thefts and the fencing of stolen goods.

The already difficult situation of Roma children has become even more precarious in a paradoxical way since 1 January 2007, when Romania and Bulgaria joined the European Union. This has meant that Romanians and Bulgarians may now circulate freely in Europe. However, in France such persons may stay for more than three months. The control and enforcement of their legal stay in France is proving complicated. The result is that many more poor Roma families with children are arriving in France than before. Often they are staying on illegally in destitute circumstances. As a member of the association, *Roms Europe*, noted: 'begging in France is five or six times more lucrative than working as an agricultural labourer in Bulgaria' (*Le Monde*, 21 August 2007).

## Concluding remarks

In this chapter we have discussed the magnitude and seriousness of the problems of poverty facing immigrant children in France. We have stressed the emerging new legal frameworks that are believed to compromise the access of these children to proper health care and education in their childhood, and to proper housing and employment later.

We noted that poor immigrant children, especially the Roma, suffer from economic and financial disadvantage. Their poverty situation is worse than that of French citizens, which retards their later development in life, leading to cumulative disadvantages. This is made even more damaging by the fact that their access to education and health services is relatively limited. In addition, discrimination against them (especially against the Roma) in the housing and job markets as well as in the health sector hinders the development of capabilities discussed in Chapter 1. For example, immigrant children's lack of access to primary, secondary and higher education stands in the way of accumulating knowledge capital, which puts them at a further handicap in the job market when they enter it. Finally, their segregated life, often in ghettoes, and racial discrimination minimize their chances to develop social and cultural capital.

The increasingly strict new French immigration laws have significantly worsened an already bad situation for such children. The progressive substitution of economic criteria for humanitarian ones, which prospective immigrants are now expected to meet for family reunification, has put in doubt their children's realistic chances of naturalization and citizenship. The new laws have also resulted in many families having no realistic chances of resuming a life together with their children and other family members.

When the above factors are considered against the backdrop of human rights legislation generally and children's rights in particular (legislation incorporated in international and regional charters that France has endorsed) discussed in Chapter 1, we can conclude that many current and relatively recent policies concerning immigrant children are in violation of France's political, economic and social commitments and responsibilities.

# 6
# Housing Poor Immigrant Children in France

Poor housing is one of the most important chronic problems faced by immigrant children in France besides declining naturalization possibilities, inadequate access to proper health care, unemployment, school violence and delinquency, which all deeply affect the development of their capabilities discussed in Chapter 1. In this chapter we examine this situation in detail.

In 2007, nearly 6 million people in France suffered from inadequate housing (Merlot, Gabel and Gaudron, 2007; Abbé Pierre Foundation, 2008). Over 3.5 million people lived in crowded lodgings and 1.15 million housing units were without bathroom and heating (Abbé Pierre Foundation, 2007). It is true that the housing situation in France has improved steadily over the last 35 years.[1] The National Office for Urban Renewal (ANRU) has made substantial progress in reducing the share of outmoded high-rise social housing (HLM). Moreover, the National Agency for the Improvement of Housing (ANAH) has continued to provide important financial assistance to those owners' associations (*'copropriétés'*) which have not been able to afford the onerous costs of bringing older buildings up to current housing norms. The Paris municipality has also multiplied its housing aid programmes, such as Assistance to Mono-parental Families (*Aide pour Familles Monoparentales*), Paris Family Shelters (*Paris Logement Familles)* and the Solidarity Fund (*Fond de Solidarités)*. However, despite these efforts, the present housing situation in France remains extremely problematic for poor immigrant families and children, as we discuss below. However, before turning to the housing problems of immigrant families and children, we discuss the general housing situation in France.

## The general housing situation

Poor families in France, like any other families, need to find 'appropriate housing', defined as accommodation that is sanitary (for example, it includes indoor plumbing), safe (for example, it has no lead paint peeling from walls) and sufficiently spacious to satisfy family needs. Some progress was made between 1988 (when roughly 88 per cent of such families had indoor toilets) and 2003 (when that proportion had risen to 92 per cent). However, even in 2003 serious problems were encountered with respect to humidity, heating and proper repairs (CERC, 2004, p. 82). Furthermore, roughly a quarter of families suffered from overcrowding, defined by INSEE as housing below the standard norm for the number of rooms (see footnote to Table 6.2).

Housing is particularly crowded for families with three or more children. However, public housing (when available) is less crowded than private housing (INSEE, 2002, cited in CERC, 2004, p. 83). As we discuss below, such overcrowding can have adverse effects on children's education, health and social well-being, thus substantially decreasing their capacities and capabilities as persons.

Poor families find it almost impossible to secure appropriate housing because of the substantial price rises or rental costs in the different Paris housing markets (*Le Monde*, 9 January 2008).[2] Most often, these families are unable to acquire sufficient public financial support for purchasing houses or for renting them. For example, in 1980 45 per cent of low- and middle-income families and 51 per cent of high-income families owned houses. However, according to the annual report of the Research Centre for the Study of Living Conditions (CREDOC), by 2007 the ratio had dropped to 33 per cent for low-income families. It had risen to 46 per cent for middle-income families and 70 per cent for high-income families (cited in Rey-Lefebvre, 2007).[3]

Public support programmes exist to assist low-income families to buy houses at low prices (for example, in rural areas support for purchasing a modest house of about $90\,\mathrm{m}^2$ for about 112,000 euros with a very low down-payment of between 0.7 to 0.4 per cent of annual income at no interest). However, a study by the National Agency for Information on Housing (ANIL) (2007) showed that in the Paris region the majority of those benefiting from this social housing programme, or housing loans without interest (PTZ), were not the people of modest incomes (those earning less than 23,700 euros annually) for whom this programme was created. Rather, the majority were either single persons or childless couples with a decent lifestyle. Moreover, even when immigrant families are able to demonstrate eligibility for various housing assistance programmes such as the PTZ, very often preference is given to so-called 'nationals', an instance of what has been called the 'national preference reflex' (van Eeckhout, 2007, p. 36).

Failing to find affordable houses, the next best solution for a family is to qualify, if possible, for subsidized quasi-permanent social housing (that is, an apartment in an HLM). If a poor family is unable to qualify for permanent municipal or HLM lodging, it might look for temporary housing. There are three main possibilities: to be admitted (1) temporarily to an HLM or to lodgings for persons in difficulty, (2) to accommodation and resettlement centres (CHRS), or (3) to emergency shelters. However, admission to municipal housing requires proof of three years of stable residence. Very poor immigrant families are unable to provide such proof.

In 2005, one-third of the population of single-parent families and one-third of that of immigrant families were estimated to fall below even the very low level of income, that is, the qualifying level for subsidized housing. Incomes of roughly 65 per cent of the poor do not reach the required minimum to qualify for social housing. The most affected are single-parent families with more than one child and immigrant families from non-EU countries. A much smaller proportion of single mothers own houses compared to couples with children (INSEE, 2007a). Single mothers with children often share housing with others or 'stagnate' in temporary and insalubrious housing intended only for emergency purposes.[4]

According to an in-depth study of inadequate housing over the last 16 years (CERC, 2004), the so-called 'right to housing' (*Loi Besson*) introduced in May 1990 remains largely unenforced. The National Housing Agency (ANPL) has not succeeded in inducing the government to increase the supply of affordable public housing despite repeated government promises to do so. Indeed, the government has decreased its allocation to this budget item. Thus, despite occasional improvements the general situation remains quite bad (ONPES, 2008, pp. 121–42).

## The Canal Saint-Martin incident

We now focus more sharply on the housing situation in France by presenting a brief case study. As we did in the case of the Cachan incident in Chapter 5, here we describe a similar situation that occurred just months after that incident. We call it the 'Canal Saint-Martin incident'; it enables us to highlight the main elements in the current problems of poor housing, especially in the Paris metropolis.

### Box 6.1   The Canal Saint-Martin incident

On 19 December 2006, the widely respected French association, *Médecins du monde* (MDM), published a special report on the typical homeless person camping in the Paris streets (Bissuel, 2006a). This was an appropriate gesture on the part of this organization, since in 2005 MDM had already initiated a small programme to distribute tents to some Paris people without fixed residence (SDF). The idea was to dramatize the plight of such homeless persons. However, the result was simply to mobilize many hitherto comfortable and quietly sedate neighbourhoods in the interest of expelling the agitated and noisy 'SDF campers' from their pavements. Nonetheless, the programme did provide MDM with sufficient information to sketch a portrait of such homeless persons by the end of 2006. Among them were a number of poor immigrant children. Living with homeless persons had appreciably affected their health and school results.

In general, the persons concerned were between 30 and 50 years old. They had been living in the streets on average for roughly five years. They frequently exhibited serious health problems (especially respiratory and dermatological problems), which often remained untreated. One out of two was dependent on alcohol. Fifteen per cent suffered from AIDS. Roughly one-third suffered from serious psychiatric difficulties (Bissuel, 2006b). Ninety-four per cent expressed the wish to leave the streets if a decent and durable solution were available. Most complained of the recurring problems of insecurity, personal hygiene and violence. Average life expectancy for an SDF was 43 years.[5] However, MDM did not provide a portrait of the many children who were regularly to be found, mainly with female SDF.

These were the kinds of persons for whom, in early December 2006, a new organization dedicated to helping the homeless, *Les Enfants de Don Quichotte* (EDQ), provided new tents.[6] The tents were for settling down along the Quai de Jemmapes of the Canal Saint-Martin, not far from the Gare du Nord and the Gare de l'Est, where many homeless people (including many children and young persons) continue to congregate, and just north of the Place de la République near the Hôpital Saint Louis in Paris's Xth Arrondissement, where some medical help was available. Among the EDQ's several practical objectives were raising the consciousness of Parisians to a level that would increase political pressures so that an acceptable settlement could be found for the urgent problems of the Paris homeless (see Philibert, 2006). (In 2002 the socialist presidential candidate, Lionel Jospin, had promised 'zero SDF' by 2007.)

The then Prime Minister, Dominique de Villepin, announced new emergency measures for housing the SDF persons who were still camping in tents along the Quai de Jemmapes – many of them newcomers replacing those for whom decent housing had now been found. He also announced a government proposal to provide supplementary budgeting of 850 million euros for the construction of public housing between 2007 and 2009 (*Le Figaro*, 23 February 2007).

Further, the government not only passed new legislation concerning the right to decent housing but also added important amendments.[7]According to this legislation (February 2007), all French persons (non-French persons whose situation is irregular were excluded) were to have the right to decent and independent housing ('the right to a decent and independent housing is guaranteed by the State to anyone who is a regular resident of the French territory, who does not have the means to acquire it or maintain it') (cited in Philibert, 2007). Now, any SDF person who had been received in any 'emergency shelters' could stay on indefinitely rather than be forced to leave the next day, as had been the rule until that point (Bissuel, 2007).

Procedures were also spelled out. Thus, any person concerned by this law would (1) have to contact a mediation commission at the level of the department, which would then investigate their case. If the commission were to pronounce in favour, then (2) the department's Prefect would have to find suitable housing in the department for the person concerned in no less than three months. Should the Prefect fail, then (3) the person could formally bring a lawsuit against the state in an administrative tribunal. And if the suit were successful, then (4) the state would be condemned to pay damages to the person concerned (Philibert, 2007).

No details were given, however, about how the several million poorly housed persons in France, not to speak of those without any housing (for example, the SDF), were expected to manage such a complicated and lengthy process successfully. And no provisions were made to accommodate the many poor immigrant children living among the SDF.

So, many SDF remained both sceptical and recalcitrant in the face of many measures that offered only short-term relief rather than any long-term solutions. Moreover, the new government elected in June 2007 had increasing difficulties in keeping the past government's commitments, given the persistence of France's serious problems concerning financing as well as necessary social reforms.

*Table 6.1*  Poor housing for French immigrants by nationality and type of housing (2005) (%)

| Nationality | Type of housing | | | | Share of households without comfortable housing (%) |
|---|---|---|---|---|---|
| | Private ownership | Public housing | Private rented housing | Free housing | |
| French by birth and naturalization | 61.4 | 6.4 | 21.2 | 11 | 9.3 |
| European Union | 46.3 | 9.8 | 29.2 | 14.6 | 8.9 |
| Other Europe | 26.2 | 15.1 | 34.3 | 23.6 | 9.8 |
| Algeria, Tunisia, Morocco | 22.8 | 16.1 | 35.3 | 25.8 | 13.5 |
| Other Africa | 0 | 7.4 | 45.2 | 47.3 | 8.5 |
| Cambodia, Vietnam, Laos | 0 | 100 | 0 | 0 | 4.8 |
| Other | 11.5 | 12.9 | 42.2 | 33.3 | 8.4 |
| Total | 59.2 | 6.9 | 22.1 | 11.8 | 9.4 |

*Source*: Grand Council for Integration (2007) – Statistical Report for 2005.

## The housing problems of immigrants and their children

As we discuss below, the general housing situation of most immigrant families and their children is extremely bad. This situation depends on the type of households and the kind of employment of adult household members (for example, children living in a non-working or a working mono-parental family, those living with a non-working couple, or with a couple where only one or both work and so on).

The general housing situation remains very serious for many immigrants coming from the Maghreb (Algeria, Morocco and Tunisia) and other parts of Africa compared to immigrants from within Europe. Twenty-two per cent of the households from the Maghreb and Africa suffer from poor housing conditions owing to a lack of one or more amenities (for example, hot running water, central heating or a WC – see Table 6.1). This high proportion compares unfavourably with 13.3 per cent for immigrants from Asia (Cambodia, Laos, Vietnam and so on) and over 9 per cent for the total population. Nearly 2 per cent of the immigrant households have no WC compared to 0.8 per cent of non-immigrant households (see Table 6.2). Nearly 6 per cent of immigrant households are without central heating compared to 7 per cent non-immigrant households.

*Table 6.2*  Characteristics of housing in France for immigrant, non-immigrant and mixed households

| | All households | Non-immigrant households | Mixed households | Immigrant households |
|---|---|---|---|---|
| *Sanitary comfort* | | | | |
| Without water or running water only (%) | 0.8 | 0.8 | 0.3 | 1.3 |
| Water and WC but without sanitary fittings (%) | 0.8 | 0.9 | 0.3 | 0.5 |
| Water, sanitary fittings but no WC (%) | 0.9 | 0.8 | 0.3 | 1.8 |
| WC, bath but no central heating (%) | 6.9 | 7.1 | 6.1 | 5.6 |
| WC, bath and central heating (%) | 90.6 | 90.5 | 93.0 | 90.8 |
| Total | 100.0 | 100.0 | 100.0 | 100.0 |
| *Size of lodging* | | | | |
| Average no. of persons per household | 2.4 | 2.3 | 3.2 | 2.9 |
| Average surface area (m$^2$) | 89.6 | 90.6 | 92.7 | 75.1 |
| Average area per person (m$^2$) | 37.5 | 39.2 | 29.3 | 26.1 |
| Average no. of rooms | 4.0 | 4.0 | 4.1 | 3.5 |
| Average no. of rooms per person | 1.7 | 1.7 | 1.3 | 1.2 |
| *Indicator of overcrowding* (%)* | | | | |
| Below average | 72.0 | 74.9 | 65.2 | 41.4 |
| Average | 21.0 | 20.1 | 24.4 | 30.2 |
| Above average (overcrowding) | 7.0 | 5.0 | 10.4 | 28.4 |
| Total | 100.0 | 100.0 | 100.0 | 100.0 |

*Note*: *'Overcrowding' is defined as housing below the standard norm for the number of rooms: two rooms for a single person or a couple, plus one room for two children of the same sex or one room per child if children are of different sex.
*Source*: INSEE (2005), p.145.

This lower figure for immigrants is hard to explain considering that they generally have much lower incomes and cannot easily afford housing at high rents. Perhaps the figures refer to public housing, which is partly subsidized by the state. Still INSEE (2005, p. 144) notes that immigrant households declare twice as often as non-immigrants that they suffer because their lodgings are cold. It further notes that, in 2002, one-third of immigrant tenants in households in private housing were in this situation. This raises doubts about the accuracy of the figures in Table 6.2.

Most poor immigrant families live in social housing of one sort or another, in HLMs. But whatever the difficulties such families face in enjoying access to social housing – and there are very many, ranging from arbitrary selection practices to waiting lists sometimes stretching 20 years into the future – most families within which very poor immigrant children live do not qualify for any social housing.

Forty-two per cent of immigrant families with the lowest incomes rent social housing compared to 23 per cent of non-immigrants and 39 per cent mixed families in which one parent is an immigrant. In this poorest category, only 23 per cent of immigrants owned private houses compared to 41 per cent of non-immigrants. Overall, 58 per cent of non-immigrants owned private houses compared to 33 per cent of immigrants (see INSEE, 2005, p. 141). The latter generally live in rented social housing, invariably apartments. This is true particularly of immigrants from the Maghreb, sub-Saharan Africa and Turkey.

The housing difficulties of poor immigrant children from Mali living with their families is especially noteworthy. In June 2008, the French Immigration Ministry paid special attention to the large population of Malian immigrants in France. About half of the 250 hostels for immigrant workers around Paris in the Ile-de-France region (of about 700 such hostels in France as a whole) are occupied by young Malian men. These hostels are very basic, with nothing more than beds crammed into all available space. However, as in the Bara hostel in Montreuil in the Paris peripheral department of Seine-Saint-Denis, the hostel may house up to 1,000 persons, including families living in miniscule rooms. In order to counter some of the negative effects of such crowding on the present and future capabilities of the impoverished children, the Bara hostel complex is organized in the form of a Malian village. Thus, the Immigration Ministry reported that at Bara one finds children looking on while a barber shaves heads, a jewellery-maker toils away, women do outdoor cooking and many men, just back from their jobs as garbage men and street cleaners, sip tea under several scraggly trees.

Young immigrants over 18 years of age more often live with their parents than those who are French by birth. Most are from Algeria, Morocco and Tunisia. Those who live with friends (because their parents are still living in their countries of origin) are generally out of the labour market (Grand Council on Integration, 2007, pp. 124–5). Immigrant women are generally married and live with their children; or, frequently, they are single-parent heads of households. The Maghreb accounts for 10 per cent of the single-parent families in France, Africa 12 per cent and French households by birth or naturalization, 6 and 8 per cent respectively (*ibid.*, p. 126).

Immigrants spend a greater proportion of their disposable incomes on housing than non-immigrants. As a result they have less income for meeting their children's other basic needs such as food, education and health. The disposable income of immigrants is also much lower compared with that of non-immigrants: in 2002, it was 21,200 euros per immigrant compared to 27,600 euros per non-immigrant (INSEE, 2005, p. 142).

In general, young persons are obliged to pay higher rent for smaller accommodation, at least 40–50 per cent higher than that for bigger accommodation. This is because of a higher turnover in smaller apartments, which allows for an increase in rent every time a new tenant moves in (Abbé Pierre Foundation, 2006, p. 17). The higher cost of housing means that a larger proportion of a young person's income is spent on shelter, leaving less for other needs. The young have to make hard choices and they tend to cut down on expenditures for food and health services (*ibid.*, p. 34).

Poor immigrant families are often shunted back and forth between different government agencies often with similar responsibilities for assisting them in gaining access to proper housing. These agencies are located at different levels of government: federal, regional, departmental and municipal. Consequently, families looking for suitable housing have to make their way through an administrative labyrinth. They face further problems trying to resolve some of the contradictions between the different sets of regulations in different semi-autonomous housing associations governing access to HLMs. A combination of the bureaucratic maze and the contradictions between different housing associations often discourage many poor immigrant families from looking for proper housing altogether.

In France, if individuals lack proper official papers (for example, proof of having gained legal entry, '*attestation d'acceuil*') and, especially, valid immigration visas, they are excluded from being considered for social housing whatever their social and economic situation. In order to alleviate this long-standing problem, in 1970 the French government began a construction programme dedicated to providing 'modern' social housing of a temporary nature for poor immigrant families. These multiple housing units were called transitional housing blocks ('*cités de transit*').

Unfortunately, however, they quickly became quasi-permanent slum dwellings for immigrant families who had originally been segregated into provisional housing while waiting for proper papers and access to more permanent housing.

In short, the housing situation of at least some immigrants is much better than that of poor immigrants without French nationality:

1. Those immigrants who have acquired French citizenship (see INSEE, 2005, p. 140) often own houses rather than renting them. It may be that they are considered better integrated into French society and are thus subjected to less discrimination. Racial discrimination is prevalent mainly against people from the Maghreb, Africa (Malians and Senegalese) and Turkey, who suffer especially from particularly bad housing conditions (Erba, 2007, pp. 41–64).
2. Immigrants from within the EU and the rest of Europe, namely, Italians, Spaniards and Portuguese, do not suffer from any racial discrimination. Usually, they migrated much earlier than other non-EU immigrants.
3. Mixed households in which one parent is an immigrant whereas the other is French often enjoy satisfactory housing. In contrast, immigrant children without French nationality, and especially poor immigrant children in France, suffer inordinately from indecent and sub-standard housing.

Housing problems of poor immigrant children and their parents can be examined either in terms of a single problem, overcrowding, for example (see below), or in terms of a number of related problems, for example, space, noise, sanitary conditions and so on. However, even when there are no apparent housing problems, sufficient space may not be available for children to do their homework, to receive friends and so on. Below we briefly discuss social implications of overcrowded housing.

**Overcrowded housing**

We noted above that many French and immigrant families live below the minimum level of income required to qualify for social housing. One consequence of low incomes is that a large proportion of poor families are forced to live in overcrowded conditions (for example, fewer than two rooms for a single person or a couple, which is considered standard). Immigrants and their children usually live in social housing (HLMs) and in smaller apartments/houses than non-immigrants.[8]

Table 6.2 shows that over 28 per cent of immigrant households live in overcrowded housing compared to only 7 per cent non-immigrants. The smaller size of accommodation and a larger number of persons per immigrant household lead to overcrowding, which has adverse consequences for the health and education of immigrant children. Overcrowding aggravates the incidence of common colds among children. It also affects their normal study conditions and environment, and hence their relative success or failure in school.

Poor housing conditions, insufficient floor space and lack of privacy in co-habitation (with family and friends) militate against raising a family, devoting adequate time to studies and professional pursuits and so on. Children living in poor families in overcrowded housing are much more exposed in their daily lives to such serious inconveniences as insecurity, excessive noise, vandalism and surrounding violence. This is particularly true of the suburban ghettoes.

## The Nanterre housing movement

The government policy of building transitional housing blocks mentioned above led to a proliferation of sub-standard housing (for example, the '*Gutenberg cité*', one of the four *cités de transit* in Nanterre) in the early 1980s. Today, these housing blocks are in various stages of degradation and are completely separated from the normal neighbourhoods and social life of the city. Inadequate drainage provisions, omnipresent mud, crumbling walls, frequent fires, uncollected garbage and poor children playing in the midst of it all – this was already the scene in the early 1970s when one of the authors walked from the train station to the newly constructed university in the midst of nowhere. Everyday conditions were such that imagining oneself in a shantytown in Rio rather than in a Parisian suburb was not so difficult. Today, the situation is worse.

By the mid-1980s many of the children had become young adults. These persons began to revolt against the unacceptable transitory housing arrangements that by now were threatening an entire generation. Forming a galaxy of neighbourhood associations, the Nanterre youth allied themselves with street theatre groups and high-school students to organize rock concerts in order to mobilize the entire population of the *cités de transit*. They also succeeded in influencing the government construction association, the Sonacotra, charged with the task of administering the *cités*, to plead their cause with the government and to insist on the importance of mixed neighbourhoods instead of ethnic segregation in implementing public housing policies.

The Nanterre movement spread quickly to other *cités* elsewhere, as 20 years previously the Nanterre student revolts of 1968 had spread just as quickly. The major result was that the Nanterre mayor's office finally abandoned its previous discriminatory policies of treating poor immigrant families as 'nomads' (a derogatory term in French now being used to describe the Roma) or as 'unsociable', that is, as 'unadapted' for living properly in normal social housing. Suddenly, many poor immigrant families still living in 20-year-old decaying temporary housing units were now enrolled, not on the rigid *cités de transit* lists, but on the much more flexible lists of the 'poorly housed' (*mal-logés*).

By February 1985 many hitherto obscure questions about fairness of segregated immigrant housing were being openly discussed. However, it was not until December 2000 that a new comprehensive law governing social housing was to be voted in, the law on Urban Renewal Solidarity (*Solidarité de Renouvellement Urbain*). This law required all municipalities larger than 3,500 inhabitants to dedicate at least 20 per cent of its new housing construction to public housing. In January 2006 this law was amended to make the 20 per cent quota more flexible, allowing, for example, those units in HLMs purchased with government help by their inhabitants to count towards fulfilling the quota. However, many municipalities continued either to postpone any implementation of the new legislation, or to interpret the new legislation in such a way as to avoid any new construction initiatives for social housing. In July 2008 the Ministry of Housing issued its three-yearly report that showed more than 300 municipalities still in violation of the law, with worst marks for the wealthy suburb of Neuilly, of which President Sarkozy had been mayor for several years.

## Homelessness

Lack of adequate housing and the incapacity of many poor families to pay for it has partly led to the phenomenon of homelessness. It is difficult to obtain reliable information on the exact number of homeless immigrant children (legal or illegal) in France (Marpsat, 2008a, pp. 413–32). Similar difficulties are encountered in determining the number of homeless people in Europe generally (Edgar *et al.*, 2007). Although estimates for homeless immigrants and children are not available, it may be safe to assume that a large proportion of the homeless are immigrants, as we noted in Chapter 5, Box 5.1, on the Cachan expulsions.

INSEE estimated the number of the homeless in France in 2001 (the last time any official estimate of homeless people was undertaken) at about 80,000 persons. The Abbé Pierre Foundation (2008, p. 270) estimated their number at 100,000. Estimating the number of homeless persons, including that of immigrant children, remains difficult for three main reasons. First, the subject of homeless people remains politically very sensitive. Second, for the most part the homeless remain invisible in the sense that they appear nowhere on official computer screens. Even the number of calls to emergency housing centres has proved to be an unreliable indicator of the actual number of homeless people. Finally, despite the growing use of so-called 'itinerant survey teams', questioning the homeless directly continues to raise practical and ethical problems. Questioning them against their will violates their personal dignity and privacy.

Understanding what homelessness means in France requires some sense of the different kinds of precarious situations that many 'non-homeless' persons have to endure. Before one is considered 'a homeless person', one's situation has to be worse than the precarious situations of at least three different groups of people who have serious problems with housing.

The first group consists of those persons who are living in a 'short- or medium-term genuinely fragile housing situation' (*situation de réelle fragilité à court ou moyen terme*). The second group consists of those who have no personal domicile (*'domicile personnel'*), including many immigrant women and children living in insalubrious hotel rooms, cabins, or mobile homes on camping grounds. The third group of persons facing serious housing problems consists of those who are living in what are called 'very difficult housing conditions' (*'des conditions de logement trés difficiles'*). Taken together, these three groups of persons number about 5.9 million.

## Housing aid

Poor immigrant families in Paris or in the nearby suburbs may sometimes be able to benefit from their children qualifying for social welfare assistance. This programme has a special municipal budget, part of which goes towards lodging (understood as somewhat different and less satisfying than independent housing). However, few rooms are available.[9]

The French government provides various kinds of social welfare assistance, including housing aid to about 6 million households (Volovitch, 2007, pp. 267–73; ONPES, 2008, pp. 60–9). This assistance amounts to about 14 billion euros, annually distributed as follows: the social welfare programmes, 7 billion euros; the state, 5 billion euros; and the newly controversial social deductions from companies (1 per cent housing deduction), 2 billion euros. The housing component of these programmes allows households to reduce their costs of renting or purchasing principal residences.

In its annual report of February 2007, the French government's highest accounting agency, '*La Cour des comptes*', highlighted gross inefficiencies as well as injustices in social housing support for households. The personal financial assistance for housing had risen from around 6 billion euros in 1988 to 13.8 billion euros in 2005. Yet in 1988 the same persons were spending 12.7 per cent of their resources for housing, while in 2002 they were spending 16.2 per cent. Moreover, 19 per cent of these persons, in 1988, were living below the poverty line, whereas, in 2002, the figure was 25.7 per cent. Among them were many poor immigrant families with children. These figures, published by *Cour des Comptes*, raise the basic issues of fairness and equity, as well as social and moral justice in the distribution of public goods.

Housing aid benefits between 74 and 77 per cent of households, whatever their nationality. Generally, the poorest households (see 1st quartile in Table 6.3) are the largest beneficiaries since they cannot afford to pay high rents for their lodgings. As the majority of immigrants belong to the lowest rung of the economic and social ladder, they are more likely to qualify for housing assistance than those with higher incomes (for example, those in the 3rd and 4th quartiles). Overall, 53 per cent of immigrant households benefit from housing aid compared to 30 per cent of non-immigrant households and 30 per cent of mixed households.

Between 2002 and 2006, rental costs in France increased by 16.4 per cent, that is, 7 per cent more than the increase in the consumer

*Table 6.3*   France: share of households benefiting from housing aid classified by level of income (%)

| Level of income | All households | Non-immigrant households | Mixed households | Immigrant households |
|---|---|---|---|---|
| 1st quartile | 76.4 | 76.7 | 74.4 | 75.5 |
| 2nd quartile | 37.7 | 37.6 | 31.4 | 42.0 |
| 3rd quartile | 7.4 | 7.2 | 10.1 | 8.5 |
| 4th quartile | 1.8 | 1.5 | 3.1 | 7.8 |
| All | 32.1 | 30.0 | 30.0 | 53.1 |

*Source*: Grand Council for Integration (2007) – Statistical Report for 2005.

price index during the same period. Also regular utility charges, especially for heating, increased significantly. Despite the extensive social programmes, housing assistance did not keep pace with these large increases. The result was that more and more people were excluded from decent housing for a lack of adequate incomes and sufficient guarantees.

## Housing of Roma children

The housing situation of Roma children is even worse than that of other immigrant children discussed above. It is characterized by an extremely small living space in a van with no privacy and only occasional outdoor water and toilet facilities. The van usually stands in a cluster of other small vans and larger camping vehicles on the polluted and noisy margins of highways in the outskirts of small to medium-sized cities. However, the van remains parked for short periods only since the Roma often suffer from expulsions by the authorities. This has been the pattern, especially in one of the most important housing areas for the many Roma children, not only on the margins of the superhighways leading to Paris, but also in the outskirts of France's second- and third-largest cities, Lyon and Marseilles.

Such precarious housing conditions and illegal activities reinforce the sense of isolation, segregation and social ostracism. According to social psychiatrists, one consequence of very poor housing conditions of the Roma is the great difficulty faced by their children in settling, even when decent housing is made available. The cumulative results of poor housing are such that the psychological and cultural prerequisites for leading a settled life are often lacking (Mohacsi, 2008).

We can summarize the 'poor housing' of Roma children in terms of four distinct housing categories. First, a small minority of poor Roma families involved in seasonal occupations sometimes find temporary housing, for example, in Marseilles, in the lowest categories of dilapidated public hotels. Sometimes some accommodation, even if insalubrious, is available here for families with children. However, such sub-standard housing is extremely limited since poor families from North Africa already occupy much of this accommodation.

Second, poor Roma families who cannot find any housing in such hotels live on the edges of highways in the vans and campers described above. Still lower on the housing hierarchy are the shacks and temporary shelters to be found in hastily constructed shantytowns around Lyon, for example. Neighbouring municipalities regularly bulldoze this type of construction.

Third, another precarious type of temporary housing for many Roma children is the 'squat', that is, an unlit and dark, unheated, severely degraded and abandoned housing unit that is illegally repossessed for short periods by drug addicts and mentally disturbed people. The Roma squatter population, with its many children, continues to grow despite government efforts between 2004 and 2006 to build new housing and to make it more widely available than before. Roma immigrant families from such countries as Romania, Slovakia, the Czech Republic and Hungary suffer from greater discrimination than that experienced by poor immigrant families from outside the EU.

Finally, Roma families crowd into campsites on the edges of highways surrounding the several major cities in France, especially around Paris. These sites have neither running water, nor electricity, nor sanitary facilities. Newcomers lack the vans that other Roma often use for housing. Instead, they settle precariously in shanties stacked together with debris from roadside construction. Roma families thus become '*Gens du voyage*'. However, unlike them, almost none of these recent immigrant Roma families have proper official papers, not to speak of French nationality. Consequently, when Roma campsites are razed, many Roma are simply 'evacuated' (the French administrative jargon) to their home countries (see Landrin, 2007).

The Roma squatter population continues to grow. In its third comprehensive report on France for 2004, the European Commission against Racism and Intolerance (ECRI) observed that, despite its detailed recommendations in its previous report, France had made no substantial progress combating discrimination in housing (ECRI, 2005, p. 13). ECRI found that racial discrimination against immigrants and visible minorities continued to affect both the sale and rental of housing.

Moreover, ECRI explicitly noted that 'the perpetrators of such discrimination may be either private individuals and entities (private owners or estate agencies) or social lessors, such as some of the public agencies administering low-rent housing' (HLM) (ECRI, 2005, p. 23).

ECRI's accusation regarding public administration entities is particularly telling in the light of our arguments in Chapter 1 that evidence exists for finding France in violation of its legal commitments as well as of many of its moral engagements. In June 2008, the High Commission for the Struggle Against Discrimination and for Equality (HALDE) reported that the private sector continued to discriminate against poor immigrants seeking housing and regular employment (HALDE, 2008).

Roma families and children are often expelled by the authorities from their camping areas. These local expulsions are often followed by expulsion from the French territory altogether under the guise of 'humanitarian repatriation'. For example, from August to December 2007, the French authorities repatriated 866 Roma to their countries of origin, mostly to Romania. However, once repatriated many Roma have tried to return to France for various reasons. In order to prevent those repatriated from returning (and perhaps trying to claim a further repatriation bonus), authorities have planned to institute a strict system of biometric controls (Rodier, 2002). Moreover, France has set higher quotas for overall expulsions from its territory from 25,000 in 2007 to 26,000 in 2008 and to 28,000 in 2010 (van Eeckhout, 2007). Such controls, like the notorious new DNA controls for some immigrants, are subject to increasing challenges in French constitutional courts and the French Assembly.

## The riots in Paris suburbs

The poor housing situation of immigrant children in France, together with such other factors as very high unemployment, limited educational opportunities, family instability and chronic lack of suitable health care (Chapter 5), were major factors in the disastrous suburban riots during three weeks in the late autumn of 2005 and during one week in late November 2007. Box 6.2 describes some of the catastrophic social consequences of overcrowded housing in urban ghettoes and persisting poverty among many immigrant children living in them.

Whatever the final verdict on the suburban violence among mainly teenage immigrants, the violence of the Villiers riots coming only two years after the prolonged Clichy riots of 2005, showed that something quite fundamental was and remains seriously wrong with the French social order.[10] Originally from Morocco and someone who grew up in a housing project near Valence, Hamid Senni understands 'the hopelessness and anger behind the riots', and believes that unrest was sparked by allegations of 'police harassment' as well as 'exclusion and joblessness'. He has noted three basic sources of income in the high-rise districts around Paris: (1) for a very small minority, hard work and education lead to a good living, (2) support through welfare benefits and (3) an extensive underground economy of drugs and crime. High rates of unemployment among immigrant youth in these districts imply that hard work and good educational qualifications do not enable them to earn a decent living. Therefore, it is not surprising that many people slip into alternatives (2) and (3) (Senni, 2007).

---

### Box 6.2   Recurrent riots in Paris suburbs

Some Paris suburbs offer an example of the overcrowded housing and the kinds of social problems that eventually lead to social alienation, helplessness and violence. On 25 November 2007, in the rundown suburb of Villiers-le-Bel just north of Paris, near Charles de Gaulle airport, two 15-year-old immigrant boys illegally speeding on a mini-motorbike unauthorized for use on city streets crashed into a police car said to be slowly patrolling the chronically depressed area. Rescue services were at the scene within minutes. However, despite their efforts, both boys died very quickly.

A mob of mainly immigrant teenagers set fire to garbage bins and parked cars. The riots continued most of the night and resulted in more than 40 police and firemen being hospitalized. The number of teenage immigrants also hospitalized was not known. The actual details of the accident were disputed in court cases brought by the victims' families.

On 26 November, once again immigrant teenage gangs began rioting across the suburb. They now burned many more cars, including some police cars. Using walkie-talkies, ringleaders mobilized nine- to 11-year-olds to signal the whereabouts of anti-riot forces so as to maximize the success of their hit-and-run tactics.

Paris was not burning. But despite its name Villiers-le-Bel was not a pretty place either. In fact, it never was. From the early 1950s this small suburb, like so many other similar economically and socially depressed areas around Paris, had become almost a ghetto for immigrant families which included many jobless, under-nourished, under-educated and poorly housed immigrant youth (Ternisien, 2007). At roughly the same time, at the end of October and early November 2005, riots in the largely immigrant Paris suburb of Clichy-sous-Bois had gone on for three weeks. The immediate cause again was the death of two immigrant teenage boys, electrocuted accidentally while fleeing from police and hiding in an electrical power shed.

Many promises were made to solve the pressing social problems in the Paris suburbs through proper nourishment, education, health care, jobs and, especially, proper housing. However, despite a good deal of money spent, a number of major incidents continued to occur. The mayors of six of the nearby suburbs were quoted as saying that nothing substantial had been done in two years to improve the situation before the new and more violent riots broke out in late November 2007.

> The first set of riots that lasted three weeks in Clichy-sous-Bois in 2005 was the culmination of a long series of increasingly inadequate government efforts at different levels to help poor people living in Paris suburbs, especially young immigrants. These riots were also the starting point for a number of other violent disturbances in nearby Paris suburbs and elsewhere in France. By contrast, the second set of riots lasted but three days, and they were confined to Villiers-le-Bel.

Some sociologists (for example, Souliez, 2007) have scrutinized the suburban outbreaks of violence by impoverished immigrants. No clear consensus has emerged on their multiple causes, although a certain pattern in these riots is noticeable. President Sarkozy offered the following explanation. He said: 'What happened at Villiers-le-Bel had nothing to do with a social crisis and everything to do with the reign of thugs [*la voyoucratie*] . . . with rootless [*destructurés*] thugs and drug traffickers ready for anything' (*Le Figaro*, 30 November 2007). He went on to add: 'I refute every form of "angelism" that aims at finding in every delinquent a victim of society, in every rioter a social problem' (*Le Monde*, 1 December 2007). He reminded the audience that his 'Marshall Plan for the Suburbs' was due out before the end of January 2008. But now, given the Villiers riots, the plan was not going to be launched. 'The response to riots', he said, 'is not more taxpayers' money. The response to riots is arresting the rioters' (*loc. cit.*).

President Sarkozy's views are not widely shared (Sopo, 2007). In fact, what is needed most is an understanding of immigrant children's poverty in terms other than 'thuggery'. We subscribe to the view that overcrowded housing in urban ghettoes with its associated social problems largely explains frequent riots there.


## Concluding remarks

We pointed out in this chapter that the housing situation of poor immigrant families and their children has substantially worsened even though the general housing situation in France has significantly improved over the past decades. In many cases, their housing conditions are unsafe, insalubrious and overcrowded, particularly for families coming from Africa and the Maghreb. The main reason for this situation has been the failure of successive governments to respect poor people's right to proper housing by ensuring them adequate access to accommodation. Successive governments have also permitted unsuitable persons to remain settled in social housing units for very long periods, and sometimes failing to detect blatant cases of fraud.

We showed that housing aid is neither adequate nor evenly distributed. Poor immigrant families most at risk are those of the Roma, who suffer from almost universal discrimination in housing. No social housing blocks are willing to accept these families as regular residents, even if they are Europeans and are legal residents in France.

In general, the lack of sufficient and decent housing stock, the affordability of even rental accommodations, the very low financial resources of poor immigrant families, and especially the extremely overcrowded conditions of housing – all hinder the development of poor immigrant children's capacities and capabilities.

The ongoing and painful story of the homeless in France generally, and in Paris in particular, raises questions of fair and equitable distribution of public goods, which is our concern in this book. Poor housing not only prevents the development of capabilities of poor immigrant children but it also deprives them of personal dignity.

We have shown how current housing policies in France continue to violate the rights of immigrant children to decent housing. In early June 2008, the European Committee on Social Rights made public two official determinations, which formally charged France with repeated violations of some of its commitments under the Charter, particularly its continuing failure to uphold the treaty's prescriptions regarding housing. The EU committee's charges arose from a thorough examination of the French government's new legislation conferring on its citizens the so-called 'right to housing'. This new measure will eventually allow certain persons to bring legal suits against their municipalities for not having provided them with urgently needed social housing.

Among the EU committee's charges were that France repeatedly violated the treaty's requirements regarding the prevention of improper expulsions from rented accommodation, failing to provide proper housing for low-income households for the poorest of the poor individuals, and the general mediocrity of the French social housing policies.

Our conclusion is that the poor immigrant children's housing situation in France is a case of persisting social injustice. The successive French governments (since at least the time of France's signing the revised EU Charter on Social Rights in 1996) (see Chapter 1 for details) have repeatedly violated major provisions of the Charter concerning housing for poor families.

# 7
# Switzerland vs France: A Comparative Perspective

Having examined poverty among immigrant children in Switzerland and France in Chapters 4 to 6, in this chapter we present a comparative picture of the two countries. Both Switzerland and France are rich countries of Western Europe. According to Table 2.1 in Chapter 2, Switzerland ranks as the second richest country in Western Europe, and France the eighth. However, the gap between the two countries was much narrower in 2004 in terms of GDP per capita in PPP$ than the nominal dollar GDP per capita would suggest (see Table 7.1). The two countries are also similar with respect to such social indicators as infant mortality rates, adult literacy rates, public expenditures on education and health and annual population growth.

However, there are also striking differences between the two countries with respect to maternal mortality rates: during 1990–2004 this rate in France was twice that in Switzerland. Other differences pertain to the magnitudes of immigrant and refugee populations. An average for 1996–2000 shows that immigrants in Switzerland formed 19 per cent of the population whereas they represented only about 6 per cent in France. This may partly explain why anti-immigrant and xenophobic tendencies have grown in Switzerland during the past two decades.

A prolonged economic recession (which lasted over a decade) in Switzerland is reflected in an insignificant annual growth of GDP per capita (1990–2004 average was 0.2 per cent compared to nearly 2 per cent in France).[1] The 2006 OECD *Economic Survey of Switzerland* noted: 'Switzerland is still a prosperous country, but it is stuck in a low-growth trap and is facing growing fiscal policy problems' (OECD, 2006b, p. 12). This factor may also explain an anti-immigrant sentiment in Switzerland. Many Swiss nationals feel that immigrants take away their jobs, a view that is somewhat exaggerated considering that the total unemployment rate in the country was only 4 per cent compared to 10 per cent in France. Also the long-term unemployment and youth unemployment rates are much lower in Switzerland than in France (see Table 7.1).

Since 2006 the economic and employment situation in Switzerland has improved. According to the Chief Economist of Credit Suisse, 'the momentum of growth for the first semester of 2007 was significantly greater than that of the European Monetary Union (EMU), as is demonstrated by higher growth rates in new orders, production, exports and capital expenditure' (*Bulletin, Credit Suisse Magazine*, no. 4, October/November, 2007, p. 44). The booming Swiss economy accounts for phenomenally high rates of capacity utilization (94 per cent) in the mechanical engineering, electric and metal industries. It also explains the existence of a serious shortage of highly qualified professionals and specialists.

The general economic situation in France over the last six to seven years was similar to that in Switzerland. France also had to recover from a recession in 2001–2. This recovery was achieved by 2004. However, since 2004 the economic situation in France, unlike that in Switzerland, has varied from one financial quarter to another, sometimes continuing to improve and at other times falling back once again. Thus, in 2005, 2006 and 2007 France's GDP grew by 1.7 per cent, 2.2 per cent and 1.9 per cent respectively (OECD, 2007a). Those estimates were revised downwards at the end of June 2008 with the onset of the banking and economic crisis.

As the most recent OECD *Economic Survey of France* (2007) noted, 'The French economy seems ... to have been unable to benefit fully from the stabilization of both domestic and foreign demand' (*ibid.*, p. 22). This failure of the French economy to stabilize sufficiently has led to an increasing uneasiness among large parts of the population.

One result, as the OECD *Economic Survey* points out, is the further development of poverty and social exclusion despite France's extensive system of social protection (*ibid.*, pp. 47–86). The French government continues to face problems in tackling structural reforms of its central institutions such as the labour markets, the educational system and the health system (Le Boucher, 2007).

Short-term economic prospects for France are not encouraging: OECD forecasts for 2008 and 2009 are 1.8 per cent and 2 per cent economic growth rates respectively. The long-term prospects are unusually uncertain (INSEE, 2007b), and so are such prospects for France's large immigrant population (Guélaud, 2007).

In the following section, we discuss how the above socio-economic similarities and differences have shaped the nature and contents of immigration policies in the two countries.

*Table 7.1*  Switzerland vs France: some key economic and social indicators

| Indicator | Switzerland | France |
|---|---|---|
| GDP per capita (US$) (2004) | 48,385 | 33,896 |
| GDP per capita (PPP$) (2004) | 33,040 | 29,300 |
| Annual growth of GDP per capita (1990–2004) (%) | 0.2 | 1.7 |
| Population (2004) (million) | 7.2 | 60.3 |
| Annual population growth rate (1975–2004) (%) | 0.5 | 0.5 |
| Population under 15 (million) (2004) | 16.8 | 18.2 |
| Population: dependency rate | 47.2 | 52.9 |
| Population victimized by crime (% of total) (1999) | 18.2 | 21.4 |
| Adult literacy rate (% of 15 and older) (2004) | 99.0 | 99.0 |
| Life expectancy at birth (years) (2004) | 80.7 | 79.6 |
| Infant mortality rate (per 1,000 live births) (2004) | 5 | 4 |
| Maternal mortality rate (per 1,000 live births) (1990–2004) | 5 | 10 |
| Refugees by country of asylum (thousands) (2005) | 48 | 137 |
| Proportion of immigrants (1996–2000) (%) | 19.1 | 5.6 |
| New asylum-seekers per 100 foreigners (beginning of 2001) | 1.5 | 1.4 |
| Naturalization rate (no. of naturalized persons per 100 foreigners at the beginning of the year (1996–2000) | 1.6 | 4.2 |
| Births to mothers under 20 | 1.3 | 1.9 |
| Total unemployment rate (% of labour force) (2005) | 4.1 | 10.0 |
| Unemployed people (thousands) (2005) | 179.2 | 2,742.2 |
| Long-term unemployment (as % of labour force) (2005) | 1.6 | 4.3 |
| Youth unemployment (% of labour force ages 15–24) (2005) | 8.8 | 22.8 |
| Unemployment benefits expenditure (as % of total government expenditure) | 0.4 | 3.2 |
| ***Public expenditure on education (% of GDP) (2002–4)*** | 5.4 | 6.0 |
| *Current public expenditure on education by level (% of all levels)* | | |
| Pre-primary & primary (2002–4) | 34.3 | 31.9 |
| Secondary | 38.7 | 49.5 |
| Tertiary | 24.0 | 17.2 |
| *Net enrolment ratio*(as % of relevant age group) | | |
| – Primary (2004) | 94 | 99 |
| – Secondary (2004) | 83 | 96 |
| ***Public health expenditure (% of GDP) (2003)*** | 6.7 | 7.7 |
| Private health expenditure (% of GDP) (2003) | 4.8 | 2.4 |
| Per capita expenditure on health (PPP$) (2003) | 3,776 | 2,902 |
| ***Population below income poverty line (%) (50% of median income (1994–2002)*** | 7.6 | 8.0 |
| Overall relative poverty (%) | 7.6 | 8.9 |
| Absolute poor children (%) | 1.6 | 17.3 |
| Relative poor children (%) | 6.3 | 9.8 |

*Sources*: World Bank, 2006; UNDP, 2006; Bradbury and Jäntti (2001) and Chapter 2, Table 2.1; Park and Sandefur (2004).

## The immigration policies

Swiss immigration policy has generally been considered more restrictive than that of France. Foreigners/immigrants have found it more difficult to obtain naturalization in Switzerland than in France, which explains the much larger size of foreign population in the former. In studies of different models of immigration policy (for example, Castles and Miller, 1993) France is considered as part of the group of social democratic countries including Denmark, Norway and Sweden. Castles and Miller (1993) present the following three categories of countries with respect to their immigration policies: (1) *Exclusionary*: Switzerland, Belgium and Germany; (2) *Republican*: France and the UK; and (3) *Multi-cultural*: Australia, Canada and the UK.

However, this three-fold grouping is not watertight. One may argue that France can just as well be included in the third category since it has a large number of Muslim immigrants from such former colonies as Algeria and Tunisia, as well as from Mali, Mauritania, Senegal and Côte d'Ivoire. Therefore, we need to discuss the situation in each country in greater detail, which we do below.

### Switzerland[2]

In Switzerland, attitudes towards foreigners and asylum-seekers have hardened during the past few decades. This is especially true of the Swiss-German cantons, which is hardly surprising considering that foreigners form nearly one-fifth of the Swiss population. Table 7.2 on the initiatives and national referendums concerning foreigners and the results of the popular vote bear this out. In 1970, Schwarzenbach's '*Aktion*' called for limiting the total number of foreigners in each canton to 10 per cent of its native population. In view of Geneva's international character, an exception was made to allow the ratio to go up to 25 per cent in the canton (Steinberg, 1976, pp. 92–3). Swiss industrialists and business-men (concentrated mainly in the German-speaking part of the country) were alarmed at this growing feeling against 'guest workers', whom they considered indispensable for the Swiss economy. They started an anti-Schwarzenbach campaign to demonstrate to the Swiss public how important foreign workers were to Switzerland.

The new Swiss immigration policy (following the September 2006 referendum on foreigners and asylum-seekers) made immigration to Switzerland (entry and establishment) more difficult. The Federal government of Switzerland put the proposed change in the Foreigners Law of 2005 to a popular vote, which it won handsomely. In a national

*Table 7.2*  Switzerland: popular initiatives concerning foreigners and asylum-seekers

| Year | Initiative concerning foreigners and asylum-seekers | Results of the popular vote |
| --- | --- | --- |
| 1965–88 | Several initiatives against high proportion of foreigners. The Schwarzenbach campaign which exploited the issue of foreign workers to political advantage | The Schwarzenbach initiative was narrowly defeated in June 1970 |
| April 1981 | Initiative to abolish the system of seasonal workers (*saisonniers*) started by the *syndicats chretiens* (Christian Labour Unions) | Initiative was defeated by a large majority |
| June 1982 | The Swiss Federal Parliament recommended to the Federal government a complete revision of the 1931 Law on Foreigners | The proposal was narrowly rejected (50.4% voted against) |
| April 1987 | Partial revision of the 1931 Law on Foreigners to allow for the internment of foreigners/asylum-seekers prior to their expulsion | Accepted by 67% 'yes' vote. |
| December 1994 | The Federal Law concerning restrictions on foreigners. | Approved by 73% vote. |
| 1995 | The Swiss Social Democratic Party started an initiative in favour of a reasonable asylum policy | The Swiss Parliament invalidated the initiative on the grounds that the text violated international law. |
| December 1996 | First initiative of the Swiss People's Party (UDC) against illegal immigration | The initiative was voted by 54% in favour |
| June 1999 | Emergency measures against the abuse of law of 1998 concerning foreigners and asylum-seekers | The measures were approved by 71% of the votes. |
| May 2000 | Bilateral agreement with the EU concerning free movement of people from 2002 onwards | The agreement was approved by 67% of the votes. |
| September 2000 | Popular initiative for curbing immigration | Rejected by 64% of the votes. |
| September 2002 | Federal Law concerning accelerated naturalization of second-generation immigrant children and automatic citizenship to third-generation young immigrants | Rejected by 57% and 52% of the votes respectively |
| September 2006 | The Federal government put to a popular vote the amended 2005 Law concerning foreigners and asylum-seekers. The Law restricts immigration of non-EU foreigners to highly qualified professionals | Approved by nearly 68% of the vote |

referendum on 24 September 2006, all the cantons and nearly 68 per cent of citizens voted in favour of the new Federal Law, which applies mainly to non-Europeans (the situation of foreigners from within the EU countries is regulated by a different treaty with the EU).

The new law, which came into force on 1 January 2008, is intended to link immigration to economic conditions and the labour market, and to curb illegal immigration and employment. In the future, foreigners from outside Europe will be accepted as immigrants only if they are highly qualified and show a potential to contribute to the Swiss economy.[3]

The new law has become so strict that it may encourage asylum-seekers to go underground. Many observers believe that the more restrictive the laws regarding immigration the greater the tendency for the illegal immigrant population to grow. The law does not exempt the sick or children from detention if they are denied asylum. Detention of children under 15 for violating the law contravenes the Convention on the Rights of the Child discussed in Chapter 1.

The new restrictive features of the Swiss immigration policy are summarized below:

1. Effective from January 2008, only highly qualified professionals from non-EU countries are allowed into the country, and even then only if Swiss employers failed to find such personnel from within Switzerland or the EU countries.
2. The clause concerning 'people without identity papers' has been made more restrictive. Birth certificates and driving licences will no longer be accepted as sufficient for establishing legal identity.
3. Immigration control measures (for example, police powers and restriction of civil liberties) have been reinforced. The legal maximum length of detention for insubordination has been raised from nine months to two years. Furthermore, with the consent of the person concerned, the legal control within 92 hours is delayed till the eighth day. A special 20-day detention can be ordered by the Federal Office of Migration in case of expulsion from the centre for registration. Those considered unsuitable will be forbidden to leave a particular territory under penalty of three years of prison sentence.
4. The law on asylum-seekers has been further tightened. Their personal distress and exemplary behaviour will no longer be taken into account in granting a residence permit.
5. The new law concerning asylum-seekers introduces exclusion from social benefits without exception for applicants considered unsuitable.

6. Foreigners living in Switzerland are no longer entitled to bring their children over 12 years of age into the country on the previously sufficient grounds of family reunification. A guarantee of income and adequate housing is now obligatory for family reunification.
7. Second-generation and third-generation children of immigrants will no longer be able to acquire citizenship easily. This change follows the rejection by referendum of the Federal government proposals to accelerate the naturalization of second-generation immigrants and to grant automatic citizenship at birth to third-generation immigrant children (see below).

The new Swiss immigration policy will further restrict family reunification, especially for nationals of non-European countries. This will cause social hardships and separation of immigrant parents from their wives and children. Already the European Commission on Racism and Intolerance (ECRI) (2000a, p. 15) had expressed concern that the rights to family reunification prevailing then were somewhat strict, ambiguous and subjective. It noted the case of a canton which allowed such reunification only when certain criteria were fulfilled, such as the assessment of the family in question as 'success oriented'! It further deplored the Swiss referendum in which the population rejected the proposal to facilitate the naturalization of young people living in Switzerland (see below).

ECRI's concerns in 2000 have turned out to be even more fully justified today. In cases where certain criteria are formulated in such ambiguous terms as an immigrant family's 'success orientation', the room for interpretation is too large and hence potentially very damaging. This is the case because such broad scope for interpretation leaves open too many opportunities for ad hoc and arbitrary administrative judgements. Vague criteria for fundamental matters such as family reunification are among the kinds of phenomena that we criticized in Chapter 1 as legally, socially and morally unacceptable.

The victory of the anti-immigration far-right Swiss People's Party (UDC) in the national vote on 21 October 2007 does not augur well for the future of immigrant children and their parents in Switzerland. The UDC launched a racist campaign with infamous posters showing a white sheep kicking a black sheep off the Swiss map. Such a campaign clearly implied the wilful violation of the fundamental human and children's rights incorporated in the United Nations Universal Declaration of Human Rights. The campaign led to riots between opposing parties in the streets of Berne, a rare scene in a generally calm and placid society, although nothing like the outbreaks of violence in the Paris suburbs in 2005 and 2007.

Although the shift to the right in Swiss politics may not have led to any immediate shift in immigration policy – the policy had already become stricter even before the general election – the longer-term social forecast looks alarming. In the future Switzerland is likely to be even more unwelcoming to immigrants, particularly non-Europeans and their children. As we noted in Chapters 4 and 5, the reunification of children with their parents and other family members in both Switzerland and France has become much more difficult.

In Chapter 4 we discussed the education of children of illegal/ clandestine immigrants in the Geneva canton. We noted that Geneva is perhaps the only canton that has officially recognized its obligation to provide clandestine children access to public schools. In a circular of 19 March 1991, the Federal Office for Foreigners in Switzerland concerning education of clandestine immigrant children ('*Scolarisation des enfants étrangers clandestins*') exhorted the individual cantons (which are responsible for implementing educational policy) to be generous in accepting these children in public schools. The circular also recommended that schools should avoid discriminating against them. This circular was followed up by a recommendation of the Conference of Swiss Cantonal Directors of Public Education (24 October 1991) that all children (including clandestine immigrant children with a foreign language as their mother tongue) should be integrated into Swiss public schools. This matter was further taken up by the Federal authorities in April 2003. Despite these frequent recommendations, very few cantons except Geneva have implemented federal recommendation. Public education is the only domain in which a coordinated national/federal policy exists vis-à-vis illegal immigrants. But this policy recommendation is not being implemented.[4]

Increasingly, the rightist political parties and the majority of people equate unskilled immigrants with rising unemployment and crime.[5] In its *Second* (2000a) and *Third* (2004) reports on Switzerland, ECRI warned the authorities against prejudicial treatment of refugees and asylum-seekers. It noted in 2004 that 'even if these persons are illegal they should not be treated as criminals' (p. 15). Furthermore, the rightist parties argue that immigrants and asylum-seekers put a very heavy burden on social welfare services. Xenophobic tendencies are growing; they result from a fear that the size of the foreign population is exceeding an acceptable limit. Thus one of the main objectives of the new policy is to stabilize the migrant population by making new admissions very strict.

The recent economic boom in Switzerland has generated a significant shortage of highly qualified manpower. A similar shortage also exists in France, but for different reasons. Such shortages can be overcome not by unrealistic measures such as raising the birth rates in both countries, but instead by accepting greater immigration than at present (Bernard, 2002). However, this is unlikely in the current political climate, which explains why the highly pertinent question of linking immigration to economic policy is rarely discussed. As we discussed in Chapter 4, immigrant youth and immigrants in general are at a disadvantage in the labour market. Yet qualified young immigrants can be an economic asset in a high-growth economy, as indeed they were during the 1970s.

Switzerland's bilateral agreement with the European Union (EU) on the free movement of persons (which came into effect in 2002) has meant a reduction of the inflow of manpower from non-EU countries. Apart from such industrialized countries as Australia, Canada, New Zealand and the USA, persons immigrating from other non-EU countries (mainly developing countries of Africa and Asia) are considered 'culturally distant' and thus difficult to assimilate (see Chapter 4).[6] In a referendum on 8 February 2009, Switzerland extended (by 59.6 per cent votes) the earlier agreement to two new EU members, Bulgaria and Romania. Immigrants from these countries will further reduce labour inflows from non-EU countries.

*Referendums on (young) immigrants*

The new law discussed above includes measures to facilitate the integration of immigrants' children. For example, parents will be encouraged to invite their children to live with them within the first five years of their entry into Switzerland, after which their reunification with parents would be allowed only in exceptional circumstances. Furthermore, language and integration courses for foreigners would become compulsory. However, the Socialist Party and other critics believe that the Law discriminates against non-European immigrants compared to those from the European Community.

Earlier, in a referendum held on 26 September 2004, Swiss voters rejected two Federal government proposals, which would have facilitated the naturalization of second-generation young immigrants.[7] They would have also granted automatic citizenship at birth to those third-generation children whose parents grew up in Switzerland. The proposal concerning an accelerated naturalization of second-generation immigrant children required that they should be between 14 and 24 years of age, have had at least five years of compulsory schooling in Switzerland and should be holders of a residence permit (*permis de séjour*). This proposal did not cover children of asylum-seekers, who were not entitled to such residence permits.[8]

The proposals (which were approved by the Swiss Parliament) were based on the premise that they would promote the integration of immigrant children with the local population. Their rejection by the Swiss citizens is particularly disappointing considering that 14 cantons (for example, Geneva, Vaud, Jura, Neuchâtel, Fribourg and Zurich) had already in place a process of accelerated naturalization of these children. Swiss citizens in many of the 14 cantons that facilitate the naturalization of second-generation immigrant children also voted against the Federal proposal.[9]

Does the negative vote in the national referendum invalidate the policy of accelerated naturalization in the 14 cantons? The answer is no. In Switzerland, the cantons are very autonomous. However, the negative vote in the national referendum means that the 12 cantons that do not offer accelerated naturalization will continue to stick to their old policy.

The situation of immigrants and their children described above raises questions of fairness, human rights and dignity, and social justice, as discussed in Chapter 1. Traditionally, Switzerland has been known to be generous to immigrants. But recent developments smack of a violation of such basic principles as equal treatment before the law, equality of economic opportunity and fundamental human rights. It would appear that the new legislation violates Article 2 of the Convention of the Rights of the Child, which states that appropriate measures should be taken 'to protect the child against all forms of discrimination'.

In 2008, the Swiss Conservative Party (CDU) proposed, in a popular initiative ('democratic naturalizations'), that local municipalities should decide citizenship applications in a secret ballot as has been done in the past in a few Swiss-German municipalities. In a national referendum held on 1 June 2008, the Swiss people (and cantons with the sole exception of Schwyz) overwhelmingly rejected this proposal. According to the Swiss legal experts, this proposal 'appeared to breach the Swiss Constitution, several United Nations conventions and the European Human Rights Convention' (*International Herald Tribune*, 2 June 2008). The Swiss Federal government rightly believed that the above proposal was discriminatory and arbitrary, and denied a judicial recourse to potential applicants.

### France

How does the new French immigration policy compare with the new Swiss policy discussed above? Although it is too early to give details, several points may be noted.

First, in the past the naturalization of French immigrants was much simpler than that in Switzerland. Moreover, it has also been easier for immigrant children (those born to foreign residents in France) to obtain citizenship. Therefore, the rate of naturalization has generally been higher in France (see Table 7.1). Immigrant children have been able to choose to become citizens at the age of 18. The French Nationality Code has allowed automatic citizenship to these children as in the UK and the USA.[10]

Second-generation immigrant children were obliged to profess allegiance to France in order to reinforce their supposed French identity. Moreover, for any child to qualify for French citizenship, he or she must have lived in France for at least five years.

The French government has proposed a complete overhaul of its immigration system since the election of Nicholas Sarkozy (of the Centre Right Party) as President in June 2007. Immigration into France of adults and their children has become much more difficult. This overhaul has led to the creation of a new ministry under the controversial title of a Ministry for Immigration and National Identity. The new government has also drafted more restrictive laws under the campaign plank of France requiring a carefully calibrated annual immigration quota rather than merely continuing to accept uncontrolled immigration haphazardly (the memorable slogan of *immigration choisie, pas immigration subie*).

In fact, important changes in the French immigration legislation and institutions have been taking place since May 2003, when a new 'reception and integration contract' was established for newly arriving foreigners. Furthermore, in June 2006, for humanitarian reasons, Mr Sarkozy requested the French prefects to 'regularize' the situation of those immigrant parents with children (who lacked proper immigration papers) already enrolled in French schools for at least two years. The situation seemed to be improving for poor immigrant adults as well as their children.

But then came the 'Second Sarkozy Law' of 2006. This legislation imposed more restrictive conditions for immigrants to obtain a proper residence permit either by marrying French citizens, or by coming to France on the grounds of being reunited with other family members (estimated as constituting almost 80 per cent of yearly French immigration). Much stricter conditions were imposed on those wishing to migrate to France and others hoping to have their illegal status regularized.[11]

The new immigration laws have introduced a residence permit of 'indeterminate validity' (that is, it need not be renewed although it could be revoked). It may be obtained if an immigrant makes a formal request for the new permit on the expiry of his/her former permanent residence permit after ten years. Further, an immigrant whose asylum request is refused at France's borders may now file an appeal, which was not possible earlier. Finally, legal immigration status may be awarded to a foreigner who is able to produce a valid work offer in a profession and in a geographical zone of France experiencing recruitment difficulties (*Le Monde*, 9 November 2007).

In France, immigration policy is based on the premise that everyone is French and, therefore, well integrated into the French value system. Debates in the country about secularism (*'laïcité'*) and the banning of Islamic headdress (*foulard*) in school classrooms illustrate the systematic pursuit of 'Frenchness' and the separation of religion from education and politics. Neither the *foulard* debate nor the secularism quarrel is new. Both also took place earlier, notably in 1989 when three Moroccan high-school girls decided to wear headscarves in the classroom. The Liberals at that time supported the principle of ethnic minorities' freedom of expression, whereas the Republicans favoured the principle of secular authority.

France does not yet explicitly recognize the rights of immigrant minorities. This led ECRI (2000b) to recommend that the French authorities should ratify the European Charter for Regional Minority Languages and to sign and ratify the Framework Convention for the Protection of National Minorities. But the statements made in the *Third Report* made by ECRI (2005) suggest that France failed to accept its recommendations. According to the response of the French authorities, the 'recognition of collective rights (of minorities) would be contrary to the principles of indivisibility, equality and unity on which the French Republic is based' (*ibid.*, p. 3).

On the other hand, in Switzerland ethnicity is very much in the forefront of all studies on immigrants, who are treated as 'foreigners' resident in Switzerland only temporarily rather than as settlers. They are considered as having different ethnic and cultural backgrounds. The existence of different mountainous and isolated communities with their own languages and customs and a confederal political system do not promote the sort of national cultural identity that exists in France.

A draft immigration bill (June 2007) requires families of immigrants in France to learn basic French and to acquaint themselves with French history and customs. It also requires immigrants to sign a contract agreeing to promote the integration of their families into French society, and to prove that they could support family members without state aid (*International Herald Tribune*, 13 June 2007). In situations of inadequate knowledge of French, the applicants would be required to undertake language training on the spot for a period of at least two months.

Proof and attestation of such training would be an essential prerequisite for the granting of a visa to enter France. Parents would be expected to give an undertaking to ensure a proper integration of their newly arrived children. Family and child benefits could be suspended in cases of non-compliance.

Families already in France of any prospective immigrants are now required to fulfil three conditions. First, they must prove that their family resources are between 1 and 1.2 times the actual French minimum monthly income (SMIC), which was 1,308 euros before tax at the end of the second quarter of 2008.[12] Second, parents of such immigrants must also prove that they and their children are following courses on their rights and responsibilities as residents of France. Third, they have to prove that they are fully complying with all French requirements regarding compulsory education of children up to a certain age.

We discussed above the broad contours of immigration policies in France and Switzerland. We now discuss similarities and differences between the two countries regarding income poverty of immigrant children as well as their non-income poverty through lack of access to the education, job and housing markets. However, first we digress a little to discuss briefly the age structure of the population in the two countries.

## Age-structure of child population

The age structure of the population of children in Switzerland (age groups five to nine years, ten to 14 years and 15–19 years) changed between 1993 and 2003. Since 1998 the number of children in the five to nine age group has been steadily declining, whereas that in the 15–19 age group has been steadily rising. The number of children in ten to 14 age group followed a different trend. For a few years the number rose, then it remained the same, started increasing again and then flattened out in 2002 and 2003 (see Figure 7.1). Information on the age distribution of immigrant children in Switzerland covers only two age groups, namely: birth to 14 and 15–19, which does not allow a full comparison between immigrant children and all children (see Figures 7.2 and 7.3). However, the trend for the 15–19 age group shows that the numbers of these children from within Europe (which was substantially larger than from any other region) started declining since 2000, whereas those of children from Africa, Asia and Latin America remained low and stable throughout the 1995–2006 period (see Figure 7.2). This suggests that the rise in the number of children in this group noticed in Figure 7.1 pertains almost entirely to the Swiss children.

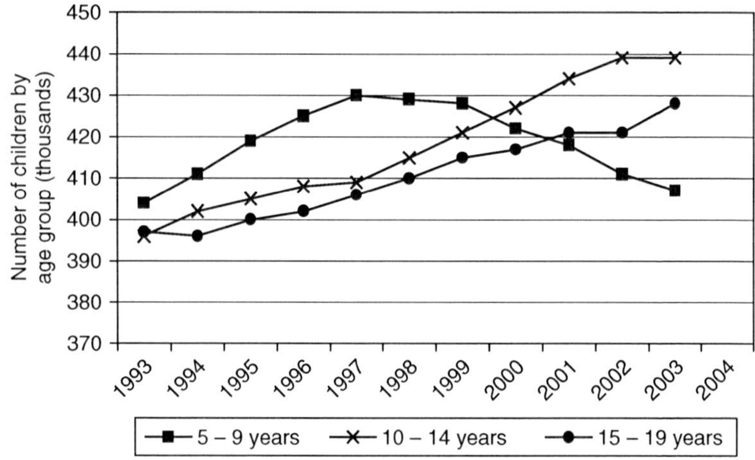


*Figure 7.1*   Trends in child population by age group in Switzerland (1993–2003)
*Source*: Based on data from the Swiss Federal Statistical Office (OFS).

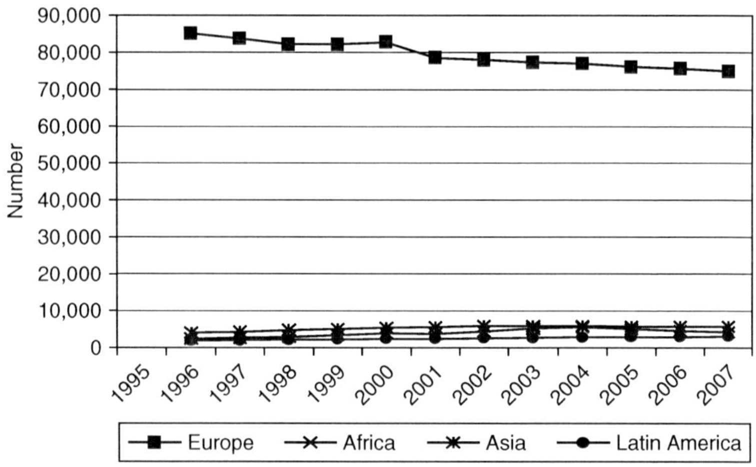


*Figure 7.2*   Trends in the number of immigrant children (15–19) in Switzerland, from different regions (1995–2006)
*Source*: Based on data from the Swiss Federal Statistical Office (OFS).

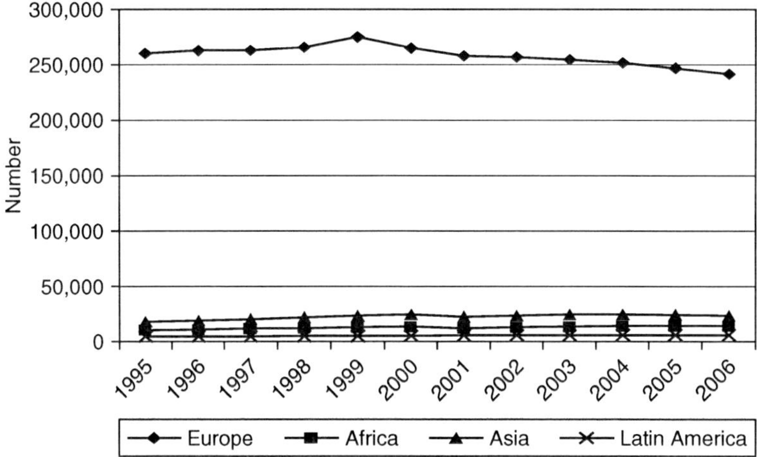


*Figure 7.3* Trends in the number of immigrant children (birth to 14) in Switzerland, from different regions (1995–2006)
*Source*: Based on data from the Swiss Federal Statistical Office (OFS).

The number of immigrant children in France in the age group birth to nine years was the largest in 1990, well above those of the other two age groups (viz. ten to 14 years and 15–19 years). But it declined rapidly till 1997, before rising again. Since then the numbers of children in the three groups have converged.

We argued in Chapter 5 that this decline is due largely to the tightening of child immigration to France under the now much more restrictive legislation concerning 'family reunification'. Immigration laws have also been tightened in Switzerland, which may have slowed down entry of immigrant children of all ages into the country.

The changing age distribution has implications for demands and pressures on school and apprenticeship systems. For example, the number of Swiss children in age groups corresponding to secondary school-going age and that for apprenticeship increased steadily during the past decade, which must have put pressures on the existing educational/training facilities.

### Income child poverty

The overall poverty rates are similar between France and Switzerland. But the share of absolute child poverty is significantly higher in France: over 17 per cent compared to 2 per cent in Switzerland (see Table 7.1). As we discussed in Chapter 4, there is a much higher proportion of poor people among immigrants than among Swiss nationals. Quantitative estimates of poverty rates among immigrant children in Switzerland (see Chapter 4) show that they are persistently poorer than Swiss children because of the larger number of children per household, lower skills of parents and higher unemployment rates among them.

The poverty situation is particularly bad among immigrant children in single-parent families and the Roma children. Bradbury and Jäntti (2001, p. 78, Table 3.3) estimates for child poverty show that, in Switzerland, the poverty rate of children living with single mothers (21 per cent) is four times the rate for children in two-parent families (5 per cent). In France it is more than thrice (25 per cent) the rate for children living with two parents (8 per cent). A single-mother household includes a mother with at least one child but no other children or adults over 18 years. Two parents include a household head and a spouse with one or more children. As we noted in Chapter 4, single-parent households are less common among immigrants from outside the EU and from such Southern EU countries as Spain and Italy. Thus, the negative effect of single-parent households is likely to be less severe among immigrant children than among native children.

The poor legal status of immigrant parents (short-term residence and work permits) adds to their precarious situation, limiting their access to the job market and income-earning opportunities. This is true also of immigrant youth in France. Temporary residence/work permits in France, valid for one year, 'give limited access to employment to certain categories of applicants' (Schuerkens, 2005, p. 30). There is also discrimination against immigrant youth in the housing market. However, we have not come across any evidence to suggest that this discrimination was due to their precarious legal status rather than their ethnic origin.

In France, income poverty among immigrant children is higher among those from Turkey and the Maghreb. It is the highest (50 per cent) in households characterized by a couple without a job and parents from outside the EU. As in Switzerland, single-parent households without a job show high rates of child poverty (36.5 per cent) (see Chapter 5, Table 5.2). Immigrant child poverty is particularly high in large households with four or more children. It is higher in households from outside the EU (for example, Maghreb and Turkey) than those from within the EU. Immigrant households suffering from unemployment and underemployment are particularly hard hit. High levels of unemployment among immigrant youth (15–24 years) is caused, *inter alia*, by a low level of education and low social status. Cases have been reported of discrimination against such youth in the job market. As in Switzerland, the precarious legal status of immigrant parents and discrimination against them in the job market in France may also affect child poverty adversely.

Data limitations in both countries (but particularly, Switzerland) have prevented a systematic analysis of immigrant child poverty in the past. In Switzerland, interest in poverty in general and child poverty in particular is very recent. Is it the affluence of the country that accounted for this neglect of a growing economic and social problem? Attention is finally being paid to the subject but mainly by academic and charity institutions rather than the Federal government.

## Non-income child poverty

### Educational access

In France, immigrant children have full rights to attend a school regardless of their legal status. The French Constitution of 27 October 1946 states: 'The State guarantees a child's and adult's equal access to education, vocational training and culture. Free public education is the responsibility of the State.' A circular of 20 March 2002 (no. 2002–063) stipulates that the enrolment of foreign pupils in French public schools should not be made contingent upon the production of a residence permit. This circular is similar to those issued by the Swiss authorities. However, what seems fine in theory does not appear to be valid in practice. The implementation of the above circulars leaves much to be desired. In its *Third Report on France* (ECRI, 2005, p. 13) the European Commission against Racism and Intolerance recommends that the French authorities should 'take all necessary measures to ensure that these circulars are thoroughly implemented throughout French territory'.

The *Second* (2000b) and *Third* (2005) ECRI reports on France have noted a disproportionate representation of pupils of immigrant origin in certain schools. This problem seems to persist because of the phenomenon of urban ghettoes and a policy of enrolling a child in a locality where he or she resides. The creation of areas with special educational needs (ZEP) may have improved the educational situation but it has failed to tackle the problem of disproportionate representation (ECRI, 2005, p. 12).

Furthermore, a ban in state primary and secondary schools on the wearing of religious signs (such as the headscarf worn by Muslim girls) (law of March 2004) is seen by some observers as discriminatory against Muslim immigrants, who may feel alienated and excluded. This may have the negative effect of radicalizing the Muslim community in France. In Switzerland, there is no such ban on the wearing of religious symbols.

In France, allegations have been made that in some cases the school authorities refuse to enrol children of illegal immigrants (*ibid.*). The situation is similar in Switzerland. Some cantons do not allow illegal immigrant children any access to schooling, as discussed above and in Chapter 4. Illegal children belong to seasonal workers and other immigrants holding temporary and short-term permits. Education is a cantonal subject under the Swiss Constitution, which means that the Federal government is powerless to overrule cantons.

In its *Third Report on Switzerland*, ECRI (2004, p. 19) recommends that 'further steps be taken to ensure that children of immigrant origin enjoy equal opportunities in education'. It further recommends that the Swiss authorities undertake to impart (1) further training for teachers in dealing with diversity in their classes and (2) financial and logistic support for teaching in the language and culture of children of immigrant origin.

Studies exist on the academic performance of immigrant and native children in primary and secondary schools. For example, the PISA 2000 study cited in Chapter 4 suggests that immigrant children generally lag behind native children in educational performance. We also noted in that chapter that immigrant children in Switzerland suffered from inequality in access to education compared to Swiss children. In France, assessments of the academic performance of immigrant and native children were undertaken using data from the 1989 French National Education Longitudinal Study, which covered about 18,500 pupils in primary and secondary schools (for example, see Vallet and Caille, 1996a, 1996b; Vallet 1996, 2005). The assessments used various criteria: child's nationality and place of birth; number of years of schooling outside France; language spoken at home; and the length of parents' stay in France. A comparison of standardized test scores (ranging from zero to 100) shows that immigrant pupils in secondary schools on average obtained 8.7 fewer points in French and 6.1 fewer points in mathematics (Vallet, 2005). Differences in socio-demographic characteristics between foreign and French pupils largely explain this performance gap. However, when a regression analysis was undertaken controlling for these characteristics of pupils and their families, surprisingly the results were reversed. To quote Vallet (2005, p. 16), 'the academic careers of immigrants' children in the French lower secondary schools were therefore better than those of their school mates, who in other respects, possessed similar social background and family environment'. Thus, it is possible that immigrant pupils overcome their social and cultural handicaps over time. Vallet further argues that strong educational aspirations of immigrant parents and families enable children to persevere for educational success in the face of all difficulties.

Given the same social origins, immigrant children perform differently in different countries depending on the organization of schooling, curricula, gender, parents' education and occupation, and family characteristics (for example, size and income status).

The share of children with tertiary education in France is much higher than that in Switzerland. Fewer Swiss children pursue higher studies. They are streamed into apprenticeships and vocational training after secondary school. In tertiary education wide variations in performance are noticed among different immigrant youth. For example, immigrant youth born and naturalized in Switzerland perform better than those who are born abroad and are not naturalized. This is not surprising considering that those born in Switzerland are likely to have longer years of Swiss education and knowledge of one of the local languages. There are variations among ethnic groups: while Italians, Serb-Croatian-speaking Yugoslavs and Croatians perform better than the Swiss (30 per cent), those from Kosovo, Portugal and Turkey are close to the Swiss average. Non-naturalized youth have fewer chances of reaching tertiary education, even if they are born in Switzerland (see Fibbi, Lerch and Wanner, 2007, p. 1130).

*Access to employment*

In France, youth unemployment was particularly high in 2005: 23 per cent of the labour force between ages of 15 and 24 compared to 9 per cent in Switzerland (Table 7.1). The EUROSTAT figures for October 2007 show that 19.3 per cent of French young men and women below the age of 25 were without work compared with the 14.7 per cent average in the 27 European Union countries (*Le Monde*, 8 January 2008).

The general unemployment rates are particularly high among Algerians and Moroccans (30 per cent among men and 40 per cent among women). The rate of unemployment is lower among Portuguese immigrants (8 per cent), who generally work for their compatriots, compared to 12 per cent for Spanish, 30 per cent for those from the Maghreb and 35 per cent for Turks (Bernard, 2002, p. 149).

The unemployment rate for immigrant children must be higher still. A study based on the National Institute of Demographic Studies (INED) survey showed that 11 per cent of youth of French origin were unemployed in 1992 compared to 40 per cent of youth of Algerian origin (*Ibid.*). Unemployment is particularly high among recent immigrants, particularly youth, who are not well integrated into the French society. Such factors as poor social origins, lack of training and education (in France 45 per cent of foreigners are without a diploma compared to 35 per cent of French) and racial discrimination may explain unemployment among immigrant youth.

Failing to find gainful employment, disenchanted and frustrated immigrant youth, particularly from North Africa (mainly from Algeria), tend to return to their Islamic roots. This may partly explain the recent urban riots in Paris neighbourhoods (see Chapter 6). In France, the problems of immigrants are linked closely to the urban ghettoes and their concentration in suburban areas. This is much less so in Switzerland, where immigrant populations are more dispersed.

In Switzerland also, immigrant youth (20–4 years) have higher unemployment rates than non-immigrants. Swiss youth have the lowest unemployment rate and Serb/Croatian speaking ex-Yugoslavs (whether naturalized or not) born in Switzerland have the highest rate, followed by Turks. Swiss employers discriminate against these groups in the labour market, which explains the higher rates (Fibbi, Kaya and Piguet, 2003).

*Access to housing*

There are differences between the two countries regarding the housing situation of immigrants and their children. As noted in Chapter 6, in France poor housing of immigrants has received far more attention than in Switzerland. As discussed there, the French authorities provide subsidized social housing to many but not all immigrant and native families. Housing aid benefits over 75 per cent of French households regardless of their nationality. As is to be expected, the poorest households are the major beneficiaries. Since immigrant households are more likely to be poor, they may benefit as much if not more than French or mixed households.

Apart from the extreme poverty limiting immigrants' access to housing, open discrimination against them in France is also a factor. ECRI (2005, p. 13) notes that 'the general shortage of housing for people with low levels of income is compounded by difficulties arising from racial discrimination in the case of immigrants, persons of immigrant origin and other visible minority groups'. Private property owners, estate agents and public agencies administering low-rent (HLM) housing discriminate against immigrants. ECRI (2005, p. 14) mentions allegations that some municipal mayors have tried to block the sale of property to immigrants within the municipal boundaries.

Similar cases of discrimination may exist in the housing market in Switzerland (see Chapter 4). The fact that ex-Yugoslavs and Turkish immigrants rarely own houses or apartments may suggest the existence of this phenomenon. However, we have no definitive and clear-cut evidence on this point. What is clear is that the poor legal status of immigrants reflected in short-term permits is an important factor explaining their lack of access to housing.[13]

## Social and political participation

As discussed in Chapters 1 and 2, the notion of immigrant child poverty defined in this book encompasses both material and non-material aspects such as social participation and human rights. The European Commission attaches particular importance to social participation and inclusion in its work on child poverty. Poverty is defined as deprivation of not only basic goods and services but also opportunities to participate in social and political life.

The participation of Swiss immigrants in public debates on issues concerning immigration and ethnic relations is very limited: only 6 per cent compared to nearly 13 per cent (see Giugni and Passy, 2004, p. 68). This lack of legitimacy implies immigrants' weak links with the host country and continued strong links with their countries of origin.

A study was undertaken in five European countries covering France, Germany, the Netherlands, Switzerland and the United Kingdom within the framework of a project on Mobilization on Ethnic Relations, Citizenship and Immigration (MERCI) (see Giugni and Passy, 2003). It is based on information collected from daily newspapers covering the period 1990–8. For case studies of France and Switzerland, the study relied on *Le Monde* and *Neue Zürcher Zeitung* respectively. A political claim is defined as any intervention, verbal and non-verbal, made on behalf of a group. The results of the study show that in France the bulk of political claims concerning ethnic relations are made by the Maghrebian/North Africans and the Jews. On the other hand, in Switzerland it is the ex-Yugoslavs and Turkish/Kurdish people, more recent immigrants, who make the major claims. For example, Italians who are far greater in number do not account for any significant claims (see Table 7.3). This may be because they are already well-integrated, having migrated much earlier. Alternatively, they may have access to other channels for making their demands.

Public participation of immigrant youth and adults in France must be low for the ECRI (2005, p. 3) to recommend 'that the French authorities sign and ratify the Convention on the Participation of Foreigners in Public Life at Local Level'. One observer notes: 'the active civic participation

*Table 7.3* France and Switzerland: distribution of claims by immigrants and ethnic minorities by nationality/ethnicity (1990–8) (%)

| Nationality/ethnicity | Country |
| --- | --- |
| | *France* |
| Maghrebian, North African | 22.3 |
| Jewish | 18.7 |
| Other African | 4.2 |
| Turkish, Kurdish | 3.0 |
| Other nationality/ethnicity | 2.5 |
| Country of residence/nationality | 7.2 |
| No specification of nationality/ethnicity | 42.0 |
| Total | 99.9* |
| Number in sample | 471 |
| | *Switzerland* |
| Turkish, Kurdish | 32.6 |
| (Former) Yugoslavian | 17.1 |
| Jewish | 7.2 |
| Tibetan | 4.9 |
| Albanian | 4.2 |
| Tamil | 4.2 |
| Italian | 2.7 |
| Other nationality/ethnicity | 6.4 |
| Country of residence/nationality | 10.2 |
| No specification of nationality/ethnicity | 11.0 |
| Total | 100.5* |
| Number in sample | 264 |

*Note*: Includes both verbal and non-verbal claims.
* Figures do not add up to 100 due to rounding.
*Source*: Giugni and Passy (2004), p. 67.

of immigrants of the first generation in France is rather low compared to the majority of the population. The largest factor influencing this result is the absence of the right to vote, even if a local consultative vote has been installed in several towns' (Schuerkens, 2005, p. 49). He further notes that there was 'a hiatus in France between the rights of foreigners in the enterprises and the rights to represent and to participate in public life' (*ibid.*, p. 4). The membership of immigrants in trade unions is limited.[14]

In Switzerland, public participation of immigrants improved when five cantons (namely, Fribourg, Geneva, Jura, Neuchâtel and Vaud) allowed them to vote in local elections. Two cantons, namely, Appenzell and Grison, leave it to the local communes to decide whether to grant the right of vote to foreigners in local elections. However, foreigners are generally not allowed to vote in the cantonal elections.[15] There are only two cantons out of 26 (namely, Jura and Neuchâtel) that allow foreigners the right to vote in cantonal elections. Foreigners are eligible to vote only if they have stayed in the canton for at least five years in the case of Jura and ten years in the case of Neuchâtel.

Under Swiss law, a distinction is made between the right of a foreigner to vote at the communal and cantonal levels and the right of being eligible for an elected office. While several cantons grant the right of vote, only Jura grants the right to be elected to an office.[16]

A Swiss citizen over the age of 18 is entitled to vote. In the case of foreigners, both young persons (18–24) and adults are granted by many cantons the right to vote as discussed above. Therefore, there is no specific provision for foreign youth to participate in political affairs. Political participation of foreigners is an essential element in the process of their integration into Swiss society and for the promotion of social cohesion between Swiss and foreigners who form a significant proportion of the total population.

## Discrimination and racism

There is discrimination against immigrant children and youth in Swiss schools and the labour market as discussed above and in Chapter 4. There may also be cases of discrimination in the housing market. As we noted in Chapter 5, similar discrimination exists against immigrant children in France, especially the Roma.[17] Although discrimination against immigrant youth in the job market is hard to prove, HALDE investigation has provided some evidence (see Chapter 5). As we noted in Chapter 5, discrimination regarding access to education and housing seems less marked.

In France, a law against racism was passed in 1972, which prohibited racial incitement and discrimination in employment and public places.[18] But the enforcement of the law leaves much to be desired; there is no special enforcement body (Dubet, 2006). Perregaux and Togni (1989, p. 53) note that the national law against racism is sometimes violated by the local authorities with impunity. They further note that the Municipality of Paris in 1983 (when Jacques Chirac was the mayor) introduced discriminatory regulations concerning the enrolment of immigrant children in schools.

There is discrimination against Algerians (especially *harkis* of Algerian origin who fought on the French side during the war). The *harkis* migrated to France in much worse economic and social conditions than the *pied-noirs* who are of French origin. To this day the *harkis* and their children suffer from extensive racial discrimination. They continue to suffer also from financial discrimination: at the end of the war their army pensions were fixed at a much lower rate than those for non-Algerian regular French army soldiers and officers.[19]

During an official visit to France in December 2007, the President of Libya, Mouammar Kadhafi, commented, 'before speaking of human rights (in Libya), one needs to verify that immigrants to France benefit from respect for *their* human rights' (*Le Monde*, 13 December 2007; our emphasis). He could have been referring to the legally and morally unacceptable situation at Roissy, where during his stay more than 100 persons, most of them Chechens, were being held, according to the National Association for Assistance to Foreigners at the Borders (ANAFE), in 'inhuman conditions' (*Le Monde*, 30–31 December 2007).

Social movements against racism have grown in France, for example, *SOS Racisme* and the *Mouvement contre le racisme et pour l'amitié entre les peuples* (MRAP) and *Groupe d'information et de soutien des travailleurs immigrés* (GISTI). But they do not deal particularly with immigrant children. We do not know of any social movements in Switzerland for the support of immigrants. However, as noted in Chapter 4, some NGOs (for example, OSEO, Swiss Labour Assistance) deal with child poverty in general and may be concerned indirectly with immigrant children.

In Switzerland, the law against racism was passed in 1994, more than 20 years after the French law was adopted. This law opens an opportunity of redress for Swiss immigrants. But it may be too early to tell whether the anti-racism law will appreciably curb racial discrimination, especially that experienced by Muslim immigrants from Turkey and ex-Yugoslavia.[20] ECRI (2004) recommendations to Switzerland suggest the existence of discrimination against persons living there without residence and work permits (*sans papiers*).[21] The non-citizens are known to be very vulnerable since they enjoy only limited or no access to health care. They are exploited in the labour market, female workers being particularly at risk (cited in *ibid.*, p. 25).

Growing anti-immigrant rhetoric and movements are common to both France and Switzerland. The rise of the National Front in France and the growing popularity of its leader, Jean Marie Le Pen (who defeated the socialist presidential candidate Lionel Jospin in the first round in 2002) parallels the popularity in Switzerland of Schwarzenbach in the 1970s and Blocher in the 21st century.

In Switzerland, foreigners were always treated as temporary residents, more a liability than an asset. In France, immigrants were seen as less of a liability not only because of the French republicanism (as Hollifield, 1994 and 2004) claims, but because their share in the total population is much smaller (see Table 7.1). But even in France the anti-immigrant sentiment and the growing strength of the National Front forced various governments to curb civil rights of immigrants and asylum-seekers. In the 1990s, the Pasqua law required immigrants and foreign students to wait for two years instead of one before being allowed to bring their families. However, it was difficult to curb family reunification because of legal and constitutional constraints.[22]

## Well-being of children

In Chapter 1 we discussed the concepts of poverty and well-being as they relate to children. In the light of that discussion we now present some empirical support for those concepts. The indicators considered are both material or economic (poverty) and non-material (social, educational and health), as we discussed in Chapters 4 to 6.

### Well-being indicators

The UNICEF Innocenti Research Centre (2007) has made a bold attempt to quantify non-economic indicators such as death due to maltreatment and perception of children about their own well-being (see below). Its analysis covers the following six dimensions of well-being: material well-being or poverty, health and safety, educational well-being, behaviour, risk and subjective well-being. The OECD countries for which data are available are ranked on the basis of these indicators. Switzerland figures in the top third (with one exception) and France in the bottom third. The comparative data for the two countries are presented in Table 7.4, which shows that Switzerland scores better than France with respect to many indicators. For example, although rates of child income poverty are similar in the two countries, Switzerland suffers from lower deprivation measured by income and educational criteria. The ill-being of children owing to lack of employment of a parent is much greater in France than in Switzerland. The unemployment rate in France is quite high, which explains this result. Health well-being of children is similar in France and Switzerland.

The UNICEF Innocenti Research Centre (*ibid.*, pp. 7–8) measures deprivation by the following three indicators: percentage of children with low

*Table 7.4*   Indicators of well-being of children in Switzerland and France

| Indicator | Switzerland | France |
|---|---|---|
| *Child income poverty* (% of children 0–17 years in households with equivalent income less than 50% of the median) | 6.8 | 7.3 |
| *Deprivation* | | |
| 1. % of children (11, 13 and 15) reporting low family affluence | 13.1 | 16.1 |
| 2. % of children (aged 15) reporting less than six educational possessions | 22.7 | 25.4 |
| 3. % of children (aged 15) reporting fewer than 10 books in the home | 10.9 | 9.1 |
| *Lack of employment* | | |
| % of working-age households without an employed parent | 1.8 | 6.2 |
| *Educational well-being* | | |
| 1. Students aged 15–19 as % of the population of 15–19 years old | 83.1 | 87.2 |
| 2. % of 15–19 year-olds not in employment or education | 8.0 | 14.0 |
| *Health well-being* | | |
| 1. Deaths from accidents and injuries per 100,000 for under 19 years (three-year average) | 12.3 | 12.5 |
| 2. Infant mortality rate (per 1,000 live births) | 4.3 | 3.9 |
| *Family structure* | | |
| % of children (11, 13 and 15) living in single-parent families | 12.5 | 11.0 |
| % of children (11, 13 and 15) living in step-family structure | 6.7 | 9.7 |
| *Child deaths through maltreatment* | | |
| No of child (under 15) deaths due to maltreatment | 56* | 756* |
| Annual number of deaths of children under 15 per 100,000 children | 0.8 | 0.5 |
| Annual number of deaths of children under 15 per 100,000 children, including those 'of undetermined intent' | 0.9 | 1.4 |

*Sources*: UNICEF Innocenti Research Centre (2007). *UNICEF Innocenti Research Centre (2003).

incomes and family affluence, less than six educational possessions and fewer than ten books in the home. On the basis of the first and second, Switzerland scores better than France, whereas France scores better with respect to the third indicator (Table 7.4).

The educational well-being of children is higher in Switzerland than in France. Switzerland ranks 14th among OECD countries, whereas France ranks 18th and is at the bottom of the ranking table. The three component indicators of this dimension of well-being are: (1) average achievement in reading, mathematical and science literacy at age 15, (2) percentage of children aged 15–19 years remaining in education and (3) percentage of children in 15–19 age group not in education, training or employment.

The UNICEF Innocenti Research Centre (2007) measures educational well-being in terms of (a) students aged 15–19 years as a proportion of population of 15–19 year-olds and (b) the proportion of 15–19 year-olds not in employment or education (see Table 7.4). However, other equally useful and more qualitative indicators have not been considered: for example, proximity and quality of schools, school drop-out rates and pre-school facilities.

Poverty indicators expressed in terms of educational criteria should aim at cross-classifying immigrant children who are income poor and are at the same time below a certain educational poverty line. Such a norm may be defined in terms of basic knowledge (or capacities) as an absolute minimum (CERC, 2005, p. 19).

## Child maltreatment

Child maltreatment is one of the indicators of child well-being or ill-being. Therefore, it may be worth discussing it here. Deaths owing to maltreatment and child abuse are very small in Switzerland compared to France. This is understandable considering that Switzerland's population of children under 15 is also much smaller. Therefore, a more accurate indicator is the annual number of deaths per 100,000 children. This ratio (a five-year average) is slightly higher for Switzerland (see Table 7.4). However, the result is reversed if 'deaths of undetermined intent' are included. The ratio becomes 0.9 for Switzerland and 1.4 for France (UNICEF Innocenti Research Centre, 2007, p. 4).

In principle, child maltreatment and abuse is a useful indicator of children's ill-being because it is associated with other symptoms of this state such as poverty and deprivation, single parenthood, family breakdown, unemployment and drug abuse. However, in practice it is difficult to determine the causes of maltreatment. Any single factor noted above is unlikely to explain maltreatment in isolation of other factors. Nevertheless, whatever the causal factors, maltreatment and violence experienced by children at home at the hands of parents and other family members can leave long-lasting scars on their adult lives. Children experiencing violence suffer from post-traumatic stress disorder; they are also at greater risk of catching allergies and asthma. Invariably they will suffer from depression and anxiety. Very young children (at primary school, for example) may have greater difficulties at school in concentrating on classes and schoolwork. Abused children are more likely to get addicted to drugs and alcohol than other children who have not experienced abuse (UNICEF, 2007, p. 24). Vulnerability of children resulting from abuse, maltreatment and domestic violence can be long lasting. It can retard the development of their capacities and capabilities, as discussed in Chapter 1.

It is poverty and mental stress resulting from, for example, unemployment, single parenthood (as discussed earlier), stress and low incomes that may raise the risk of child abuse (Gelles, 1989). A 1993 US survey shows that risk of maltreatment decreases with an increase in the incomes of children's families (cited in UNICEF Innocenti Research Centre, 2003, p. 18). Less contact with government health and welfare services at higher income levels may conceal the existence of child abuse at this level. On the other hand, child abuse is more likely to be uncovered among members of poor families who are in closer and more frequent contact with welfare services.

We do not have separate data for domestic violence affecting immigrant children. But a *priori*, these children may be worse off because of the more precarious living and working conditions resulting from abject poverty.

## Family relations and subjective well-being

There are wide differences in the ranking of France and Switzerland in respect of the dimensions of family relations and subjective well-being (see Table 7.5). This is quite surprising. How can one explain these differences? Clearly, the quality of family relations is something very difficult to measure. UNICEF Innocenti Research Centre (2007) measures it on the basis of data on family structures and children's responses to such survey questions as: eating main daily meals with parents, frequency of communication with parents and finding peers kind and helpful. As Table 7.5 shows, family structures, in terms of the share of single-parent families, are similar in France and Switzerland. However, the share of children in step-family structure is lower in Switzerland. The divorce rates, an indicator of family breakdown, are also similar in the two countries. Therefore, it would appear that the vast difference in the ranking is explained largely by how children responded to the above three questions.

*Table 7.5*   Ranking of Switzerland and France by different dimensions of child well-being

| Dimension of well-being | Switzerland | France |
| --- | :---: | :---: |
| Material well-being | 5 | 9 |
| Health and safety well-being | 9 | 7 |
| Educational well-being | 14 | 18 |
| Family and peer relations | 4 | 12 |
| Behaviours and risk | 12 | 14 |
| Subjective well-being | 6 | 18 |
| Average ranking for all six dimensions | 8 | 13 |

*Source*: UNICEF Innocenti Research Centre (2007).

In Chapter 1, we discussed the perceptions of children regarding their own well-being. These subjective judgements turn out to be vastly different in France and Switzerland. Is it because of the greater affluence of Swiss families or children? Or are there other factors at work to explain Swiss children's optimism about their own well-being? The UNICEF Innocenti Research Centre (2007) constructed this index by asking children how they rated their health, whether they liked their schools and how they regarded their personal well-being. The disillusionment of French children may be explained by the economic and social malaise in France, compounded by slow economic growth (similar to the economic situation in Switzerland) and prolonged high rates of unemployment (which are much lower in Switzerland). But can children in their teens be expected to be so sensitive to the economic malaise in their country? Highly unlikely; rather, they are more likely to be sensitive to their parents' economic situation and to what their parents tell them about the state of their financial burdens.

# 8
# Some Conclusions

Does the well-being of immigrant children coincide with that of children in general in Europe? This question requires further scrutiny. We discussed in the earlier chapters that immigrant children have a more disadvantaged status than non-immigrant children. Apart from their social and economic status, their uncertain legal status and short-term resident and work permits may often worsen their poverty situation.

Analyses of the nature and magnitude of immigrant child poverty suffer from a serious lack of adequate and comparable statistics on children by age group, sex, nationality, level of income and access to health, education and the job market. Such an analysis is essential before a meaningful strategy for poverty alleviation can be designed and implemented. The Swiss Federal Commission for Children and Youth has recognized this lacuna. The French National Statistics Office (INSEE) has also begun to revise its present inadequate procedures for measuring poverty among poor immigrant children.

The tightening of measures against immigration in Europe (including France and Switzerland; see Chapters 3 to 5 and 7) violate the human rights of children. Moreover, some provisions in the new French measures violate the French Constitution. Children enjoyed these rights under the earlier, more liberal immigration policy when family reunification was the norm and children of up to 21 years of age could freely join their parents and other family members in the countries concerned.

The liberal immigration policies in the past were pursued in the interest of maintaining economic growth during the boom periods of the 1970s and 1980s. It is important to remember that there are many low-paid occupations, which the native populations are unwilling to pursue. These low-paid occupations are mostly undertaken by immigrants, especially in agriculture, construction and various types of services.

Therefore, immigration of low-skilled workers is a necessary evil, if not an economic asset. It is most unlikely that nationals of European countries will suddenly be prepared to do the menial jobs that they have avoided doing for so long. And it is not always possible to mechanize or automate most service-sector jobs in which immigrants are generally engaged.

## Economic, legal and political status of immigrant children

In this book we have discussed issues of poverty of immigrant children in the midst of the affluence of local children and the population in general. We have shown that, in general, immigrants are income-poorer than the local population. This is particularly true of non-European immigrants from Africa, Asia and Latin America. The non-income indicators of poverty and ill-being are also weighted against immigrant children. Their access to basic goods and services, be it access to housing, health, education or the job market, is restricted by many legal, social, economic and cultural barriers. Many of these barriers are created artificially by an overly strict government immigration policy or by local people's perceptions (often false) that immigrants and their children tend to be criminals and drug addicts. Shifts in the political landscape of many European countries (especially France and Switzerland) to the right (socialist parties in these countries, which were hitherto vocal supporters of the basic human rights of immigrants, have now become much weaker) will further harden people's attitudes towards foreigners.

We summarize the poor overall situation of immigrant children in Table 8.1, which shows that they enjoy poor economic, social and legal status compared to non-immigrant children. However, the situation of mixed children is somewhat ambiguous. Children of refugees and asylum-seekers in a precarious legal situation are likely to be particularly vulnerable. We showed in Chapters 4 and 5 that in both Switzerland and

*Table 8.1*   Overall situation of immigrant children in France and Switzerland

| Status | Immigrant children | Non-immigrant children | Mixed children |
|---|---|---|---|
| Economic status | Poor | Good | Poor/good |
| Social status | Poor | Good | Poor/good |
| Legal status | Poor | Very good | Poor/good |
| Political status | None | Very good | Poor/good |

France child poverty among immigrants may be explained partly by the precarious legal status of their parents rather than low incomes per se. Those with short-term and temporary residence permits are particularly disadvantaged. They are discriminated against in school and in the job and housing markets.

One witnesses a rather paradoxical situation in Europe today. At the European level, laws, regulations and resolutions are being passed to uphold the rights of foreign immigrants and asylum-seekers. The European Commission against Racism and Intolerance (ECRI) is working hard to curb the forces of growing xenophobia in Europe. Through its regular country reports it makes strong recommendations against racial discrimination and intolerance of immigrants. Yet at the national level, in a growing number of European countries the plight of immigrants is becoming worse and new admissions of children and their parents are being more strictly controlled. In other words, the recommendations of the above Commission and other international bodies (such as UNICEF and the UN) are being largely ignored by individual countries. A growing divergence between policies at the European level and those at the national levels is increasingly disturbing for both the human rights bodies and enlightened individuals within countries. The above situation reinforces the need for a common European immigration policy towards economic immigrants, refugees and asylum-seekers and their children. Such a common policy needs to be based on the principles of fairness and social justice discussed in Chapter 1 and alluded to throughout this book.

## Social justice and immigrant children

Social justice and the human rights of the child is a central theme of the book. In Chapter 1, we outlined the main articles of the UN Convention on the Rights of the Child, which has been ratified by a very large number of member countries. Yet we maintain that many articles of the Convention are being violated in individual countries, including France and Switzerland, with the formulation of the new discriminatory immigration policies. We noted in Chapters 4 and 5 that, in theory, clandestine children are entitled to attend a public school regardless of their legal status. But, in practice, in both the countries these children suffer from discrimination except in the Canton of Geneva. We also noted that this is especially the case for poor immigrant Roma children. Can there be social justice in Europe if individual member countries continue to violate the basic principles of human rights and the protection of an immigrant child?

In December 2007, the UN celebrated the 60th anniversary of its Universal Declaration on Human Rights. Also on the eve of the signing of the new comprehensive EU treaty, the Presidents of the European Commission and the European Parliament once again proclaimed the importance of the EU Charter of Fundemantal Human Rights.

The EU first adopted this Charter in Nice on 7 December 2000. The new EU treaty explicitly 'recognizes' that this Charter has the same juridical value as all other EU treaties. But the EU Charter itself enshrines the essential fundamental human rights of the individual as already formulated and adopted in the UN Universal Declaration of Human Rights. Among these essential fundamental rights, as we have stressed in this book, is the primacy of personal dignity and worth of all human beings, including that of impoverished immigrant children.

An improvement of the rights of immigrant and other children will require a national strategy for the alleviation of child poverty. Neither France nor Switzerland at present has such a strategy in place.

In Chapter 2 we noted that studies on child poverty are based on the assumption of equitable income and food sharing within the household. This assumption is unrealistic since income sharing and food sharing are in fact unequal among boys and girls and among younger and older siblings. Marlier *et al.* (2007, p. 126) note that 'the policy analysis does not take the gender dimension fully into account. Analyses based on survey data typically treat the household as a unit assuming an equal sharing of financial resources within households.' The gender dimension of poverty was also noted by the European Commission in its discussion of social indicators.

In Switzerland the problem of child poverty has finally been recognized with the publication by the Federal Commission for Children and Youth of a report entitled *Young and Poor* (2007).[1] This publication will certainly create an awareness on the part of the Swiss public and policy-makers of the seriousness of the problem. However, it will do little to alleviate child poverty until a coherent strategy with well-defined goals and objectives is formulated and implemented. Such a strategy will need to combat not only income poverty but also lack of access of children (especially immigrant children) to the basic human needs and rights discussed in this book. Non-income poverty can only be removed by designing measures to improve access to health, education and employment. For example, at present in Switzerland there is a missing link between nursery schools and compulsory schools. A similar problem exists in France. The Swiss Federal Commission mentioned above recommends the establishment of a compulsory school for four-year-old children to ensure a smooth and flexible transition from nursery to formal compulsory schools.

In Chapter 1 we discussed the issues of social justice, capability and well-being in the context of the plight of immigrant children in Europe. Social injustice faced by poor immigrant children occurs when they are treated, both as individuals and as social groups, in morally inappropriate ways. In other words, many of the 'rules of the game' that govern the institutions concerned with poor children are unfair. For example, take the case of their parents' eligibility for low-income social housing discussed in Chapter 6. As immigrants they do not qualify for such housing. What is sometimes worse is that the rules do apply, but in a substantially different and discriminatory manner.

Immigrant children suffer from different kinds of unfairness. There is unfairness in the rules that govern the distribution of common goods, 'those arrangements that promote the flourishing of everyone in the community' (Murphy, 2005). There is unfairness in the rules that govern procedures. And there is also unfairness in the betrayal of legitimate normative expectations, what has been called 'unfairness-as-betrayal' (Cullity, 2004, p. 116).

Most immigrant children do not suffer from unfair wages or from unfair prices, as few actually hold jobs and even fewer actually have any money to spend. These children suffer mainly from persistently unequal treatment without any good reasons.

Given the uncertain and at times shaky economic, social and political situation of even affluent European countries, and given that these countries do have many important social programmes in operation, why is such persisting inequality socially and morally reprehensible? The basic reason is that these wealthy countries usually try to provide suitable means for alleviating the unacceptable poverty situation of immigrant children without providing strong juridical sanctions for the social programmes, which fail to produce fully satisfactory results (Wuhl, 2007). An even more basic reason is that all too often many European governments persistently fail to institutionalize appropriate means for assisting immigrant children.

We recognize that understanding practical issues concerning social injustice is not easy. We also accept that historically there are many competing conceptions of the fraught relations between theory, practice and moral reasoning (Dworkin, 2006). As one political scientist has written:

> the idea of social justice has two faces. One looks toward the distribution of the benefits of social life; the other, toward the allocation

of its burdens. Justice is about both distribution and contribution. The subject of social justice is difficult partly because the two problems interact and must be faced simultaneously, even though they implicate moral ideas that are to some extent distinct. (Beitz, 2001, p. 120)

But however difficult the subject, there are cogent arguments for attempting such an understanding.

Many investigators show that immigrant children in Europe continue to have unequal access to basic goods largely on the grounds of different natural abilities and different social situations, which are both arbitrary. Hence, we argue that such a situation where successive governments fail to distribute public goods, including wealth, is socially and morally unjust.

In brief, tolerating debilitating inequality among immigrant children is socially and morally reprehensible because the evident and quite serious disadvantages of natural gifts and circumstances, particularly among those living in the midst of knowledgeable, powerful and plentiful societies, disadvantage them unfairly (Simmons, 1992).

In summary, we have not written the earlier chapters either from a justice-as-fairness approach to immigrant child poverty or from a capability approach to child poverty. Rather, our approach to elucidate immigrant child poverty is from the perspective of social justice understood mainly in moral rather than in merely legal terms. In other words, social justice here is a matter of principle (Dworkin, 1985).

This perspective is even more fundamentally an ethical one. That is, our perspective here is not mainly a moral one of duties, obligations, even of rights alone, but of values, goods and responsibilities. Yet this ethical and not just moral perspective is, finally, neither just an ethics of responsibility, like Weber's *Verantwortungsethik*, nor an ethics of ultimate ends like his *Gessinungsethik*. Rather, our perspective is an ethical one in the stricter sense of what Weber called, a *Vornehmheitsethik*, an ethics of human dignity, integrity and nobility.

We conclude with the hope that this book might contribute in some small way to the governments of the European countries (including France and Switzerland) upholding the principles of legal, social and moral justice, as well as the human rights and the personal dignity of children. After all, Europeans countries have committed themselves to doing so.

# Notes

## 1  Child Poverty and Well-Being

1. Comprehensive studies on child poverty include: UNICEF Innocenti Research Centre (2007), McGillivray (2006) and Bradbury, Jenkins and Micklewright (2001a).
2. On the general juridical details of these difficult issues see the relevant articles in Bouchet-Saulnier (2006). On our particular concerns here, the rights of children, see Martinetti (2002) and Dekeuwer-Défossez (2006).
3. English philosophical usage today of the expression 'well-being' remains somewhat tributary to several remarkable investigations in the history of philosophy chief among which is Aristotle's discussion in Book X of the most important of his several ethical and political works, the *Nichomachean Ethics* (Aristotle, 2000). There, Aristotle details his general theme of *'eudaimonia'*, which is often rendered in English as 'well-being' or 'happiness'. However, Aristotle's notion of well-being is not suited to our enquiry into a person's well-being or lack of it. Despite its suggestiveness for indicating a person's living a good life in the sense of living well and doing well, the word *eudaimonia* has a different connotation in Greek than the term 'well-being' has in English. As one philosopher writes, *eudaimonia* 'can be diminished by events after the subject's death, and [impossibly for our concerns] it is not a state that children can possess. It is complete and self-sufficient, to be attained for no other end than itself, so it includes all other ends that are pursued for themselves. Therefore it includes pleasure, but goes beyond it' (Blackburn, 2005b, p. 122).
4. A number of studies on well-being are now available. For example, see Boarini, Johansson and d'Ercole (2006) and McGillivray and Clarke (2006).
5. For a representative standard description of utilitarianism, see Brock (1999).
6. The literature on Rawls is very extensive. An excellent bibliography of and on Rawls divided by themes can be found in Freeman (2003), cited hereafter as *Companion*.
7. On Sen's idea of poverty as 'capability-deprivation', see especially his *Development as Freedom* (1999, pp. 20, 87–110), cited hereafter as DF. A selective but extensive bibliography of Sen's work is to be found in Vizard (2006, pp. 256–8). Several critical appreciations of Sen's work with replies can be found, for example, in special issues of the journals, *Economics and Philosophy* 17 (2001), and *Feminist Economics* 9/2–3 (2003), and in Basu, Pattanaik and Suzumura (1995).
8. See also Sen 'Utility and Well-being' and 'Well-being, Agency and Freedom' in his 1986 Royer Lectures at Berkeley, dedicated to Kenneth Arrow (Sen, 1987). For a brief and recent overview of how Sen developed his capabilities approach, see Éloi Laurent, *'Biens premiers et capacités'*, in Mesure and Savidan (2006).
9. To ensure the widest dissemination, UNICEF decided to publish the complete text of the 1989 Convention in French together with a simple commentary

in an easily accessible paperback edition in 2002 at the cost of only 2 euros (Martinetti, 2002).
10. We follow here Runciman's reconstruction of Weber's views, which are often difficult to articulate precisely.


## 2   Immigrant Child Poverty in Europe

1. As Sen (1993) has pointed out, richer African Americans in the USA have lower chances of reaching advanced ages than the poorer Chinese and Indians in Kerala.
2. A large body of literature exists on adult poverty in Europe and other industrialized countries. For example, see Atkinson (1998).
3. In Spain nearly 90 per cent of young people between the ages of 20 and 24 years, and more than half of those between 25 and 29 years continue to live with their parents (Cantó and Marcader-Prats, 2001, p. 215).
4. Cantó and Marcader-Prats (2001, p. 217) note that 'Spain is one of the European countries with the highest proportion of individuals in the working-age population not at work because of either unemployment or inactivity.'
5. The EU-SILC was started in 2004. The questions concerning intergenerational transfer of poverty were asked as part of the 2005 SILC. Respondents were aged 25 to 65 and were asked questions pertaining to their experiences as teenagers (between the ages of 12 and 16) (CSO, 2007).


## 3   The European Immigration Debate

1. Spain has had the most entries with 683,000 immigrants arriving in 2005. Germany had 573,900 entries, the UK 473,800 and France 134,800 during the same year. However, even these numbers may not be sufficient to counterbalance these countries' normal loss of population owing to deaths and to low birth rates (Day, 2007).
2. The number of immigrants without papers arriving on the shores of Spain's Canary Islands went up six-fold from 2005–6, with 31,000 such immigrants arriving in 2006 alone. And between 11 May and 14 May 2007, more than a thousand Africans without papers were intercepted trying to land on the beaches of the Canaries (*Le Monde*, 29 December, 2007).
3. Deaths of immigrants trying to enter Europe have become a serious problem. For example, between 1993 and 2007 the number of documented deaths was 8,855 (*Le Monde*, 10 October, 2007). In 2006, 2,088 persons died while trying to enter the EU illegally. In 2007 the number of those who died was 1,861 persons, including 1,684 who died at sea. December 2007 was one of the worst months recorded so far when 243 persons died, including 120 in the Aegean Sea (*Le Monde*, 9 January, 2008). However, no one knows the number of people who actually died during the last few years while trying to reach Europe. The numbers of drowned persons washed up on the shores of Italy and Spain alone from 2005–7 would suggest a far larger number than the number of documented deaths.

4. Parsons and Smeeding (2006, p. 14) note that the European welfare programmes 'were originally premised on worker–retiree ratios well above 5:1'.
   This ratio has now gone down to 4:1, and is expected to fall to 2:1 by 2040.
5. In the 1980s, 15 such multilateral groups have been noted: the Rhodes group,
   the Schengen group, the Trevi group, 'the *ad hoc* immigration group', the
   Berlin group and so on (see Collinson, 1993).
6. By 2007, 13 countries had signed the Schengen Agreements, including two
   countries that were not members of the European Union (Norway and Iceland). On 21 December 2007 nine more countries signed the agreements to
   form a new total of 21 signatory states (Nies, 2007). Cyprus is expected to
   join this Schengen group in 2008, while Switzerland, not a member of the
   European Union, will also join in 2008. Romania and Bulgaria are expected to
   join in 2011. Current EU treaties now require all EU member states eventually
   to become members of the Schengen group.
7. The law was adopted by 369 votes in favour, 197 against and 106 abstentions
   (Brothers, 2008).
8. The principle of a common EU policy for asylum and immigration was first
   established in the Treaty of Amsterdam (1998). At the Tampere summit the
   European Council declared that 'the separate but closely related issues of
   asylum and migration call for the development of a common EU policy'.
9. In 1964, Switzerland concluded a bilateral agreement with Italy, which
   improved the legal status of Italian workers who accounted for 70 per cent of
   all foreigners at that time (Afonso, 2005, p. 658).

## 4   Immigrant Child Poverty in Switzerland

1. Dr Jean-Marc Falter, Economics Department, University of Geneva, and
   Ms Sybille Bayard of the Jacobs Centre for Productive Youth Development,
   University of Zurich, gave useful comments on an earlier draft of this chapter.
2. Foreigners from non-EU countries accounted for 5 per cent of the total in
   1976; this figure rose to 14.6 per cent in 2005 (OFS, 2007, p. 25).
3. Between 1993 and 1998, the shares of immigration into Switzerland for family reasons declined from 41 per cent in 1993 to 30 per cent in 1998; and
   those for skills category increased from 26 per cent in 1993 to 33 per cent in
   1998 (Coppel, Dumont and Visco, 2001).
4. Permit A for seasonal workers (*les saisonniers*) was abolished in 2002 when
   Switzerland signed a bilateral agreement with the EU. This measure was
   considered inconsistent with the EU rules and regulations.
5. One needs to distinguish between active and non-active immigrants. While
   the former are in the labour market or seeking employment, non-active
   immigrants include school children and students, with whom we are mainly
   concerned, spouses and very small children (who enter under family reunification clause), retired persons, foreign spouses of Swiss nationals and
   asylum-seekers and refugees. In Switzerland, spouses and children represent about 50 per cent of the total population of non-active immigrants (see
   Piguet, 2005, pp. 79–80).
6. Provisional admission status was granted to 25 per cent of asylum-seekers to
   stay in the country while their applications were being processed. However,

many stayed in unsatisfactory conditions for several years. Only 10 per cent of all asylum-seekers were granted recognized refugee status (Moret, 2006).

7. Headcount ratio can be misleading as it does not show whether some poor people live just below the poverty line or far below it. For this reason alternative measures, namely, the poverty-gap ratio and the Foster-Greer-Thorbecke (FGT) index, have been developed. These are measures of poverty intensity rather than its incidence. They show: (a) difference between the average income of poor people and the poverty line distinguishing poor and non-poor and (b) poverty by population sub-groups. The FGT index is additively decomposable with population share used as weights. For more details, see Bhalla and Qiu (2006), Appendix to Chapter 1 on 'The Measurement of Poverty'.

8. We owe this point to Ms Sybille Bayard of the Jacobs Centre for Productive Youth Development at the University of Zurich, Switzerland.

9. There are 250,000 poor children, 604,400 poor adults during working life (19–64 years) and 196,000 poor after retirement (65+ years). Adding all three figures one obtains an estimate of about 1 million poor in Switzerland, which came to about 14.3 per cent of the total population in 2003 (see Kehrli and Knöpfel, 2007, p. 52).

10. This policy of forced expulsion of Roma is followed by France (see Chapters 5 and 6) and other European countries, which raises questions about the human rights of these people and about social justice in Europe.

11. A study commissioned by the Federal Social Insurance Office estimated that workload with two children amounted to 195 hours per month, which translates into 5,070 Swiss francs per month at an hourly rate of 26 Swiss francs.

12. The Basle study by Drilling (2004; 2007a; 2007b) was based on data obtained from various sources, viz. social welfare statistics, residents' registration offices and welfare case files. Based on this data factor analysis was undertaken using variables covering economic, social and cultural capital.

13. There are about 50,000–300,000 foreign clandestine persons in Switzerland (IMES-ODR-AFD, 2004, p. 5). According to Professor Schneider of the University of Linz, about 90,000 are foreign clandestine workers, which is one-third more than ten years ago (cited in *Ibid.*).

14. Federal policy for regularizing the status of undocumented immigrants followed a case-by-case approach. The Federal government refuses to regularize their status collectively. However, the policy varies at the cantonal level. The Canton of Geneva considered the possibility of regularizing the status of illegal immigrants by granting them residence permits. A few years ago, two motions were studied at the cantonal level. The first proposal presented by the left parties was to regularize on a collective basis (Kaya, 2005). The second proposal presented by the right parties was to do it on a case-by-case basis. The Municipal Council of Geneva City supported the first option. However, the collective regularization option was not adopted. The final motion accepted by the Geneva Cantonal Parliament (*Grand Conseil*) was an improved version of the right-wing motion. The canton of Zurich rejected collective action: it was in favour of the expulsion of undocumented immigrants.

15. The comfort and decency of housing may be assessed by the existence of a kitchen or a kitchenette. In general, 1.4 per cent of single foreigners in

Switzerland are without this facility compared to 0.5 per cent of Swiss. But the proportions are much higher for Portuguese (17 per cent), ex-Yugoslavs (16.4 per cent) and Turks (11.7 per cent) (Wanner, 2004, p. 51).

16. In 2003, ex-Yugoslavs constituted nearly 24 per cent, Portuguese over 10 per cent and Turks over 5 per cent of all permanent residents.

## 5   Immigrant Child Poverty in France

1. A number of studies exist on the general nature of poverty in France, for example, ONPES (2008); ONPES Travaux (2008); Chauvel (2007). The general economic, political and social contexts of poverty in France are available in numerous places, notably in Duboys-Fresney (2006), which includes excellent selected bibliographies and generally up-to-date numbers on demography, health, the economy, the workplace, education and culture, family, society and the information society.

2. Any immigrant entering France is required to submit a valid medical certificate along with his/her application for an entry visa. Refugees staying in a 'reception centre for asylum-seekers' (CADA) have to undergo a medical examination.

3. The procedures governing 'expulsions' are particularly fluid, especially with the imposition of new annual quota for expulsions, which was 25,000 in 2007. These quotas have been challenged.

4. With respect to an immigrant's entry into France, the number and nature of the documents required – all to be presented in officially notarized (and expensive!) French translations only – is particularly striking. While perhaps generally justifiable, a partial list of such documents may nonetheless serve as an example of the great difficulties that prospective immigrants need to overcome. Official documents are required to prove the person's identity, a particularly sensitive matter ever since the new legislation at first required the use of DNA testing, although in certain cases only and under certain conditions, to verify a person's claim to his or her identity. The French constitutional court later invalidated this requirement.

5. Those employed at least seven months out of 12 in a year but not earning enough to keep them above the poverty level are defined as the 'working poor' (*travailleurs pauvres*).

6. CERC (2004, p. 45) notes that over 32 per cent of poor single-parent heads of households were unemployed and 22 per cent were in part-time employment. Only 13 per cent were in full-time employment.

7. CERC (2004); this note refers to the importance of the nationality factor.

8. See the tables in CERC (2004, p. 47).

9. On 31 August, 2006, the French weekly, *Le Point*, chose the issue of school violence for its cover and its lead articles. The French government introduced its draft law on delinquency and violence for debate in the Parliament on 13 September 2006. See especially the excellent interview with the Pontoise judge, D. Peyrat (see Peyrat, 2006). Peyrat provides careful numbers, for example, the population of minors in France today – 'minors' here refers to young people between the ages of 13 and 25 – is about 8 million. More importantly, he also offers a very careful sociological and partly philosophical reflection

on the nature of violence and delinquency of minors, including remarks on poverty and immigration.

10. The so-called 'syllable method' is a method for teaching children reading by regularly dividing work into syllables to be pronounced and first read as units.

11. The Directorate for the Legal Protection of Youth (PJJ) provides another estimate of minor children involved in judicial cases. The PJJ estimates that 2,700 minors were known to the public prosecutor's office (*parquets*) and another 1,800 to the various PJJ departments, bringing the total to 4,500. Immigrant minors were newly put at risk in the summer of 2008 when the Ministry of the Interior decided to combine and extend existing computer bases of all those in France already with criminal records or known to be susceptible to criminal association or activity. The new comprehensive computer system is known as 'Edvige' (*Exploitation documentaire et valorisation de l'information générale*).

12. In 2001, there were 3,568 minor children under its charge. Their number tripled between 1999 and 2001 (Etiemble, 2004, p. 16).

13. In its Annual Report, the Committee for the Rehabilitation of Displaced Persons (CIMADE) (June 2008) has called attention to the unfair conditions in which prospective immigrants, including children, are received at the prefectures.

14. The actual number of the Roma people in France today is not known. Nor is the exact number of Roma children. Nonetheless, studies based on investigations of the umbrella association, 'Romeurope', estimate that between 220,000 and 250,000 Roma are in France among the approximately 6–8 million Roma in Europe as a whole. In late November 2007, however, new estimates put the number of Roma in the European Union at between 7 and 9 million and on the continent as a whole at between 12 and 15 million persons ('Romaphobie', Editorial, *Le Monde*, 27 November 2007). After the inauguration of the 'Decade for the Inclusion of the Roma in Europe' in 2005, UNICEF noted in 2006 that 'the Roma population constitutes Europe's largest and most vulnerable minority' (UNICEF, 2006, p. 24). It further noted that Roma have very limited education and low skills and that they suffer from discrimination in the labour market. Roma children suffer the most. Forty-one per cent of Roma workers are not qualified, and nearly 39 per cent of the Roma are illiterate (Manea, 2007).

15. The Italian Interior Minister, Mr Roberto Maroni, has proposed to fingerprint the Roma and their children living in camps in Italy as part of a campaign to curb street crime. The proposal has been criticized in Italy and abroad as smacking of racism and discrimination (*International Herald Tribune*, 30 June 2008). In July 2008, the programme was further developed despite official protests from the Italian Conference of Bishops, the European Commission and the European Parliament (*Le Monde*, 6–7 July 2008).

16. From 2002 to mid-2007, 100 or so Roma children, mostly under 12 years, have been repatriated. The main grounds for repatriation, besides difficulties with school access and family violence, were economic problems, according to the head of an association working with minors in the Ile-de-France (*Le Monde*, 21 August 2007). For humanitarian reasons, a number of Romanians with their children (361 in 2005 and 397 in 2006) who were in a precarious situation in France were repatriated. Of these, in 2006 there were 21

minor children. In the first nine months of 2007, 262 Romanian children were repatriated on humanitarian grounds. On repatriation ANAEM offered a repatriation grant of 153 euros per adult and 46 euros per accompanied minor child (ANAEM, 2007, p. 62). The repatriation also included Roma families (see also below) from Romania (68 persons in 2006) and street children. ANAEM returns them to their families in Romania or to the Romanian National Authority for the Protection of the Rights of Child. This was done within the framework of the previous bilateral agreement between France and Romania signed in October 2002.

17. However, the numbers of Romanians granted entry to France between 1998 and 2006 were already very low. The numbers, especially of the Roma, will be even lower in the future.


## 6   Housing Poor Immigrant Children in France

1. For example, today less than 2 per cent of all available housing lacks any bathroom facilities, compared with roughly 39 per cent three decades ago.
2. According to the National Association of Real Estate Agents (FNAIM), in the Paris housing market prices rose by 140 per cent between 1997 and 2007.
3. This situation may have led Christine Boutin, the Minister of Housing in March 2008, to call for substantially reducing the admissibility threshold for poor families' access to public housing (HLM). She also called for changing the regulations governing such housing in such a way as to reserve HLM for the poorest of the poor.
4. The 'insalubrity' of tenement housing in Paris is often a euphemism for outright mortal danger. Just a few days after the Cachan expulsions, for example, and one year after 18 people lost their lives in a fire in a rundown HLM in L'Haÿ-les-Roses, another community of the Val-de-Marne (*Le Monde*, 7 and 13 September 2005 and 6 September 2006), still more people were burned alive in another 'insalubrious' tenement in Paris. Since 2001, the Paris municipality offices have identified more than 1,000 such buildings in Paris itself. One hundred and fifty of these have been transferred to the courts for injunction orders against the landlords requiring immediate repairs on the buildings. Paris has also set up what it calls an *'Observatoire du logement insalubre'*. The socialist mayor of Paris, M.B. Delanoë, set up a fund of 200 million euros to be expended before the end of his mandate in 2007 for razing some buildings, evacuating others, expropriating still others and relocating as many families still in such buildings as possible (see <www.ps-paris.org>).
5. Anthropological, literary and photographic presentations of such lives can be found in Rahnema (2003), Banier (2006) and de Luca (2006).
6. See the website <www.lesenfantdedonquchotte.com>.
7. In fact, the French Assembly passed the new legislation on 21 February with six amendments, which included a new list of priorities for housing, effective from 1 December 2008.
8. The average surface area for immigrant households is $75\,m^2$ compared to $91\,m^2$ for non-immigrants (Abbé Pierre Foundation, 2008).
9. The government uses the same private hotels to house some foreign families who have been denied exile or who are waiting for administrative decisions

about their exile requests and who cannot be placed in the already full government-run 'reception centres for asylum-seekers' (CADA), or in the ominously named 'administration detention centres' (CRA). Moreover, most of the rooms available are decrepit and overcrowded. Cooking and making use of supplementary heating are not allowed.

10. Some French economists and sociologists make a direct link between housing difficulties and the recent emergence of two distinct youth cultures in the Paris riots of autumn 2005 and spring 2006, suburban youth (*'la jeunesse des banlieues'*) and student youth (*'la jeunesse étudiante'*). For background information, see Cohen (2007), and France's *Académie des sciences morales et politiques* collective publication, *La France prépare mal l'avenir de sa jeunesse* (Paris: Seuil, 2007) with summary essays by two of France's former prime ministers, Raymond Barre and Pierre Messmer in *Le Figaro*, 18 January 2007, the important essay of J. Roman on the current difficulties for integrating France's young people into French society, *Eux et nous* (Paris: Hachette, 2006) and the problems of housing specifically for young people at <www.jeudinoir.org> and at <www.aieulsdailleurs.org>. An important correlation also seems to hold between housing difficulties and the very high rate of youth suicide, which is the second cause of mortality among French youth between the ages of 15 and 24 (see Faure, 2007).

# 7  Switzerland vs France: A Comparative Perspective

1. The OECD *Economic Survey of Switzerland* (2006b, pp. 38–41) notes that Switzerland has been suffering from slow growth in production and per capita income. One explanation for this slow growth may be insufficient demand especially in the early 1990s; another may be structural factors such as a weakness of productivity gains compared with other countries.

2. For a detailed account of the Swiss immigration policy, see Kaya (2005); Afonso (2005); and Piguet (2006).

3. Employers shall have to prove that no Swiss national or national of the EU countries can fill those vacancies for which a non-European is to be hired. Non-European workers have been indispensable in the past in occupying many agricultural and service jobs. Most of these jobs are menial and low-paid ones which Swiss nationals would not occupy. A significant demand exists for their services in these occupations. But in future it will not be possible for non-Europeans to seek the above types of employment.

4. An IMES-ODR-AFD report on illegal immigration (2004, p. 30) notes: 'Very few cantons have included in their laws the right to schooling of children who do not have a legal residence status. Their admission to a school of higher education or apprenticeship poses more problems than their attendance in compulsory schools.'

5. With the successive victories of the Swiss People's Party, the argument linking immigration with security and crime in Switzerland seems to have won the day. It is pertinent to note that the Federal Councillor in charge of immigration and national security was no other than Mr Blocher of the Swiss People's Party, a right-wing political party.

6. It is surprising that a ban was imposed on Yugoslav workers even though they were accepted by Switzerland for several years. They are culturally not that different from Swiss citizens. Such attitudes and policies have been deplored by Swiss employers as well as human rights groups (Afonso, 2005, p. 663).

7. The first proposal concerning second-generation immigrant children was defeated by 57 per cent against and 43 per cent in favour. It is interesting to note that most French-speaking cantons voted in favour. The second proposal on the third-generation immigrant children was defeated by 52 per cent of the voters in favour and 48 per cent against. Here again the majority of French-speaking cantons voted in favour. This linguistic divide is quite common in many popular votes, which may reflect greater conservatism on many issues in the German-speaking cantons.

8. The cantons voted as follows: Geneva (68 per cent), Vaud (67 per cent), Neuchâtel (65 per cent), Jura (55 per cent) and Fribourg (51 per cent). By contrast, almost all the German-speaking cantons voted against: Berne (55 per cent), Lucerne (68 per cent), Zurich (56 per cent), Uri (73 per cent), Schwyz (76 per cent) and St Gallen (69 per cent).

9. Argau, Glaris, Grison and Solothorn, all German-speaking cantons, heavily voted against the proposal, whereas all the French-speaking cantons voted in favour. This suggests that the public opinion in German-speaking cantons is against the cantonal policy. The French-speaking cantons voted as follows: Geneva (71 per cent), Vaud (72 per cent), Neuchâtel (71 per cent), Jura (62 per cent) and Fribourg (58 per cent).

10. In the 1980s the Chirac conservative government attempted to revise Article 23 of the Code to revoke automaticity. The proposed legislation, which targeted the Franco-Algerians in particular, had to be withdrawn in the face of stiff opposition and protests from the Republican right and left.

11. In September 2006, Mr Sarkozy announced that of the roughly 35,000 immigrant parents of children already being schooled in France who had applied for 'regularization' (in accordance with the conditions of the June Circular), no more than 6,924 were deemed to qualify for legal residence permits. Nothing was said of their children.

12. According to the regularly increased government grants for the so-called 'social minimums', in the third quarter of 2007 persons satisfying conditions for the first category of SMIC were receiving 1,280 euros per month before tax deductions.

13. In Switzerland, no study or data exist on the housing conditions of immigrants and their children. The OFS study on the housing situation (Gerheuser, 2004) has no separate section or sub-section on immigrants.

14. In the 1970s only 10 per cent of immigrants were members of trade unions compared to 20–5 per cent of French workers. Under-representation of immigrants was particularly marked in the car industry in which a large number of immigrants worked (Schuerkens, 2005, p. 21).

15. The subject was discussed in the canton of Vaud but its Executive Council rejected a proposal to grant foreigners the right to vote at the cantonal level (*Le Matin* online, 15 January 2008).

16. In April 2005, the electors in the canton of Geneva granted foreigners the right to vote in the commune elections if they had lived in the canton for

at least eight years. However, they rejected the right of eligibility to hold an elected office.

17. ECRI (2005, p. 2) notes that 'immigrants and asylum-seekers (in France) still meet with difficulties and are sometimes as a group perceived as "cheaters"'; it encourages the French authorities to improve the situation of minority groups including 'Travellers, Roma and Muslims as well as immigrants, persons of immigrant origin and asylum seekers'. It recommends 'that the French authorities sign and ratify the United Nations Convention on the Protection of the Rights of All Migrant Workers and Members of their Families' (*ibid.*, p. 4).

18. Perrigeaux and Togni (1989, p. 51) note: 'A few years ago the MRAP succeeded in persuading the French National Assembly to vote in favour of a law condemning racist practices. We would like to see this law passed in Switzerland.'

19. President Sarkozy has promised the surviving *harkis* that he will bring their now pitiful army pensions fully into line with other regular French army pensions today. But despite the formal and public promise, the details of the agreement, as some have been all too content to note, remain murky, the financing uncertain and the timing unsettled. Like many other subjects touching on the discrimination against visible minorities in France, the situation of immigrants, whether the pensions of the *harkis* or the access of poor immigrant children to proper education, health care and housing, remains precarious. The demands of legal, social and moral justice may be quite clear in most cases, but dealing with such matters effectively still proves to be very problematic.

20. However, after a three-day visit to Switzerland, an emissary of the Organization of Security and Cooperation in Europe (OSCE) noted in November 2007 that the Muslims were better treated in Switzerland than in France, the Netherlands and the United Kingdom. They also have better training and better economic and social situation, as they are not housed in urban ghettoes (see Gumy, 2007).

21. The passage of a restrictive immigration law concerning foreigners and asylum-seekers in Switzerland (see Chapter 4) is considered a victory for Blocher and his anti-immigrant position in the Swiss Federal Council and the Parliament.

22. From 1968 till 1990, family members of immigrants constituted from 21–9 per cent of the total number of immigrants (see Hollifield, 1994, Table 5.2).

## 8   Some Conclusions

1. It may be worth mentioning that the best chapter in the Report, in terms of empirical richness, deals with Germany, not Switzerland, and is written by a German national! This shows that Switzerland has a long way to go in tackling child poverty and other social problems of the poor and young. The Swiss Federal Commission for Children and Youth (2007) notes that in Switzerland talking about poverty has been a taboo, which needs to be broken. The 2007 Report makes an effort in this direction.

# Bibliography

Abbé Pierre Foundation (2006, 2007, 2008) *Annual Report: L'état du mal-logement en France* (Paris: Fondation Abbé Pierre).

Adleman, L., S. Middleton and K. Ashworth (2003) *Britain's Poorest Children: Severe and Persistent Poverty and Social Exclusion*, Save the Children/Centre for Research in Social Policy (CRSP), Loughborough University, Leicestershire.

Afonso, Alexandre (2004) 'Immigration and Its Impacts in Switzerland', *Mediterranean Quarterly*, vol. 15.

Afonso, Alexandre (2005) 'When the Export of Social Problems is No Longer Possible: Immigration Policies and Unemployment in Switzerland', *Social Policy and Administration*, vol. 39, no. 6, December.

Agence Nationale de l'Accueil des Étrangers et des Migrations (ANAEM) (2007) *Rapport d'activité années 2005–2006*, Paris, April.

Alba, Richard and Roxane Silberman (2002) 'Decolonization Immigrations and the Social Origins of the Second Generation: The Case of North Africans in France', *International Migration Review*, vol. XXXVI, no. 4, Winter.

Amin, Kaushak and Carey Oppenheim (1992) *Poverty in Black and White: Deprivation and Ethnic Minorities* (London: Runnymede Trust).

Amossé, Thomas, Anne Doussin, Jean-Marie Firdion, Maryse Marpsat and Thierry Rochereau (2001) 'Vie et santé des jeunes sans domicile ou en situation précaire', *Bulletin d'information en économie de la santé*, no. 40, CREDES (Centre de recherche, d'étude, et de documentation en économie de la santé), September.

Anand, Sudhir, Fabienne Peter and Amartya Sen (eds) (2004) *Public Health, Ethics and Equity* (Oxford: Oxford University Press).

Andriani, Jean-Louis (2008a), 'De grandes inégalités dans les salaires et les budgets des ménages', *Le Monde*, 1 April.

Andriani, Jean-Louis (2008b), 'Trente ans de blues français', *Le Monde*, 1 April.

Arbour, Louise (2007) 'Droits de l'homme, un défi', *Le Monde*, 11 December.

Arend, M. (2003) 'La planification et la politique du marché du logement peuvent-elles contribuer à une meilleure intégration des migrants?', in H.R. Wicker, R. Fibbi and W. Haug (eds), *Les migrations et la suisse* (Zurich: Seismo).

Aristotle (2000) *Nichomachean Ethics*, translated by Roger Crisp (Cambridge: Cambridge University Press).

Arrow, Kenneth (1951) *Social Choice and Individual Values* (New York: Wiley).

Atkinson, A.B. (1983) *Parents and Children: Incomes in Two Generations* (London: Heinemann Educational).

Atkinson, A.B. (1990) 'Comparing Poverty Rates Internationally', WSP/53 (London: Suntory and Toyota International Centres for Economics and Related Disciplines).

Atkinson, A.B. (1998) *Poverty in Europe* (Oxford: Basil Blackwell).

Aubry, Martine (ed.) (2006) *Immigration: comprendre, construire* (Paris: l'Aube).

Audi, Robert (2004) *The Good in the Right* (Princeton: Princeton University Press).

Audi, Robert (ed.) (2005) *The Cambridge Dictionary of Philosophy*, 2nd edn (Cambridge: Cambridge University Press).

Audi, Robert (2006) 'Ethical Generality and Moral Judgment', in James Dreier (ed.), *Contemporary Debates in Moral Theory* (Oxford: Blackwell).

Auzet, Laurent, Magali Février and Aude Lapinte (2007) 'Niveaux de vie et pauvreté en France: les départements du Nord et du Sud sont les plus touchés par la pauvreté et les inégalités', *INSEE no. 1162*, October.

Banier, F.-M. (2006) *Perdre la tête* (Paris: Gallimard).

Barou, Jacques (2006) *L'Europe, terre d'immigration. Flux migratoires et intégration*, rev. edn (Saint-Martin-d'Héres: PUG).

Barou, Jacques (2007) 'Immigration: Grandes tendances', in Élisabeth Lau (ed.) *État de la France Édition 2007–2008* (Paris: La Découverte).

Basu, K., K.P. Pattanaik and K. Suzumura (eds) (1995) *Choice, Welfare and Development: A Festschrift in Honour of Amartya K. Sen* (Oxford: Clarendon Press).

Bauer, A. (2006) 'Délinquence: chiffrage non-partisan', *Le Monde*, November–December.

Bauer, Philip and Regina T. Riphahn (forthcoming) 'Heterogeneity in the Intergenerational Transmission of Educational Attainment: Evidence from Switzerland on Natives and Second-generation Immigrants', *Journal of Population Economics.*

Becker, Charlotte B. and Lawrence C. Becker (eds) (1992) *Encyclopedia of Ethics* (Chicago: St James Press).

Beitz, Charles (2001) 'Does Global Inequality Matter?', in Thomas Pogge (ed.), *Global Justice* (Oxford: Basil Blackwell).

Bellanger, Martine-Marie and Philippe Mossé (2007) 'Santé: Grandes tendances', in Élisabeth Lau (ed.) (2007) *État de la France* (Paris: La Découverte).

Ben-Arieh, Asher (2006) 'Measuring and Monitoring the Well-being of Young Children around the World', *Background paper prepared for the UNESCO Education for All Global Monitoring Report 2007-Strong Foundations Early Childhood Care and Education* (Paris: UNESCO) (2007/ED/EFA/MRT/PI/5).

Bennhold, K. (2006) 'Expulsion of Illegals Stepped up in France', *International Herald Tribune*, 2–3 September.

Bernard, Philippe (2002) *Immigration: le défi mondial* (Paris: Éditions Gallimard).

Berthoud, Richard (1998) 'The Incomes of Ethnic Minorities', *Institute for Social and Economic Research (ISER) Report 98-1*, University of Essex, Colchester, November.

Berthoud, Richard (2000) 'Ethnic Employment Penalties in Britain', *Journal of Ethnic and Migration Studies*, vol. 26, no. 3.

Bhalla, A.S. and Frédéric Lapeyre (2004) *Poverty and Exclusion in a Global World* (London: Palgrave Macmillan).

Bhalla, A.S. and Shufang Qiu (2006) *Poverty and Inequality among Chinese Minorities* (London: Routledge).

Bianchi, Suzanne (1990) 'America's Children: Mixed Prospects', *Population Bulletin*, no. 45.

Bigot, Régis (2006) *La parcours des mineurs isolés Roumains suivi par Hors La Rue et pris en charge par l'Aide Sociale à l'enfance de Paris* (Paris: Hors La Rue), 3 December.

Bihr, Alain and R. Pfefferkorn (2008) *Le système des inégalités* (Paris: La Découverte).

Birdsall, Nancy (2001) 'Why Inequality Matters: Some Economic Issues', *Ethics and International Affairs,* vol. 15.

Bischoff, A.N. (1995) *Migration and Health in Switzerland* (Geneva: HUG, Unité Médicine des voyages).

Bissuel, B. (2006a) 'Portrait-robot du SDF parisien', *Le Monde*, 20 December.

Bissuel, B. (2006b) 'Exclusion – l'hébergement d'urgence reste insuffisant', *Le Monde*, 26 December.

Bissuel, B. (2007) 'Les riverains exaspérés par les SDF du Canal-St Martin', *Le Monde*, 20 February.

Blackburn, Simon (2005a) *Oxford Dictionary of Philosophy*, 2nd edn (Oxford: Oxford University Press).

Blackburn, Simon (2005b) *'Eudaimonia'*, in S. Blackburn, *Oxford Dictionary of Philosophy*, 2nd edn (Oxford: Oxford University Press).

Blanc, Patrice (2004) 'Comment protéger les enfants migrants?', *Hommes et Migrations*, no. 1251, September–October.

Blanden, Joe and Steve Gibbons (2006) *The Persistence of Poverty across Generations: A View from Two British Cohorts* (Bristol: Policy Press).

Blauquaux, Jean, Anne Burstin and Dominique Giorgi (2005) *Mission d'analyse et de proposition sur les conditions d'accueil des mineurs étrangers isolés en France*, Rapport de l' Inspection Générale des Affaires Sociales (Paris: IGAS), January.

Blume, Kraen, Björn Gustafsson, Peder J. Pedersen and Mette Verner (2003) 'A Tale of Two Countries: Poverty among Immigrants in Denmark and Sweden since 1984', *World Institute for Development Economics Research (WIDER) Discussion Paper no. 2003/36* (Helsinki: United Nations University).

Boarini, R., A. Johansson and M.M. d'Ercole (2006) 'Alternative Measures of Well-Being', *OECD Social, Employment and Migration Working Papers*, no. 37 (Paris: OECD).

Boeri, T., G. Hanson and B. McCormick (eds) (2002) *Immigration Policy and the Welfare System* (Oxford: Oxford University Press).

Bollini, P. and H. Siem (1995) 'No Real Progress Towards Equity: Health of Migrants and Ethnic Minorities on the even of 2000', *Social Science and Medicine*, vol. 41, no. 6.

Bonnie, R.J., C.E. Fulco and C.T. Liverman (1999) *Reducing the Burden of Injury* (Washington DC: National Academy Press).

Borrel, C. (2005) 'Près de cinq millions d'immigrés à la mi-2004', *INSEE première*, no. 1098, August.

Boucher-Saulnier, F. (2006) *Dictionnaire pratique du droit humanitaire*, 3rd edn (Paris: La Découverte).

Bradbury, B., S.P. Jenkins and J. Micklewright (eds) (2001a) *The Dynamics of Child Poverty in Industrialised Countries* (Cambridge: Cambridge University Press).

Bradbury, B., S.P. Jenkins and J. Micklewright (2001b) 'Conceptual and Measurement Issues', in B. Bradbury, S.P. Jenkins and J. Micklewright (eds) *The Dynamics of Child Poverty in Industrialised Countries* (Cambridge: Cambridge University Press).

Bradbury, Bruce and Markus Jäntti (2001) 'Child Poverty across Twenty-five Countries', in B. Bradbury, S.P. Jenkins and J. Micklewright (eds) *The Dynamics of Child Poverty in Industrialised Countries* (Cambridge: Cambridge University Press).

Bradshaw, J. (1990) 'Child Poverty and Deprivation in the UK', *Innocenti Occasional Papers, Economic Policy Series* (Florence: UNICEF Innocenti Research Centre).

Bradshaw, J. (2001) *Poverty: The Outcomes for Children* (London: Family Policy Studies Centre).

Bradshaw, J. and N. Finch (2002) 'A Comparison of Child Benefit Packages in 22 Countries', *Research report no. 174, Department for Work and Pensions.*

Brandt, Richard (1979) *A Theory of the Good and the Right* (Oxford: Oxford University Press).

Brewer, M., T. Clark and A. Goodman (2002) *The Government's Child Poverty Target: How much Progress has been Made?*, Institute for Fiscal Studies, London, April.

Brink, David (1993) 'The Separateness of Persons, Distributive Norms, and Moral Theory', in R.G. Frey and Christopher W. Morris (eds), *Value, Welfare, and Morality* (Cambridge: Cambridge University Press).

Brock, Dan W. (1999) 'Utilitarianism', in *The Cambridge Dictionary of Philosophy*, 2nd edn (Cambridge: Cambridge University Press).

Brothers, Caroline (2008) 'EU Votes to Unify Rules on Detention of Migrants', *International Herald Tribune*, 19 June.

Brousse, Cécile (2005) 'Définir et compter les sans-abri en Europe: enjeux et controverses', *Genèses*, no. 58.

Brousse, Cécile , B. Euiot de la Rochère, E. Massé ( 2006) 'L'enquête sans-domicile 2001', INSEE, coll. INSEE-Méthodes, no. 116.

Brücker, H., J.R. Frick and G.G. Wagner (2006) 'Economic Consequences of Immigration in Europe', in C. Parsons and T. Smeeding (eds), *Immigration and the Transformation of Europe* (Cambridge: Cambridge University Press).

Bruniaux, C. and B. Galtier (2003) *L'étude du devenir des enfants des familles défavorisées : l'apport des expériences américaines et britanniques*, Les Papiers du Cerc, no. 1 (Paris: CERC).

Büchel, F. and J.R. Frick (2004) 'Immigrants in the UK and in West Germany – Relative Income Positions, Income Portfolio, and Redistribution Effects', *Journal of Population Economics*, vol. 17, no. 3.

*Cahiers français* (2006) 'Le modèle social français', *Documentation française*, no. 314.

Caille, J.–P. (2005a) 'Les projets d'avenir des enfants d'immigrés', in C. Tavan (ed.), *Les immigrés en France* (Paris: INSEE).

Caille, J.–P. (2005b) 'Le vécu des phases d'orientation en fin de troisième et de seconde', *Education & formations*, vol. 72.

Caisse nationale d'allocations familiales (CNAF) (1999) *Enfants pauvres, pauvres enfants*, Informations sociales, no. 9.

Callan, T. and B. Nolan (1991) 'Concepts of Poverty and the Poverty Line: A Critical Survey of Approaches to Measuring Poverty', *Journal of Economic Surveys*, vol. 5.

Cantó, Olga and Magda Marcader-Prats (2001) 'Young People Leaving Home: The Impact on Poverty in Spain', in B. Bradbury, S.P. Jenkins and J. Micklewright (eds), *The Dynamics of Child Poverty in Industrialised Countries* (Cambridge: Cambridge University Press).

Carballo, Manuel and Aditi Nerukar (2001) 'Migration, Refugees and Health Risks', *Emerging Infectious Diseases*, vol. 7, no. 3, Supplement, June.

Carreras, Laetitia et Chritiane Perregaux (2002) *Histoire de vie, histoire de papiers: du droit á l'éducation au droit à la formation pour les jeunes sans papiers* (Lausanne: édition d'en bas).

Case, A., D. Lubotsky and C. Paxson (2002) 'Economic Status and Health in Childhood: The Origins of the Gradient', *American Economic Review*, vol. 92, no. 5.

Castel, Roger (2007) *La discrimination négative: Citoyens ou indigènes* (Paris: Seuil).

Castles, Stephen and Mark J. Miller (1993) *The Age of Migration* (London: Macmillan).

Cattafi-Maurer, F., G. Abriel, P.R. Dasen, C. Lack and C. Perregaux (1998) *Vivre en précarité: L'accès à une formation professionelle des jeunes migrants en situation juridique précaire*, Faculty of Psychology and Educational Sciences, University of Geneva and Centre of Contacts between Swiss and Immigrants.

Cawson, P., C. Wattam, M. Brooker and G. Kelly (2000) *Child Maltreatment in the UK: A Study of the Prevalence of Child Abuse*, National Society for the Prevention of Cruelty to Children (London: NSPCC).

Central Statistical Office (CSO), Republic of Ireland (2007) *EU Survey on Income and Living Conditions (EU-SILC): Intergenerational Transmission of Poverty 2005*, Dublin, August.

Chatterjee, D.K. (ed.) (2004) *The Ethics of Assistance: Morality and Distant Need* (Cambridge: Cambridge University Press).

Chauvel, Louis (2007) 'Stratification sociale: grandes tendances', in Élisabeth Lau (ed.), *État de la France Édition 2007–2008* (Paris: La Découverte).

Chazal, Joëlle and Patrick Pommier (2007) 'Le chômage depuis un quart de siècle', in Élisabeth Lau (ed.), *État de la France Édition 2007–2008* (Paris: La Découverte).

Chimienti, Milena and Sandro Cattacin, in collaboration with Denise Efionayi, Martin Niederberger and Stefano Losa (2001) *Migration et santé: priorités d'une stratégie d'intervention* (Neuchâtel: Swiss Forum for Migration Studies).

Cingolani, Patrick (2005) *La précarité* (Paris: Presses universitaires de France).

Citrin, Jack and John Sides (2006) 'European Immigrants in the People's Court', C. Parsons and T. Smeeding (eds), *Immigration and the Transformation of Europe* (Cambridge: Cambridge University Press).

Clanché, François (2000) *La Rue et le Foyer* (Paris: Ined/Presses universitaires de France).

Clayton, Matthew and Andrew Williams (eds) (2000) *The Ideal of Equality* (London: Macmillan).

Clerc, Denis (2007) 'Reduire le nombre de pauvres en France: un plan en trois mesures', in *L'Économie politique*, no. 26, April, 2005; reprinted, with additions, in *Problèmes économiques*, no. 2920, March.

*Code [2007] de l'entrée et du séjour des étrangers et du droit d'Asile* (Paris: Les Éditions des journaux officiels), 22 June.

Cohen, D. (ed.) (2007) *Une jeunesse difficile: Portrait économique et social de la jeunesse française* (Paris: Editions Rue d'Ulm).

Collinson, Sarah (1993) *Beyond the Borders: Western European Migration Policy towards the 21st Century* (London: Royal Institute of International Affairs).

Comim, Flavio, M. Quizilbksh and S. Akre (eds) (2007) *The Capability Approach: Concepts, Measures and Applications* (Cambridge: Cambridge University Press).

Conseil de l'Emploi, des Revenus et de la Cohésion Sociale (CERC) (2002) *Estimer l'évolution récente de la pauvreté*, Les dossier du CERC, September.

CERC (2004) *Child Poverty in France (Les enfants pauvres en France)*, Document no. 4 (Paris: CERC).

CERC (2005) *Estimer la pauvreté des enfants*, Document no. 2 (Paris: CERC).

Conseil de l'Europe (2001) *Le conseil de l'Europe et la protection des droits de l'homme* (Strasbourg: Direction générale des droits de l'homme), November.

Coppel, Jonathan, Jean-Christophe Dumont and Ignazio Visco (2001) 'Trends in Immigration and Economic Consequences', OECD *Economic Department Working Papers no. 284* (Paris: OECD).

Corak, M., C. Lietz and H. Sutherland (2005) 'The Impact of Tax and Transfer Systems on Children in the European Union', UNICEF *Innocenti Working Paper no. 2005–4*.

Corcuff, Philippe (2007) *Les nouvelles sociologies*, 2nd edn (Paris: Armand Colin).

Cornelius, W.A., T. Tsuda, P.L. Martin and J.F. Hollifield (eds) (1994, 2004) *Controlling Immigration: A Global Perspective* (Stanford: Stanford University Press).

Cornia, G.A. and S. Danziger (1997) *Child Poverty and Deprivation in the Industrialized Countries* (Oxford: Clarendon Press).

Council of Europe (1961) *The European Social Charter* (Strasbourg: Council of Europe).

Couturier, Marie (2008) 'Les transferts sociaux atténuent les risques d'exclusion', *La Croix*, 27 February.

Crédit Suisse, *Bulletin* (2007) no. 4, October–November.

Crisp, Roger (ed.) (2000) *Well-Being and Morality: Essays in Honour of James Griffin* (Oxford: Clarendon Press).

Crul, Maurice (2007) *Pathways to Success for the Children of Immigrants*, Migration Policy Institute (Washington, DC)/BertelsmannStiftung Transatlantic Task Force on Immigration and Integration, September.

Crul, Maurice and Hans Vermeulen (2003) 'The Second Generation in Europe', *International Migration Review*, vol. 37, no. 4, Winter.

Crul, Maurice and Hans Vermeulen (2006) 'Immigration, Education and the Turkish Second Generation in Five European Nations: A Comparative Study', in C. Parsons and T. Smeeding (eds), *Immigration and the Transformation of Europe* (Cambridge: Cambridge University Press).

Cullity, Garrett (2004) *The Moral Demands of Affluence* (Oxford: Oxford University Press).

Daguet, Fabienne and Suzanne Thave (1996) 'La population immigrée: Le résultat d'une longue histoire', *INSEE no. 458*, June.

Damon, Julien (2002) *La question SDF: Critique d'une action publique* (Paris: Presses Universitaires de France).

Dancy, Jonathan (ed.) (2000) *Normativity* (Oxford: Blackwell).

Daniels, Norman (2003) 'Democratic Equality: Rawls's Complex Egalitarianism', in Samuel Freeman (ed.), *The Cambridge Companion to Rawls* (Cambridge: Cambridge University Press).

Dasgupta, Partha (1993) *An Inquiry Into Well-being and Destitution* (Oxford: Clarendon Press).

Dasgupta, Partha (2001) *Human Well-being and the Natural Environment* (Oxford: Oxford University Press).

Dasgupta, Partha (2007) *Economics: A Very Short Introduction* (Oxford: Oxford University Press).

Day, Maguy (2007) 'Immigration-natalité: le ticket prioritaire', *Le Monde: Dossiers et documents*, no. 370, December.

de Coulon, Augustin (1998) 'Wage Differentials between Ethnic Groups: Empirical Evidence from Switzerland', *Department of Economics and Politics (DEP) Working Papers* (Geneva: Faculté des Sciences Économiques et Sociales).

de Coulon, Augustin (1999) 'Disparité regional du chômage: population étrangère', *Revue Suisse d'économie, politique et de statistique*, vol. 135, no. 2.

de Coulon, Augustin, Jean-Marc Falter, Yves Flückiger and José Ramirez (2003) 'Analyses des différences de salaries entre la population Suisse et étrangère', in Hans-Rudolf Wicker, Rosita Fibbi and Werner Haug (eds), *Migrations et relations interculturelles* (Zurich: Seismo).

Degrate, A., A. Testa-Mader and N. Clerici (1999) 'Mortality in the Swiss and Foreign Immigrants in the Canton of Ticino', *Epidemia e Prevenzione*, vol. 23, no. 2.

Dekeuwer-Défossez, F. (2006) *Les droits de l'enfant*, 7th edn (Paris: Presses Universitaires de France).

de Luca, E. (2006) *Le chanteur muet de rue* (Paris: Gallimard).

de Saint Pol, Thibault, (2007) 'La santé des plus pauvres', *INSEE no. 1161*, October.

Devereux, Stephen (2001) 'Sen's Entitlement Approach: Critiques and Counter-critiques', *Oxford Development Studies*, vol. 29, no. 3.

Devereux, Stephen (2003) 'Conceptualising Destitution', *IDS Working Paper 216*, December.

Diener, E., E. M. Suh, R. E. Lucas and H. E. Smith (1999) 'Subjective Well-Being: Three Decades of Progress', *Psychological Bulletin*, no. 125.

Diminescu, Dana (2003) *Visibles mais peu nombreux (Les circulations migratoires roumaines)* (Paris: Editions de la Maison des Sciences de l'Homme).

Diminescu, Dana (2004) 'La mobilité des jeunes roumains à l'heure de l'élargissement', *Hommes et Migrations*, no. 1251, September–October.

Docquier, F. and H. Rapaport (2007) 'L'immigration qualifiée, remède miracle aux problèmes économiques européens?', *Problèmes Économiques*, no. 2937, 19 August.

Dorval, Camille (2008) '7 millions de pauvres en France', *Alternatives Économiques*, June.

Dreier, James (ed.) (2006) *Contemporary Debates in Moral Theory* (Oxford: Blackwell).

Drilling, Matthias (2004) *Young Urban Poor: Abstiegsprozesse in den Zentren der Sozialstaaten* (Wiesbaden: VS Verlag).

Drilling, Matthias (2005) 'Young urban poor: regard sur une biographie', paper presented at a Conference on Young, Adult and Poor, held in Yverdon-les-Bains, Switzerland, 24 May.

Drilling, Matthias (2007a) 'Pauvre un jour, pauvre toujours?', in Commission Fédérale pour l'Enfance et la Jeunesse (CFEJ), *Jeune et pauvre: un tabou à briser*, August.

Drilling, Matthias (2007b) 'Young Urban Poor: Capability Deprivation, Capability Enlargement, Welfare and Social Work', paper presented at the exploratory workshop Education and the Capability Approach – Towards a European perspective for Welfare Service Research, European Science Foundation, Münster, Germany, 3–5 May.

Dubet, F (2006) 'Les inégalités et les principes de justice' in Martine Aubry (ed.) *Immigration: comprendre, construire* (Paris: l'Aube).

Duboys-Fresney, L. (2006) *Atlas des Français aujourd'hui: Dynamiques, modes de vie et valeurs* (Paris: Autrement).

Dummett, Michael (2001) *On Immigration and Refugees* (London: Routledge).

Duncan, Greg (1991) 'The Economic Environment of Childhood', in A. Huston (ed.), *Children in Poverty: Child Development and Public Policy* (New York: Cambridge University Press).

Duncan, Greg and Jeanne Brooks-Gunn (2000) 'Family Poverty, Welfare Reform and Child Development', *Child Development*, vol. 71, no. 1.

Dupree, Allan and Wendell Primus (2001) *Declining Share of Children Lived with Single Mothers in the Late 1990s*, Centre on Budget and Policy Priorities Research Report.

Dworkin, Ronald (1985) *A Matter of Principle* (Cambridge, MA: Harvard University Press).

Dworkin, Gerald (2006) 'Theory, Practice, and Moral Reasoning', in D. Copp (ed.), *The Oxford Companion of Ethical Theory* (Oxford: Oxford University Press).

Edgar, Bill, M. Harrison, P. Watson and V. Busch-Geertsema (2007) *Measurement of Homelessness at European Level, European Communities*, available at <http://ec.europa. eu/employment_spocial/social_inclusion/docs/2007/study_ jhomelessmess_en.pdf>

Eggebeen, David J. and Daniel T. Lichter (1991) 'Race, Family Structure, and Changing Poverty among American Children', *American Sociological Review*, vol. 56.

Elster, Jon and John Roemer (eds) (1991) *Interpersonal Comparisons of Well-Being* (Cambridge: Cambridge University Press).

'Enfants pauvres, pauvres enfants' (2003) *Journal d'Association Suisse pour la protection de l'enfant*, no. 3, September.

Erba, Salvator (2007) *Une France pluriculturelle – Le débat sur l'intégration et les discriminations* (Paris: Librio).

Ermisch, J., M. Francesconi and D.J. Pevalin (2001) 'Outcomes for Children of Poverty', *Research Report no. 158, Department of Work and Pensions*, Corporate Document Services, Leeds.

Etiemble, Angélina (2002) 'Les mineurs isolés étrangers en France', *Migrations Etudes*, no. 109, September–October.

Etiemble, Angélina (2004) 'Quelle protection pour les mineurs isolés en France?', *Hommes et Migrations*, no. 1251, September–October.

Eurobarometer (2006) 'Les français plus tolérants vis-à-vis des immigrés que la moyenne des européens', *Centre d'analyse stratégique, Le Monde: Dossiers et Documents*, no. 370, December.

European Commission (1989) 'The Fight Against Poverty', *Social Europe Supplement 2* (Luxembourg: Office for Official Publications of the EC).

European Commission (2004a) *Joint Report on Social Inclusion 2004* (Luxembourg: Office for Official Publications of the European Communities).

European Commission, Directorate-General for Employment and Social Affairs (2004b) *The Situation of Roma in an Enlarged European Union* (Brussels: EC).

European Commission (2006) 'Technical Annex to the Joint Report on Social Protection and Social Inclusion', *Commission Staff Working Document* no. SEC (20060 523 (Brussels: EC).

European Commission, Directorate-General for Employment, Social Affairs and Equal Opportunities (2008) *Child Poverty and Well-Being in the EU* (Brussels: EC).

European Commission against Racism and Intolerance (ECRI) (2000a) *Second Report on Switzerland* (Strasbourg: ECRI).

European Commission against Racism and Intolerance (ECRI) (2000b) *Second Report on France* (Strasbourg: ECRI).

European Commission against Racism and Intolerance (ECRI) (2004) *Third Report on Switzerland* (Strasbourg: ECRI).

European Commission against Racism and Intolerance (ECRI) (2005) *Third Report on France* (Strasbourg: ECRI).

EUROSTAT (1997, 2005) *Eurostat Yearbook 1997 and 2005* (Luxembourg: Office for Official Publications of the European Communities).

EUROSTAT (2006) *Population Statistics* (Luxembourg: Eurostat).

Faas, Jérôme (2007) 'Dès la fin du mois, la mendicité devrait être illégal', *Tribune de Genève*, 2 November.

Falter, Jean-Marc (2005) *Child Poverty in Switzerland* (Geneva: University of Geneva) (mimeo).

Faure, C. (2007) *Aprés le suicide d'un proche* (Paris: Albin Michel).

Fibbi, Rosita, Bulent Kaya and Etienne Piguet (2003) 'Le passeport ou le diplôme? Étude des discriminations à l'embauche des jeunes issus de la migration', *Research Report* no. 31, *Swiss Forum for Migration and Population (SFM) Studies* (Neuchâtel).

Fibbi, Rosita and Mathias Lerch (2006) 'Familles immigrantes: modes de accultur-ation et cohésion familiale', in *L'impact de la migration sur les enfants, les jeunes et les relations entre générations* (Berne: Fonds National Suisse).

Fibbi, Rosita, Mathias Lerch and Philippe Wanner (2007) 'Naturalisation and Socio-Economic Characteristics of Youth of Immigrant Descent in Switzerland', *Journal of Ethnic and Migration Studies*, vol. 33, no. 7, September.

Fieldhouse, A.E., V.S. Kalra and Saima Alam (2002) 'A New Deal for Young People from Minority Ethnic Communities in the UK', *Journal of Ethnic and Migration Studies*, vol. 28, no. 3, July.

Fine, B. (1997) 'Entitlement Failure?', *Development and Change*, vol. 28.

Fine, B. (2001) *Social Capital vs Social Theory* (London: Routledge).

Flaherty, John, John Viet-Wilson and Paul Dornan (2004) *Poverty: The Facts*, 5th edn (London: Child Poverty Action Group, CPAG).

Fleurbaey, Mac, M. Sales and J. Weymark (eds) (2008) *Justice, Political Liberal-ism, and Utilitarianism: Themes from Harsanyi and Rawls* (Cambridge: Cambridge University Press).

Fluckiger, Y. (2000) *Intégration de la population étrangère en Suisse: Aspects économiques*, Geneva, Final Repport, PNR39/FNRS.

Fontanel, Marie, Nicolas Grivel and Valérie Saintoyant (2007) *Le modèle social français* (Paris: Odile Jacob).

Forssén, K. (2000) 'Child Poverty in the Nordic Countries', *Working Paper Series B, no. 22/2000*, University of Turku, Department of Social Policy.

Förster, Michael F., assisted by Michele Pellizari (2000) 'Trends and Driving Fac-tors in Income Distribution and Poverty in the OECD Area', *Labour Market and Social Policy – Occasional Papers* no. 42 (Paris: OECD).

Forster, Simone (1993) *Les enfants de l'immigration* (Immigrant Children at School) (Neuchâtel: Institut Romand de Recherches et de Documentation).

Freeman, Samuel (ed.) (2003) *The Cambridge Companion to Rawls* (Cambridge: Cambridge University Press).

Frey, R.G. and Christopher W. Morris (eds) (1993) *Value, Welfare, and Morality* (Cambridge: Cambridge University Press).

Freyssenet, Michel (2007) 'Travail: Grandes tendances', in Élisabeth Lau (ed.), *État de la France Édition 2007–2008* (Paris: La Découverte).

Fricker, Miranda (2007) *Epistemic Injustice: Power and the Ethics of Knowing* (Oxford: Oxford University Press).

Gabel, Shirley Gatenio and Sheila B. Kamerman (2006) 'Investing in Children: Public Commitment in Twenty-one Industrialized Countries', *Social Service Review*, June.

Gadrey, Jean and Jany-Catrice Florence (2005) *Les nouveaux indicateurs de richesse* (Paris: La Découverte).

Galasi, Peter and Gyula Nagy (2001) 'Are Children Being Left behind in the Transition in Hungary?', in B. Bradbury, S.P. Jenkins and J. Micklewright (eds), *The Dynamics of Child Poverty in Industrialised Countries* (Cambridge: Cambridge University Press).

Galland, Olivier (2002) *Les jeunes*, 6th edn (Paris: La Découverte).

Garson, Jean-Pierre (2007) *Rapport sur l'immigration 2007* (Paris: OECD).

Gaubert, Patrick (2008) 'Politique d'immigration: osons la rupture', *Le Monde*, 13 February.

Gelles, R. (1989) 'Child Abuse and Violence in Single-Parent Families: Parent Absence and Economic Deprivation', *American Journal of Orthopsychiatry*, vol. 59.

Gerheuser, Frohmut W. (2004) *Logement et conditions d'habitation: Évolution de 1990 à 2000* (Neuchâtel: OFS), October.

Giugni, Marco and Florence Passy (2003) 'Modèles de citoyenneté et moblisation des immigrés en Suisse et en France : Une approche des opportunité politiques', in Hans-Rudolf Wicker, Rosita Fibbi and Werner Haug (eds), *Les migrations et la Suisse* (Zurich: Seismo).

Giugni, Marco and Florence Passy (2004) 'Migrant Mobilization between Political Institutions and Citizenship Regimes: A Comparison of France and Switzerland', *European Journal of Political Research*, vol. 43.

Giugni, Marco and Florence Passy (2006a) *La Citoyenneté en Débat: Mobilisations politiques en France et en Suisse* (Paris: L'Harmattan).

Giugni, Marco and Florence Passy (eds) (2006b) *Dialogues on Migration Policy* (Lanham: Lexington Books).

Golder, Stephen M. and Thomas Straubhaar (1999a) 'Discrimination in the Swiss Labour Market: An Empirical Analysis', *Centre for Economic Policy Research (CEPR) Discussion Paper no. 2100* (London: CEPR).

Golder, Stephen M. and Thomas Straubhaar (1999b) *Explaining Immigrant–Native Earnings Differentials: Evidence from the Swiss Household Survey* (Hamburg: Europe-Kolleg, Institut für Integrationsforschung).

Gonzalez, Elisabeth, Marienne Némethy and Josefa Velasco (1988) *Des enfants illégaux, des enfants tolérés : les enfants sans status légal à Genève* (Geneva: Institut d'études sociales).

Goodin, R.E., P. Pettit and T. Pogge (eds) (2007) *A Companion to Contemporary Political Philosophy*, 2nd edn, 2 vols (Oxford: Blackwell).

Gordon, D., L. Adelman, K. Ashworth, J. Bradshaw, R. Levitas, S. Middleton, C. Pantazis, D. Patsios, S. Payne, P. Townsend, J. Williams (2000) *Poverty and Social Exclusion in Britain* (York: Joseph Rowntree Foundation).

Gore, Charles (1993) 'Entitlement Relations and "Unruly" Social Practices: A Comment on the Work of Amartya Sen', *Journal of Development Studies*, vol. 29, no. 3, April.

Gottschalk, Peter and Sheldon Danziger (2001) 'Income Mobility and Exits from Poverty of American Children', in B. Bradbury, S.P. Jenkins and J. Micklewright (eds), *The Dynamics of Child Poverty in Industrialised Countries* (Cambridge: Cambridge University Press).

Grand Council on Integration (France) (*Haut Conseil à l'Integration*) (2007) *Rapport Statistique 2005 de l'Observatoire Statistique de l'Immigration et de l'Intégration*, Paris, January.

Gregg, P., S. Harkness and S. Machin (1999a) *Child Development and Family Income* (York: Joseph Rowntree Foundation).

Gregg, P., S. Harkness and S. Machin (1999b) 'Poor Kids: Trends in Child Poverty in Britain 1968–96', *Fiscal Studies*, no. 20, 2, June.

Griffin, James (1986) *Well-Being: Its Meaning, Measurement and Moral Importance* (Oxford: Oxford University Press).

Gross, Dominique M. (2006) 'Immigration to Switzerland: The Case of the Former Republic of Yugoslavia', *World Bank Policy Research Paper* WPS 3880 (Washington, DC: World Bank), April.

Guélaud, Claire (2007), 'Le pouvoir d'achat progressera moins en 2008 qu'en 2007', *Le Monde*, 21 December.

Guio, A.-C. and J.M. Museux (2006) 'The Situation of Children in the EU: Comparisons between Income Poverty and Material Deprivation Approaches: What can be Learned from the New EU-SILC 2004 Data?', *paper presented at the International Association for Research on Income and Wealth 29th General Conference*, Joenssu, 20–6 August.

Gumy, Serge (2007) 'Les musulmans de Suisse bien traités, malgré des bémols', *Tribune de Genève*, 15 November.

HALDE (High Commission for Fight Against Discrimination and for Equality) (2008) 'Principales recommendations', *Rapport annuel 2007* (Paris: La Documentation française).

Hammar, Thomas (1985) *European Immigration Policy: A Comparative Study* (New York: Cambridge University Press).

Harris-White, B. (2002) 'A Note on Destitution', *Queen Elizabeth House Working Paper 86*, Oxford.

Harsanyi, John C. (1977) 'Morality and the Theory of Rational Behaviour', *Social Research*, vol. 44.

Haveman, R. and B. Wolfe (1995) 'The Determinants of Children's Attainments: A Review of Methods and Findings', *Journal of Economic Literature*, vol. 33, no. 4, December.

Héran, François (2007) *Le temps des immigrés: Essai sur le destin de la population française* (Paris: Éditions du Seuil et La République des Idées).

Hernandez, Donald J. (1993) *America's Children: Resources from Family, Government, and the Economy* (New York: Russell Sage Foundation).

Herpin, N. and L. Olier (1996) 'Pauvreté des familles, pauvreté des enfants', *INSEE première no. 499* (Paris: INSEE), December.

Herschowitz, S. (ed.) (2007) *Exploring Law's Empire: The Jurisprudence of Ronald Dworkin* (Oxford: Oxford University Press).

Herzog, Stéphane (2007a) 'Un vent d'exclusion pous les Roms vers Genève', *Tribune de Genève*, 30 October.

Herzog, Stéphane (2007b) 'Les Roms à la recherche de leurs sous confisqués', *Tribune de Genève*, 1 November.

Herzog, Stéphane (2007c) 'Le plan de lutte contre la mendicité fait fuir les Romas', *Tribune de Genève*, 16 November.

Hills, M.S. and S.P. Jenkins (2001) 'Poverty among British Children: Chronic or Transitory', in B. Bradbury, S.P. Jenkins and J. Micklewright (eds), *The Dynamics of Child Poverty in Industrialised Countries* (Cambridge: Cambridge University Press).

Hillyard, P., G. Kelly, E. McLaughlin, D. Patsios and M. Tomlinson (2003) 'Bare Necessities: Poverty and Social Exclusion in Northern Ireland: Key Findings', *Democratic Dialogue*, no. 16.

Hinsch, Wilfried (2001) 'Global Distributive Justice', in Thomas Pogge (2002) *World Poverty and Human Rights* (Oxford: Polity and Basil Blackwell).

Hix, Simon and Abdul Noury (2007) 'Politics, Not Economic Interests: Determination of Migration Policies in the European Union', *International Migration Review*, vol. 41, no. 1, Spring.

Hoelscher, Petra (2004) *A Thematic Study Using Transnational Comparisons to Analyse and Identify What Combination of Policy Responses are Most Successful in Preventing and Reducing High Levels of Child Poverty*, Final Report submitted to the European Commission Directorate General on Employment and Social Affairs, March.

Hoffmann, C., E. Nadai and P. Sommerfeld (2001) *Verstecktes Leid Unter Armut. Wie betroffene Kinder und ihre Eltern die Situation wahrnehmen und bewaltige* (Solothorn: Haute école specialisée de la Suisse du Nord-Ouest, Discussion Paper 2001-S01-01).

Hogan, Denis and Daniel Lichter (1995) 'Children and Youth: Living Arrangements and Welfare', in Reynolds Farley (ed.), *State of the Union: America in the 1990s*, vol. 2 (New York: Russell Sage Foundation).

Hollifield, J.F. (1994) 'Immigration and Republicanism in France: The Hidden Consensus', in W.A. Cornelius *et al.*, (eds), *Controlling Immigration: A Global Perspective,* 1st edn (Stanford: Stanford University Press).

Hollifield, J.F. (2004) 'France', in W.A.Cornelius, T. Tsuda, P.L. Martin and J.F. Hollifield (eds), *Controlling Immigration: A Global Perspective*, 2nd edn (Stanford: Stanford University Press).

Holly, Alberto and Mohamed Benkassmi (2003) *Health and Health Care Inequalities in Switzerland: A Brief Review of the Literature* (Geneva: UNRISD).

Holz, Gerda (2007) 'Pauvreté des enfants en Allemagne: moyens de prévention', in CFEJ, *Jeune et pauvre: un tabou à briser,* Swiss Federal Commision for Children and Youth (Berne: CFEJ).

Honderich, Ted (1981) 'The Question of Well-being and the Principle of Equality', *Mind*, vol. XC.

Honderich, Ted (ed.) (2005) *The Oxford Companion to Philosophy: New Edition* (Oxford: Oxford University Press).

Hooker, Brad (2005) 'Justice', in Robert Audi (ed.), *The Cambridge Dictionary of Philosophy*, 2nd edn (Cambridge: Cambridge University Press).

Hunt, Lynn (2007) *Inventing Human Rights: A History* (New York: Norton).

Iceland, John (2003) *Poverty in America: A Handbook* (Berkeley: University of California Press).

Iceland, John, Kathleen Short, Thesia Garner and David Johnson (2001) 'Are Children Worse Off? Evaluating Child Well-being Using a New (and Improved) Measure of Poverty', *Journal of Human Resources*, vol. 36, no. 2.

IMES-ODR-AFD (2004) *Rapport sur la migration illégale* (Berne), 23 June.

INSEE (2005) *Les Immigrés en France* (Paris: INSEE).

INSEE (2007a) *France, portrait social: édition 2006–2007* (Paris: INSEE).

INSEE (2007b) 'Indicateurs d'inégalités sociales', in *France, portrait social: édition 2006–2007* (Paris: INSEE).

INSEE (2007c) 'Redistribution: 1996–2006', in *France, portrait social: édition 2006–2007* (Paris: INSEE).

INSEE (2008) *Les Familles monoparentales, des difficultés à travailler et à se loger*, INSEE Première, no. 1195, June.

International Organization for Migration (IOM) (2002) *Trafficking of Unaccompanied Minors in the European Union*, case study on France by Mme Assia Ghrib (Geneva: IOM).

Jan-Hesse, Isabel (2007) 'Bébés mendiants, apprentis voleurs, quelle vie pour les enfants Roms ?', *Tribune de Genève*, 31 October.

Jenkins, Stephen P. and Thomas Siedler (2007) 'The Intergenerational Transmission of Poverty in Industrialized Countries', *Institute of Social and Economic Research (ISER) Chronic Poverty Research Centre (CPRC) Working Paper 75*, University of Essex, Colchester, April.

Julienne, Christian (2006) *Logement. Solutions pour une crise fabriquée* (Paris: Les Belles Lettres).

Kamerman, Sheila B., Michelle Neuman, Jane Waldfogel and Jeanne Brooks-Gunn (2003) 'Social Policies, Family Types, and Child Outcomes in Selected OECD Countries', *OECD Social, Employment and Migration Working Papers* no. 6 (Paris: OECD).

Kaya, Bülent (2005) 'Switzerland', in Jan Niessen, Yongmi Schibel and Cressida Thompson (eds), *Current Immigration Debates in Europe: A Publication of the European Migration Dialogue*, September.

Kaya, Bülent (2006) *Egalité des chances en matière de santé*, Document de réflexion, Swiss Forum for Migration and Population Studies (SFM), Neuchâtel.

Kehrli, Christin and Carlo Knöpfel (2007) *Manuel sur la pauvreté en Suisse* (Lucerne: CARITAS Suisse).

Khan, A.R. and C. Riskin (2001) *Inequality and Poverty in China in the Age of Globalization* (New York: Oxford University Press).

Khandakar, Qudrat-i-Elahi (2006) 'Entitlement Failure and Deprivation: a Critique of Sen's Famine Philosophy', *Journal of Development Studies*, vol. 42, no. 4, May.

Klassen, Stephan (undated) *L'exclusion sociale, les enfants et l'éducation: concepts et mesures* (Munich: Université de Munich).

Klugman, Jeni (ed.) (2002) *Sourcebook for Poverty Reduction Strategies*, 2 vols (Washington, DC: World Bank).

Körner, S. (1970) *Categorial Frameworks* (Oxford: Basil Blackwell).

Kosaka, K. (2006) 'Killing Many Innocent People: An Introduction to the Sociology of Well-being and Ill-being', in K. Kosaka (ed.), *A Sociology of Happiness: Japanese Perspectives* (Melbourne: Trans Pacific Press).

Kraut, Richard (2007) *What is Good and Why: The Ethics of Well-Being* (Cambridge, MA: Harvard University Press).

Kronig, Winfried (2003) *Flawed Selection – The Example of Immigrant Children in Swiss Education Systems*, paper presented at the UNESCO Conference on Intercultural Education, Jyväskylä (Finland), 15–18 June.

Krugman, Paul (2008) 'Poverty is Poison', *The New York Times*, 23 February.

Laferrière, F.J. (2002) 'Le traitement des demandeurs d'asile en zone d'attente entre théorie et réalité', in *Hommes et migrations*, no. 1238, July–August.

Lance, Mark Norris and Margaret Olivia Little (2006) 'Defending Moral Particularism', in James Dreier (ed.) *Contemporary Debates in Moral Theory* (Oxford: Blackwell).

Landrin, Sophie (2007) 'Billet simple pour la Roumanie', *Le Monde*, 12 October.

Lanfranchi, A. (1989) 'Enfants d'immigrés et leur familles' (in German), *Bulletin suisse des psychologues*, vol. 10 (in German).

Lanfranchi, Andrea, Jann Gruber and Denis Gay (2003) 'Succès scolaire des enfants d'immigrés: effets des espaces transitoires destiné à la petite enfance', in Hans-Rudolf Wicker, Rosita Fibbi and Werner Haug (eds), *Les migrations et la Suisse* (Zurich: Seismo).

Lapinte, A. (2003) 'Niveau de vie et pauvreté des enfants en Europe', *Working Paper no. 28, Directorate for Research, Studies, Evaluation and Statistics* (DREES), February.

Lau, Élisabeth (ed.) (2007), *État de la France Édition 2007–2008* (Paris: La Découverte).

Le Boucher, Eric (2007) '2008: les réformes en plat de résistance', *Le Monde*, 23–4 December.

*L'État de la France: Édition 2007–2008* (2007) (Paris: La Découverte).

*Le Monde* (2006) *La nouvelle critique sociale* (Paris: Édition du Seuil).

Leseman, Paul (2007) *Early Education for Immigrant Children*, Migration Policy Institute (MPI)/Bertelsmann Stiftung Transatlantic Task Force on Immigration and Integration, September.

Leu, R.E. and S. Burri (1999) 'Poverty in Switzerland', *Swiss Journal of Economics and Statistics*, vol. 135, no. 3.

Lichter, Daniel, T. (1997) 'Poverty and Inequality among Children', *Annual Review of Sociology*, no. 23.

Macculi, Iris (2005) *The Dynamics of Poverty among Children in Switzerland*, Department of Political Economy, University of Geneva, April.

MacCormick, Neil (2007) 'Mr Justice: Ronald Dworkin's Troubled Search for Respectful Politics, A Moral Law, and the Fundamentals of Democracy', *Times Literary Supplement* (TLS), 7 December.

Mäder, Ueli, Stefan Kutzner and Carlo Knöpfel (2003) *Working Poor in Switzerland: Ways out of Social Welfare*, PNR 45 Etat Social (Basel, Fribourg and Lucerne).

Maillard, Alain and Ueli Leuenberger (1999) *Les damnés du troisième cercle: les Albanais de la Kosovo en Suisse 1965–1999* (Geneva: Les éditions Métropolis).

Manea, N. (2007) 'Les Roms sont aussi européens!', *Le Monde*, 27 November.

Marlier, Eric, A.B. Atkinson, Bea Cantillon and Brian Nolan (2007) *The EU and Social Inclusion: Facing the Challenges* (Bristol: Policy Press).

Marpsat, Maryse (2007) 'Services for the Homeless in France', *National Institute for Demographic Studies (INED) Working Paper no. 149* (Paris: INED).

Marpsat, Maryse (2008a) 'Bilan des sources et méthodes des statistiques publiques concernant les personnes sans domicile', *ONPES Travaux, 2008*.

Marpsat, Maryse (2008b) 'L'enquête de l'INSEE sur les sans-domicile: quelques éléments historiques', *Courrier des statistiques*, no. 123, January–April.

Martin, Claude (2007) 'Familles et générations', in Élisabeth Lau (ed.), *État de la France Édition 2007–2008* (Paris: La Découverte).

Martinetti, Françoise (2002) *Les droits de l'enfant* (Paris: Librio).

Martini, J.-F. (2004) 'Mineurs sans famille en zone d'attente', in Dana Dimi-nescu 'La mobilité des jeunes roumains à l'heure de l'élargissement', *Hommes et Migrations*, no. 1251, September–October.

Martiniello, Marco (2006) 'The New Migratory Europe: Towards a Proactive Immi-gration Policy', in C.A. Parsons and T.M. Smeeding (eds), *Immigration and the Transformation of Europe* (Cambridge: Cambridge University Press).

Maurin, E. (2002) 'The Impact of Parental Income on Early Schooling Transi-tions: A Reexamination Using Data over Three Generations', *Journal of Public Economics*, vol. 85.

Maurin, É. (2004) *Le Ghetto français. Enquête sur la ségrégation urbaine* (Paris: Seuil).

McGillivray, Mark (ed.) (2006) *Inequality, Poverty and Well-being* (London: Palgrave Macmillan).

McGillivray, Mark and Matthew Clarke (eds) (2006) *Understanding Human Well-being* (Tokyo: United Nations University Press).

Merlot, Patrice, Markus Gabel and Stéphanie Gaudron (2007), 'Le mal-logement en France', in Denis Clerc, 'Reduire le nombre de pauvres en France: un plan en trois mesures', in *L'Économie politique*, no. 26 April, 2005; reprinted, with additions, in *Problèmes économiques*, no. 2920, March.

Mesure, Silvie and Patrick Savidan (eds) (2006) *Le dictionnaire des sciences humaines* (Paris: Presses Universitaires de France).

Micklewright, John (2002) 'Social Exclusion and Children: A European View for a US Debate', *Centre for Analysis and Social Exclusion Paper no. 51*, London School of Economics, February.

Micklewright, John (2003) 'Child Poverty in English Speaking Countries', in Colloque CERC-CNAF-CGP-Drees, *Les enfants pauvres en France*.

Middleton, S. (2002) 'Coping for the Children: Low Income Families and Financial Management', in *How People on Low Incomes Manage their Finances*, Economic and Social Research Council, London.

Middleton, S., K. Ashworth and I. Braithwaite (1997) *Small Fortunes: Spending on Children, Childhood Poverty and Parental Sacrifice* (York: Joseph Rowntree Foundation.

Mohacsi, Viktoria (2008) 'L'Europe, seul espoir des Roms', *Le Monde*, 8–9, June.

Moore, R. (2000) 'Material Deprivation amongst Ethnic Minority and White Chil-dren: the Evidence of the Sample of Anonymised Records', in J. Bradshaw and R. Sainsbury (eds), *Experiencing Poverty* (Aldershot: Ashgate).

Moret, Joelle (2006) 'Somali Refugees in Switzerland: Strategies of Exile and Pol-icy Responses', *Swiss Forum for Migration and Population (SFM) Studies*, no. 47 (Neuchâtel: SFM).

Morrisens, Ann (2006) 'Immigrants, Unemployment and Europe's Varying Wel-fare Regimes', in C. Parsons, and T. Smeeding (eds), *Immigration and the Transformation of Europe* (Cambridge: Cambridge University Press).

Moser, U. (2002) *Préparés pour la vie? Les compétence de base des jeunes – rapport national de l'enquête PISA 2000* (Neuchâtel: OFS).

Murphy, James Bernard (2005), 'Common Good', in Robert Audi (ed.), *The Cam-bridge Dictionary of Philosophy*, 2nd edn (Cambridge: Cambridge University Press).

Narring, Françoise, Pierre-André Michaud and Vinit Sharma (1996) 'Demographic and Behavioral Factors Associated with Adolescent Pregnancy in Switzerland', *Family Planning Perspectives*, vol. 28, no. 5, September–October.

Nies, Susanne (2007) 'L'élargissment de l'espace Schengen et l'Europe des libertés', *Le Monde*, 24 December.

Niessen, Jan (1999) *EU Policies on Immigration and Integration after the Amsterdam Treaty* (Utrecht: FORUM and the Migration Policy Group).

Nolan, B., B. Maitre and D. Watson (2001) 'Child Income Poverty and Deprivation Dynamics in Ireland', in B. Bradbury, S.P. Jenkins and J. Micklewright (eds), *The Dynamics of Child Poverty in Industrialised Countries* (Cambridge: Cambridge University Press).

Nolan, B. and C.T. Whelan (1996a) *Resources, Deprivation and Poverty* (Oxford: Clarendon Press).

Nolan, B. and C.T. Whelan (1996b) 'Measuring Poverty Using Income and Deprivation Indicators: Alternative Approaches', *Journal of European Social Policy*, vol. 6, no. 3.

Nussbaum, Martha (2003) 'Rawls and Feminism', in Samuel Freeman (ed.), *The Cambridge Companion to Rawls* (Cambridge: Cambridge University Press).

Nussbaum, Martha and Amartya Sen (eds) (1993) *The Quality of Life* (Oxford: Clarendon Press).

OECD (several issues) *International Migration Outlook SOPREMI* (Paris: OECD).

OECD (2001) *Trends in International Migration – Annual Report 2000* (Paris: OECD), Part II on 'Family Reunification'.

OECD (2004a) *Learning for Tomorrow's World: First Results from PISA 2003* (Paris: OECD).

OECD Country Note (2004b) *Early Childhood Education and Care Policy in France* (Paris: OECD Directorate for Education), February.

OECD (2006a) *Where Immigrant Students Succeed – A Comparative Review of Performance and Engagement in PISA 2003*, Programme for International Student Assessment (PISA) (Paris: OECD).

OECD (2006b) *Economic Survey of Switzerland* (Paris: OECD), January.

OECD (2007a) *Economic Survey of France* (Paris: OECD), June.

OECD (2007b) *Country Note on Switzerland* (Paris: OECD).

OECD (2007c) *Starting Strong II: Early Childhood Educational and Care* (Paris: OECD).

OECD (2007d) *International Migration Outlook: Annual Report* (Paris: OECD).

OECD (2007e) *PISA 2006, Programme for International Student Assessment (PISA)* (Paris: OECD).

Ogien, Albert and Louis Quéré (2005) *Le vocabulaire de la sociologie de l'action* (Paris: Ellipses).

Oldfield, N. and A.C.S. Yu (1993) *The Cost of a Child: Living Standards for the 1990s* (London: CPAG).

Olson, James M., C. Peter Herman and Mark P. Zanna (eds) (1986) *Relative Deprivation and Social Comparison: The Ontario Symposium vol. 4* (Hillsdale, NJ: Lawrence Erlbaum Associates).

OMISTATS (several years) *Annuaire des Migrations* 2004 (Paris: OMI/ANAEM).

O'Neill, Onora (2001) 'Agents of Justice', in Thomas W. Pogge (ed.), *Global Justice* (Malden, MA: Blackwell).

O'Neill, Onora (2004) 'Global Justice, Whose Obligations?', in D.K. Chatterjee (ed.), *The Ethics of Assistance: Morality and Distant Need* (Cambridge: Cambridge University Press).

ONPES (Observatoire National de la Pauvreté et de l'Exclusion Sociale) (2008) *Le rapport de l'Observatoire national de la pauvreté et de l'exclusion sociale 2007–2008* (Paris: La Documentation Française).

ONPES Travaux (2008) *Les Travaux de l'Observatoire national de la pauvreté et de l'exclusion sociale 2007–2008* (Paris: La Documentation Française).

Orshansky, Mollie (1963) 'Children of the Poor', *Social Security Bulletin*, vol. 26, no. 7, July.

Osberg, L. and A. Sharpe (2000) *Estimates of an Index of Economic Wellbeing for OECD Countries* (Cracow: International Conference on Income and Wealth), 27 August–2 September.

Osberg, L. and A. Sharpe (2002) 'An Index of Economic Wellbeing for OECD Countries', *Review of Income and Wealth*, September.

Osberg, L. and A. Sharpe (2003a) *Human Wellbeing and Economic Wellbeing: What Values are Implicit in Current Indices* (Ottawa: Centre for the Study of Living Standards, CSLS, Research Report).

Osberg, L. and A. Sharpe (2003b) 'Evaluer l'indice du bien-être économique dans les pays de l'OCDE', *Travail et Emploi*, no. 93, January.

Ovcharova, L.N. and D.O. Popova (2005) *Child Poverty in Russia: A UNICEF Report* (Moscow: UNICEF).

Palier, Bruno (2007) 'Protection sociale: les cinq familles européennes', in Élisabeth Lau (ed.), *État de la France Édition 2007–2008* (Paris: La Découverte).

Parfit, Derek (1984) *Reasons and Persons* (Oxford: Oxford University Press).

Park, H. and Gary D. Sandefur (2004) *Cross-national Variation in Performance Gaps in Reading Literacy between Native and Immigrant Children: A Comparative Analysis of 14 OECD Countries*, Department of Sociology, University of Wisconsin Madison.

Parsons, C. and T. Smeeding (eds) (2006) *Immigration and the Transformation of Europe* (Cambridge: Cambridge University Press).

Perregaux, Christiane and Florio Togni (1989) *Enfant cherche école: pour le droit à l'éducation en Suisse* (Carouge-Geneva: Édition Zoé).

Perret, B. (2002) *Indicateurs sociaux états des lieux et perspectives* (Paris: CERC).

Peyrat, D. (2006) 'Violence et délinquance ne sont pas des fatalités', *Le Monde*, 10–11 September.

Philibert, J.M. (2006) 'SDF: un nouveau campement sauvage relance la polémique', *Le Figaro*, 19 December.

Philibert, J.M. (2007) 'Les principales mesures prévues par la loi sur le droit au logement opposable', *Le Figaro*, 23 February.

Piachaud, D. and H. Sutherland (2000) 'How Effective is the British Government's Attempt to Reduce Child Poverty', *Centre for the Analysis of Social Exclusion (CASE) Paper 38*, LSE, London.

Piachaud, D. and H. Sutherland (2001) 'Child Poverty: Aims, Achievements and Prospects for the Future', *New Economy*, vol. 8, no. 2.

Piguet, Etienne (1999) 'Les jeunes issus de l'immigration en Suisse: caractéristiques socio-démographique et résultats de recherche', *Migrations société*, vol. 11, no. 62.

Piguet, Etienne (2004) *L'immigration en Suisse: cinquante ans d'entrouverture* (Lausanne: Presses polytechniques et universitaires romandes).

Piguet, Etienne (2005) *L'immigration en Suisse depuis 1948 Une analyse des flux migratoires* (Zurich: Édition Seismo).

Piguet, Etienne (2006) 'Economy versus the People? Swiss Immigration Policy between Economic Demand, Xenophobia, and International Constraint', in Marco Giugni and Florence Passy (eds), *Dialogues on Migration Policy* (Lanham, MD: Lexington Books).

Platt, L. (2002) *Parallel Lives: Poverty among Ethnic Minority Groups in Britain* (London: Child Poverty Action Group, CPAG).

Platt, L. (2005) *Discovering Child Poverty* (Bristol: Policy Press).

Pogge, Thomas (ed.) (2001) *Global Justice* (Oxford: Basil Blackwell).

Pogge, Thomas (2002) *World Poverty and Human Rights* (Oxford: Polity and Basil Blackwell).

Ponthieux, S. (2003) 'Les enfants pauvres: regard sur les conditions de vie', in Colloque CERC-CNAF-CGP-Drees, *Les enfants pauvres en France*.

Programme Nationale de Recherche 52 (PNR52) (2006) *Bien-être des enfants et des adolescents en Suisse et transmission des opportunités économiques entre les générations-Resumé des resultats*, Department of Economics, University of Geneva.

Rahnema, M. (2003) *Quand la misère chasse la pauvreté* (Paris: Fayard).

Rawls, J. (1971, 1999) *A Theory of Justice* (Cambridge, MA: Harvard University Press).

Rawls, J. (1982) 'Social Unity and Primary Goods', in A. Sen and B. Williams (eds), *Utilitarianism and Beyond* (Cambridge: Cambridge University Press).

Rawls, J. (1993) *Political Liberalism* (New York: Columbia University Press).

Rawls, J. (1999) *The Law of Peoples* (Cambridge, MA: Harvard University Press).

Rawls, J. (2001) *Justice as Fairness: A Restatement* (ed. Erin Kelly) (Cambridge, MA: Harvard University Press).

Raz, Joseph (2000) 'Explaining Normativity: On Rationality and the Justification of Reason', in Jonathan Dancy (ed.), *Normativity* (Oxford: Blackwell).

Rector, Robert, Kirk Johnson and Patrick Fagan (2002) 'The Effect of Marriage on Child Poverty', Heritage Foundation, *Center for Data Analysis Report no. 02–04*, 15 April.

Rey-Lefebvre, Isabelle (2007) 'Propriété: le temps des héritiers', *Le Monde*, 27 December.

Reynier, Alain (1995) 'Gypsy Populations and their Movements within Central and Eastern Europe and Towards Some OECD Countries', *International Migration and Labour Market Policies Occasional Papers*, no. 1 (Paris: OECD).

Richard, Jean-Luc (2005) 'Les immigrés dans la société française', *Problèmes politiques et sociaux*, no. 916 (Paris: La Documentation française), September.

Ridge, T. (2002) *Child Poverty and Social Exclusion: From a Child's Perspective* (Bristol: Policy Press).

Ringer, Fritz (2004) *Max Weber: An Intellectual Biography* (Chicago: University of Chicago Press).

Ringold, Dena, M.A. Orenstein and Erika Wilkens (2005) *Roma in an Expanding Europe: Breaking the Cycle of Poverty* (Washington, DC: World Bank).

Rizk, C. (2003) 'Les enfants pauvres: quartiers et qualité du cadre de vie', in Colloque CERC-CNAF-CGP-Drees, *Les enfants pauvres en France*.

Roberts, Adam (2008) 'Open Up: A Special Report on Migration', *The Economist*, 5 January.

Rodier, C. (2002) 'Zone d'attente de Roissy: à la frontière de l'État de droit', *Hommes et migration*, no. 1238, July–August.

Rosenberg, Sonja *et al.* (2003) *Intégration réussite des étrangers ? La réponse des statistiques. Les enfants et adolescents étrangers dans la système suisse d'éducation,* Le parcours scolaire et de formation des élèves immigrés à 'faibles' faible performances scolaires – une présentation du problème edited by CDIP, Emmetten, Conférence suisse des directeurs cantonaux de l'instruction publique, Berne.

Rosenvallon, Pierre and Thiery Pech (eds) (2006) *La nouvelle critique sociale* (Paris: Seuil).

Ross, W.D. (1930) *The Right and the Good* (Oxford: Clarendon Press).

Runciman, W.G. (1966) *Relative Deprivation and Social Justice* (London: Routledge & Kegan Paul).

Ruxton, Sandy and Fran Bennett (2002) *Including Children? Developing a Coherent Approach to Child Poverty and Social Exclusion across Europe,* report commissioned by EURONET Brussels.

Ryan, Alan (2003) 'The Way to Reason', in *The New York Review of Books,* 4 December.

Sachs, Jeffrey D. (2005) *The End of Poverty* (New York: Penguin).

Sancho, Brigittte (1992) *Les enfants de l'ombre: situation et scolarisation des enfants sans statut légal dans le canton de Vaud* (Lausanne: Edition La Passerelle).

Scanlon, T. M. (1998) *What We Owe to Each Other* (Cambridge, MA: Harvard University Press).

Scheffler, S. (2003) 'Rawls and Utilitarianism', in Samuel Freeman (ed.), *The Cambridge Companion to Rawls* (Cambridge: Cambridge University Press).

Schiff, Claire (2004) 'L'institution scolaire et les élèves migrants: peut mieux faire', *Hommes et Migrations,* no. 1251, September–October.

Schluter, Christian (2001) 'Child Poverty in Germany: Trends and Persistence', in B. Bradbury, S.P. Jenkins and J. Micklewright (eds), *The Dynamics of Child Poverty in Industrialised Countries* (Cambridge: Cambridge University Press).

Schnapper, D. (2007) *Qu'est-ce que l'intégration?* (Paris: Gallimard).

Schuerkens, Ulrike (2005) 'Active Civic Participation of Immigrants in France', *Country report prepared for the European Research Project POLITIS,* Carl von Ossietzsky Universität, Oldenburg, Germany.

Secretariat général du comité interministériel de contrôle de l'immigration (2006) Report (December).

Sen, Amartya (1982) 'Rights and Agency', *Philosophy and Public Affairs,* vol. 11.

Sen, Amartya (1967) 'The Nature and Classes of Prescriptive Judgments', *Philosophical Quarterly,* no. 17.

Sen, Amartya (1985) 'Rights as Goals', in S. Guest and A. Milne (eds), *Equality and Discrimination: Essays in Freedom and Justice* (Stuttgart: Franz Steiner).

Sen, Amartya (1987) *On Ethics and Economics* (Oxford: Basil Blackwell).

Sen, Amartya (1991) 'Welfare, Preference and Freedom', *Journal of Economics,* vol. 50.

Sen, Amartya (1992) *Inequality Reexamined* (New York: Russell Sage Foundation).

Sen, Amartya (1993) 'The Economics of Life and Death', *Scientific American,* April.

Sen, Amartya (1999) *Development as Freedom* (New York: Random House).

Sen, Amartya (2002) *Rationality and Freedom* (Cambridge, MA: Harvard University Press).

Sen, Amartya (2004a) 'Elements of a Theory of Human Rights', *Philosophy and Public Affairs,* vol. 32, no. 4.

Sen, Amartya (2004b) 'Capabilities, Lists and Public Reason: Continuing the Conversation', *Feminist Economics,* vol. 10, no. 3.

Sen, Amartya (2005) 'Human Rights and Capabilities', *Journal of Human Development*, vol. 6, no. 2.

Sen, Amartya (2006) *Identity and Violence: The Illusion of Destiny* (London: Allen Lane).

Senni, Hamid (2007) 'Behind the Banlieues: France's Hidden Discrimination', *International Herald Tribune*, 13 December.

Severino, Jean-Michel (2007) 'Les défis ont changé', *Le Monde: Dossiers et documents*, no. 370, December.

Sharp, K. (2003) 'Measuring Destitution: Integrating Qualitative and Quantitative Approaches in the Analysis of Survey data', *IDS Working Paper 217*.

Shelden, George (2001) *'Foreign Labour Employment in Switzerland: Less is Not More*, available at <http://www.unibas.ch/wwz/fai>.

Simon, Patrick (2003) 'France and the Unknown Second Generation: Preliminary Results on Social Mobility', *International Migration Review*, vol. XXXVII, no. 4, Winter.

Simmons, A. John (1992) 'Fairness', in Charlotte B. Becker and Lawrence C. Becker (eds), *Encyclopedia of Ethics* (Chicago: St James Press).

Smart, J.C.C. and Bernard Williams (eds) (1973) *Utilitarianism: For and Against* (Cambridge: Cambridge University Press).

Smeeding, Timothy, B.B. Torrey and M. Rein (1988) 'Patterns of Income and Poverty: The Economic Status of Children and the Elderly in Eight Countries', in J.L. Palmer, Timothy Smeeding and B.B. Torrey (eds), *The Vulnerable* (Washington, DC: Urban Institute Press).

Sopo, Dominique (2007) 'Tolérance zéro, bilan zéro', *Le Monde*, 29 November.

Souliez, Christophe (2007) *Les violences urbaines* (Paris: Presses Universitaires de France).

Spencer, Nick (1996) *Poverty and Child Health* (Oxford: Radcliffe Medical Press).

Srinivasan, T.N. (1994) 'Destitution: A Discourse', *Journal of Economic Literature*, vol. 32.

Steinberg, Jonathan (1976) *Why Switzerland?* (Cambridge: Cambridge University Press).

Steiner, Hillel (2006) 'Moral Rights', in D. Copp (ed.), *The Oxford Companion of Ethical Theory* (Oxford: Oxford University Press).

Streuli, Elisa and Tobias Bauer (2001) 'Les Working Poor en Suisse', *Info Social*, no. 5, April.

Sumner, Wayne (1996) *Welfare, Happiness and Ethics* (Oxford: Oxford University Press).

Sweeney, J. (2000) 'Pro-Employment Policies and Child Income Poverty', in *Department for Social Development/Queen's University of Belfast (DSD/QUB) Seminar Proceedings* (Belfast: Queen's University).

Swiss Federal Commission for Children and Youth (CFEJ) (2002) *Familles et migration*, Berne.

Swiss Federal Commission for Children and Youth (CFEJ) (2007) *Jeune et pauvre : un tabou à briser !*, Commission Report (Berne: CFEJ).

Swiss Federal Office of Migration (OFM) (2006) *Problèmes d'intégration des ressortissants étrangers en Suisse* (Berne: OFM).

Swiss Federal Office of Public Health (OFSP) (2002) *Migration et santé* (Berne: OFSP).

Swiss Federal Office of Statistics (OFS) (1999) *Comprendre la pauvreté, pour mieux la combattre* (Neuchâtel: OFS).

Swiss Federal Office of Statistics (OFS) (2005) *Federal Population Census 2000* (Neuchâtel: OFS).

Swiss Federal Office of Statistics (OFS) (2002) *Enquête Suisse sur la santé* (Neuchâtel: OFS).

Swiss Federal Office of Statistics (OFS) (2002–7) *Annual Statistical Yearbook* (Neuchâtel: OFS).

Swiss Federal Office of Statistics (OFS) (several issues) 'série verte' no. 2 and 'série jaune' nos. 1 and 4.

Swiss Federal Office of Statistics (OFS) (2005) *Federal Population Census 2000* (Neuchâtel: OFS).

*Swissinfo* (2003a) 'La Suisse compte trop d'enfants pauvres', 18 April.

*Swissinfo* (2003b) 'No Place to be Poor', 18 April.

*Swissinfo* (2005) *La pauvreté progresse en Suisse*, December, available at <http://lescommunistes.org/spip.php?article 781>.

*Swissinfo* (2006) 'Child Allowance Should Benefit All Children', 6 September.

Ternisien, Xavier (2007) 'Villiers-le-Bel, radioscopie d'un "ghetto social"', *Le Monde*, 30 November.

TNS Sofres (2007) 'Sondage', *Le Figaro*, 13 November.

Townsend, P. (1979) *Poverty in the United Kingdom* (Harmondsworth: Penguin).

Tribalat, M. (1995) *Faire France: Une enquête sur les immigrés et leurs enfants* (Paris: La Découverte).

*Tribune de Genève* (2007) 'Les mendiants Roms à Genève', 21 October.

UK Government, Department of Work and Pensions (2003) *Measuring Child Poverty: Preliminary Conclusions*, London.

UK Government, HM Treasury (1999) *Supporting Children through the Tax and Benefit System*, London.

UNDP (2006) *Human Development Report 2006* (New York: Oxford University Press).

UNICEF (2001) *The State of World's Children 2001* (New York: Oxford University Press).

UNICEF (2003) *The State of World's Children 2003* (New York: Oxford University Press).

UNICEF (2006) *The State of World's Children 2006: The Excluded and the Invisible* (New York: Oxford University Press).

UNICEF (2007) *The State of World's Children 2007* (New York: Oxford University Press).

UNICEF Innocenti Research Centre (2000) 'Child Poverty in Rich Nations', Report Card no. 1, June.

UNICEF Innocenti Research Centre (2001) *A League Table of Teenage Births in Rich Nations* (Florence: UNICEF).

UNICEF Innocenti Research Centre (2003) *A League Table on Child Maltreatment Deaths in Rich Countries*, Report Card no. 5, Florence.

UNICEF Innocenti Research Centre (2004) *Summary Report of the Study on the Impact of the Implementation of the Convention on the Rights of the Child* (Florence: UNICEF).

UNICEF Innocenti Research Centre (2005) *Child Poverty in Rich Countries 2005*, Report Card no. 6, Florence.

UNICEF Innocenti Research Centre (2007) *Child Poverty in Perspective: An Overview of Child Well-being in Rich Countries*, Report Card no. 7, Florence.

Vallet, Louis-André (1996) 'L'assimilation scolaire des enfants issus de l'immigration et son interprétation: un examen sur données françaises', *Revue française de pédagogie*, vol. 117.

Vallet, Louis-André (2005) 'What Can We Do to Improve the Education of Children from Disadvantaged Backgrounds?', paper prepared for the Joint Working Group on Globalization and Education of the Pontifical Academy of Social Sciences, Vatican City, 16–17 November.

Vallet, Louis-André and Jean-Paul Caille (1996a) 'Les élèves étrangers ou issus de l'immigration dans l'école et collège français, Une étude d'ensemble', *Les dossiers d'Education et Formations*, vol. 67 (Paris: Ministry of Education).

Vallet, Louis-André and Jean-Paul Caille (1996b) 'Niveau en français et en mathématiques des élèves étrangers ou issus de l'immigration', *Economie et Statistique*, vol. 293.

Vallet, Louis-André and Jean-Paul Caille (1999) 'Migration and Integration in France: Academic Careers of Immigrants' Children in Lower and Upper Secondary School', paper prepared for the ESF Conference, European Societies or European Society? Migrations and Inter-Ethnic Relations in Europe, Obernai, 23–8 September.

van Eeckhout, Laetitia (2007) *L'Immigration: Débat Public* (Paris: Odile Jacob).

Vasconcellos, Maria (2007) 'Éducation: Grandes tendances', in Élisabeth Lau (ed.), *État de la France Édition 2007–2008* (Paris: La Découverte).

Vegeris, S. and J. Parry (2003) 'Families and Children 2001: Living Standards and the Children', *Research Report 190,* Department of Work and Pensions, London.

Vizard, Polly (2006) *Poverty and Human Rights: A Review of Sen's Capability Approach* (Oxford: Oxford University Press).

Vleminckx, Koen and Timothy Smeeding (eds) (2001) *Child Well-being: Child Poverty and Child Policy in Modern Nations: What Do we Know?* (Bristol: Policy Press).

Volovitch, P. (2007) 'Organisation et fonctionnement de la protection sociale', in Élisabeth Lau (ed.), *L'état de la France Édition, 2007–2008,* (Paris: La Découverte).

Walker, R. (1999) *Ending Child Poverty* (Bristol: Policy Press).

Walsh, Patricia (2005) 'Well-being', in T. Honderich (ed.), *The Oxford Companion to Philosophy* (Oxford: Oxford University Press).

Walzer, Michael (1983) *Spheres of Justice: A Defence of Pluralism and Equality* (New York: Basic Books).

Wanner, Philippe (2001) *Charactéristiques démographiques des populations issues de l'immigration en Suisse* (Neuchâtel: OFS).

Wanner, Philippe (2004) *Migrations et Intégration: Population étrangère en Suisse* (Neuchâtel: OFS), June.

Wanner Philippe (2006) 'Indicateurs démographiques de l'enfance et des relations entre générations', *Demos: Bulletin d'information démographique*, no. 1, Neuchâtel.

Wanner, Philip et Rosita Fibbi (2002) 'Familles et migration, familles en migration', in Commission Fédérale pour les questions familiales (ed.), *Familles et migrations* (Berne: Office fédéral des assurances sociales).

Weber, Max (1976) *Wirtschaft und Gesellschaft: Grundriss der verstehenden Soziologie,* 5th edn (Tübingen: J. C. Mohr). Originally published in 1921.

Weber, René and Thomas Straubhaar (1994) *Budget Incidence of Immigration into Switzerland : A Cross-section Analysis of the Public Transfer System* (London: Centre for Economic Policy Research).

Weber, Sylvain (2005) 'Multidimensional Poverty and Cluster Analysis: An Illustration with Switzerland',paper presented at the International Conference on the Many Dimensions of Poverty, organized by IPC, Brasilia, 29–31 August.

Weber, Sylvain (2006) 'Durée de chômage et nationalité: Une analyse empirique pour la Suisse', *Revue suisse d'économie et de statistique*, vol. 142, no. 1, March.

Wellings, K. (1999) *Promoting the Health of Teenage and Lone Mothers – Setting a Research Agenda*, Report of the UK Health Education Authority Expert Working Group.

Wertheimer, Richard, Melissa Long and Justin Jager (2001) 'Children in Working Poor Families: Update and Extensions', *Child Trends Research Brief* (Washington, DC: Foundation for Child Development).

Whelan, C.T., R. Layte and B. Maître (2002) 'Multiple Deprivation and Persistent Poverty in the European Union', *Journal of European Social Policy*, vol. 12, May.

White, Howard, Jennifer Levy and Andrew Masters (2002) 'Comparative Perspectives on Child Poverty: A Review of Poverty Measures', *Working Paper no. 1*, Sussex.

*Why Life Chances Matter?* (2005) The Interim Report of the Fabian Commission of Life Chances and Child Poverty.

Wicker, Hans-Rudolf, Rosita Fibbi and Werner Haug (eds) (2003) *Les migrations et la Suisse: relations interculturelles* (Zurich: Seismo).

Williams, Bernard (1973) 'A Critique of Utilitarianism', in J.C.C. Smart and Bernard Williams (eds), *Utilitarianism: For and Against* (Cambridge: Cambridge University Press).

Willits, M. (2006) 'Measuring Child Poverty using Material Deprivation: Possible Approaches', *UK Department of Work and Pensions (DPW) Working Paper no. 28*, London.

Winkleman, Rainer (2002) 'Work and Health in Switzerland: Immigrants and Natives', *University of Zurich Socioeconomic Institute Working Paper* no. 0203, Zurich, March.

World Bank (2000) *World Development Report 2000–2001: Attacking Poverty* (New York: Oxford University Press).

World Bank (2006) *World Development Report 2006* (New York: Oxford University Press).

Wuhl, Simon (2007) *Discrimination positive et justice sociale* (Paris: Presses Universitaires de France).

Zeugin, Bettina (2007) *Où en est la politique migratoire de la Suisse?* (Lucerne: Caritas Suisse).

Zhang, M. (2003) 'Links Between School Absenteeism and Child Poverty', *Pastoral Care in Education*, March.

# Name/Author Index

# Subject Index